DECISION AND
INTERACTION IN CRISIS

DECISION AND INTERACTION IN CRISIS

A Model of International Crisis Behavior

Ben D. Mor

PRAEGER

Westport, Connecticut
London

To Orit, my wisest decision

Library of Congress Cataloging-in-Publication Data

Mor, Ben D.
 Decision and interaction in crisis : a model of international
crisis behavior / Ben D. Mor.
  p.   cm.
 Includes bibliographical references and index.
 ISBN 0-275-94371-2 (alk. paper)
 1. International relations—Decision making. 2. International
relations—Psychological aspects. 3. Israel-Arab War, 1967.
I. Title.
JX1391.M58   1993
327—dc20   92-31843

British Library Cataloguing in Publication Data is available.

Library of Congress Catalog Card Number: 92-31843
ISBN: 0-275-94371-2

First published in 1993

Praeger Publishers, 88 Post Road West, Westport, CT 06881
An imprint of Greenwood Publishing Group, Inc.

Printed in the United States of America

The paper used in this book complies with the
Permanent Paper Standard issued by the National
Information Standards Organization (Z39.48-1984).

10 9 8 7 6 5 4 3 2 1

Copyright Acknowledgments

The author and publisher gratefully acknowledge permission to reprint the
following copyrighted material:

Yehoshafat Harkabi, *Arab Attitudes toward Israel* (New York: Hart Publishing
Company, 1972).

Ben D. Mor, ''Nasser's Decision-Making in the 1967 Middle East Crisis:
A Rational-Choice Explanation,'' *Journal of Peace Research* 28(4): 359-375.

Contents

Figures

Preface

The importance of international crises in world politics is not difficult to appreciate. Even a moment's reflection on the events of this century points to the central and critical role that crises have played: a sequence of crises—Fashoda (1898), Morocco (1905–1906), Bosnia (1908–1909), Agadir (1911), and the Balkans (1913)—set the stage for World War I, whose immediate precipitant was the July 1914 crisis; the Hitler crises of the 1930s were the overture to World War II; and the Cold War featured a series of crises, in Iran (1945–46), Berlin (1948–49, 1958–62), Quemoy (1958), Cuba (1962), the Middle East (1973), Angola (1975–76), and elsewhere. In fact, according to one estimate (Brecher and Wilkenfeld, 1989: 6), between 1929 and 1985, the international system experienced 323 international (macrolevel) crises, in Africa (28%), the Americas (12%), Asia (23%), Europe (18%), and the Middle East (19%). At present, too, the disintegration of the Soviet Union is generating crises throughout its former empire.

The prevalence of crises has been matched by a voluminous literature on the topic. Scholars have produced in-depth case studies and aggregate data sets of crises, explored the phenomenon from different levels of analysis, and employed a variety of methodologies in its study. They investigated crisis initiation, escalation, management, termination, and forecasting, in isolation and in relation to other research areas. In short, barely has an aspect of crisis escaped the attention of researchers.

Whereas the output has been impressive indeed, its cumulative theoretical import has been less remarkable. The literature on international crises can boast some excellent studies, but it has yet to integrate them and produce a broad theory. In fact, rather than move in the direction of such a theory, the field has become divided to such an extent that the prospects for a general theory now seem dimmer than ever. One scholar has remarked that even major contemporary crises, such as the recent one in the Gulf, do not seem to jolt the community of crisis researchers into a thorough examination of current theories in the field (Kugler, 1991). It is not surprising, therefore, that in less dramatic circumstances, there are few attempts to bridge and integrate diverse theories of crisis.

This state of affairs has come about mainly as a result of the ongoing split between the psychological and rational-choice approaches to crisis decision making. The first point I wish to make in this book is that despite impressive achievements by both of these approaches, each has promoted a conception of crisis that is too narrow and limited to support a general theory. My second point is that the two approaches—contrary to common belief—are complementary, in the sense that the weaknesses of one are precisely the strengths of the other, and vice versa. The third point that this book makes is that the approaches are amenable to integration, and that such an integration is a requirement for the development of a general theory of crisis.

This thesis, which is presented in Chapter 1, defines the agenda that underlies the book. The remainder of the book is devoted to the development and application of a crisis model that begins to address this agenda. I emphasize the word begin, because in my view, a single book cannot possibly hope to offer a complete solution to the theoretical and methodological issues involved in the integration of the two approaches. Thus, I preferred to present the rationale for integration and then explore one possibility of pursuing it, both theoretically and empirically. My hope is that this book, whatever its shortcomings, will convince other researchers that the task of integration is worth their effort, too.

The organization of the book reflects these research objectives. Thus, after arguing the case for integration in the first chapter, I turn to the development of a crisis model in the second and third chapters. Although this model is game-theoretic, it is not strictly so: It incorporates perceptual and belief-related variables, which are conceived as contact points with the psychological approach. The model's specification also provides one possible solution to linking temporally related games, which current game theory cannot handle satisfactorily.

Chapters 4 and 5 are concerned with the application of the model to an empirical case—the 1967 Middle East crisis. The chapters provide an extensive, in-depth analysis of the crisis, and present a new perspective on Israeli—and especially Egyptian—behavior. The case also serves to test the model, expose its weaknesses, and suggest ways of improving it, with the integration agenda as the major criterion. The conclusions are given in Chapter 6, which also summarizes the major arguments of the book.

No book is written alone. Throughout my research and writing, I was fortunate to have had the advise and support of two outstanding teachers and scholars, Steven J. Brams and Zeev Maoz. Under their supervision, an earlier version of this book was completed as a doctoral dissertation at New York University. It was during my graduate studies at NYU that Steve first introduced me to game theory. My thinking about strategic issues took shape in numerous discussions with him, during which I learned to appreciate his exacting standards, relentless productivity, and devotion to students. His own work, in particular the theory of moves and its imaginative applications, has been a permanent source of inspiration, as this book attests. The book also reflects the complementary influence of Zeev Maoz, with whom I studied decision-making theory and methodology. Zeev was not only a stimulating and dedicated teacher, but also a fountainhead of ideas and suggestions that were invaluable to my intellectual development. The scope and depth of his knowledge, and the integrative quality of his work, continue to provide a standard worth aspiring to. I am grateful to Steve and Zeev for the benefit of their scholarship, and for their support and friendship over the years.

Other individuals contributed from their experience and advise at various stages of my research. Farhad Kazemi, Miroslav Nincic, and Frank C. Zagare read earlier drafts of this manuscript, and offered useful comments and suggestions. Gideon Doron engaged me in stimulating discussions of rational-choice theory and provided encouragement when I began to lose momentum. Former and present colleagues—Nasrin Abdolali, Uri Bar-Joseph, Tuvia Ben-Moshe, Michael Gross, Tansa Masoud, and Yair Zalmanovich—kept me going with goodwill and continuous support.

I am also indebted to the NYU Politics Department and Graduate School of Arts and Science for providing me with scholarships and the Dean's Dissertation Fellowship.

Finally, the support of my family was indispensable to the completion of this book. My parents accepted our long separation with grace and understanding, and encouraged my career choices every step of the way. My children—Adi, Dana, and Yaniv—provided much experience in crisis management and many hours of relief from the pressures of scholarly research. Last but foremost, I owe everything to my wife, Orit, who so efficiently and cheerfully managed her demanding career, adventurous children, and preoccupied husband. I dedicate this book to her.

1

Crisis Decision Making: Psychological versus Rational-Choice Explanations

The critical role that crises play in international relations demands that we acquire systematic knowledge about their origins, development, and termination. Why and when do states initiate crises? Is crisis initiation detrimental to the international system, or is it a necessary means of effecting a change in the status quo? What determines states' preferences in crises? How do states choose their crisis strategies? Can weak states compensate for their inferiority in power through their strategy choices? Why do some crises end in war, whereas others are resolved diplomatically? How can states escape escalation traps and induce compromise?

These are some of the important questions with which the crisis literature at large has occupied itself. Most individual studies, however, have focused on selective aspects of crisis, and have produced theories and models of restricted scope. Therefore, the conception of crisis that emerges from the literature is either narrow or disjointed. What is needed is an overarching and coherent view of crisis that specifies the continuous process linking initiation with termination—in other words, a general theory of crisis.

What has impeded the development of such a theory? The primary reason—as we shall see in the following pages—is the deep gulf that separates the two dominant approaches to crisis research—the psychological and the rational-choice. Although they share a common theoretical ancestry—decision-making theory—these approaches presently constitute two bodies of research that proceed from different assumptions, address separate agendas, and provide distinct explanations of crisis behavior and outcome.

Some might argue that this state of affairs should benefit the study of crisis—after all, competition in the marketplace of ideas promotes the development of good theory. Unfortunately, rather than engage in a mutually enriching debate, the two camps have only moved further apart over time. In fact, with few exceptions, there now seems to be a consensus that the integration of the psychological and rational-choice perspectives on crisis is a task neither desirable nor feasible. The incompatibility of the two perspectives appears to have become an article of faith, perpetuated by the selective training, if not indoctrination, to which new researchers are subjected.

This chapter seeks to explore the reasons for the ongoing division of the field. It reviews the major studies and findings on international crisis that have come from the two competing approaches, and examines the prospects for an integrative framework that would combine their respective insights. The contention of this chapter is that despite the impressive achievements of each approach, the overall result has been a restricted and disjointed conception of crisis that cannot give rise to a general theory. The chapter argues, moreover, that the two approaches are not inherently incompatible; rather, they are complementary and therefore amenable to integration, which is a necessary condition for the development of a general theory of crisis.

The chapter is organized as follows. The first section looks at the psychological approach and reviews its major findings. The second section undertakes the same with respect to the rational-choice approach. The third section offers a critique of both approaches and discusses the differences in their conception of rationality. Finally, the fourth section discusses the objectives and scope of the book.

Before we proceed, two comments should be made. First, the following review is restricted to decision-making theories of crisis. This focus does not imply that other perspectives—notably the systemic—are not productive, but it does reflect the conviction that theoretical obstacles at the intrastate level are responsible for the problems that presently afflict the field, and that these problems should therefore be addressed first. Nevertheless, neither this chapter nor the following two neglect the interstate level of analysis; on the contrary, the game-theoretic studies that will be reviewed and the game-based model of crisis that will be developed are rooted in the assumption that the interactive level is indispensable to the understanding of crisis.

Second, the purpose of the review provided in this chapter is to characterize the two approaches as competing *research orientations* to the study of crisis. Thus, the emphasis is on the basic assumptions, concerns, and preferences of these respective approaches, and in particular on the conception of crisis to which they give rise. The studies included in this review were selected in accordance with this emphasis, namely as representative of the type of research orientation that each approach promotes. Necessarily, other studies that merit attention were left out or only briefly referred to.[1]

THE PSYCHOLOGICAL APPROACH TO CRISIS BEHAVIOR

Introduction: Actor-Oriented Definitions of Crisis

Psychological theories of crisis behavior employ *actor-oriented* definitions of crisis. These definitions are rooted in the perceptual perspective of decision-making theory, as argued for by Snyder, Bruck, and Sapin (1962: 5): "It is difficult to see how we can account for specific actions and for continuities of policies without trying to discover how their operating environment is perceived by those responsible for choices." Thus, psychological theories of crisis view and define crisis in subjective terms, namely as a phenomenon whose existence depends on the perceptions of decision makers.[2] By and large, crisis definitions differ in terms of the dimensions they identify as empirically necessary for a situation to be perceived as a crisis.

Robinson's (1972) threefold definition has remained the cornerstone of perceptual definitions. He specified the following dimensions: "identification of the origin of the event (whether external or internal for decision-makers); time available for response (short, intermediate, or long); and relative importance to participants of the values at stake (low or high)" (p. 23). Hermann (1972b) then suggested a "situational cube" of three dimensions—threat, decision time, and awareness—in which one could locate various situations facing decision makers. A "crisis situation" was distinct in that it ranked high on all three dimensions: "a crisis is a situation that (1) threatens high-priority goals of the decision-making unit, (2) restricts the amount of time available for response before the decision is transformed, and (3) surprises the members of the decision-making unit by its occurrence" (p. 13).

This definition was employed by Holsti (1972) in his study of the 1914 crisis.[3] Snyder and Diesing (1977), however, excluded Hermann's second and third dimensions from their definition, arguing that these dimensions were neither logically nor empirically necessary (p. 9, fn. 7). Their definition centered on "the perception of a dangerously high probability of war" by the actors (p. 7),[4] and stressed the interactive nature of crisis. Lebow's (1981) definition (of "acute" international crises) similarly stressed the elements of perceived threat and high probability of war, but retained the perceived time constraint (pp. 7–12).[5]

Brecher (1980) built on the Hermann definition but introduced several modifications.[6] An important one was the "intra-war crisis" concept (IWC), wherein the second condition was replaced by "a perceived deterioration in a state's and/or an ally's military capability via-à-vis the enemy—that is, an adverse change in the military balance" (p. 7). The concept of IWC was at odds with Snyder and Diesing's (1977) understanding that war itself is excluded from the definition of crisis (p. 7). Another feature in Brecher's definition was the inclusion of a system-level dimension of crisis, namely the change in the external/internal environment. This change, however, still had to be perceived by decision makers in order for a crisis to occur.

Maoz (1982a) criticized the defender-oriented nature of the Hermann, Brecher, and Robinson definitions, and argued that "the elements of perceptual definitions are neither necessary nor sufficient for identification as far as crisis initiators are concerned" (p. 217). He proposed a definition that combines systemic and perceptual elements, as well as the initiation factor.[7] Lebow (1981), though employing a defender-oriented definition of crisis, developed a typology of crisis that included a category of cases—"justification of hostility crises"—where "leaders of the initiating nation make a decision for war *before* the crisis commences" (1981: 25; emphasis in original).[8]

The few definitions reviewed here, despite some important differences, nevertheless make the perceptions of decision makers their cornerstone. In this, as noted before, they stand in sharp contrast to systemic definitions, which ignore "the impact of public opinions, the effects of informal and non-governmental pressures, and the part played by the organizational, perceptual, motivational, and personality aspects of crisis behavior" (McClelland, 1972: 86).[9]

The Basic Elements of the Psychological Approach

The psychological approach is concerned with the impact of two basic groups of factors on the functioning of decision makers: personality factors (which include individuals' personality structures, belief systems, and related images) and situational variables (which refer to environmental changes and their relation to individuals' motivations and cognitive performance). Organizational roles are also examined for their impact on the preferences of decision makers and their ability to process information.

These three categories are not mutually exclusive. De Rivera (1968) notes that "decisions are a product both of facts such as role, power, the situation, and knowledge, and of the fact of the individual's personality" (pp. 165–66). The primary concern in studying the effects of these groups of factors is with their impact on the decision-making process: how various psychological factors impinge on the performance of individuals and groups in crisis decision making.

Personality Factors

This group of factors refers to personality-inherent predispositions and their effect on the performance of individuals in crisis-related decisional tasks.[10] The underlying assumption is that the characteristics of a crisis situation—particularly the need to make fateful decisions under severe stress—act as a trigger for personality predispositions that manifest themselves in individuals' behavior.

Lebow, in *Between Peace and War* (1981), provides several dramatic examples of personality predispositions triggered by crisis. Thus, for example, he argues (p. 138) that "contradictory elements of motivation and fatalism" in the character of German Chancellor Bethmann-Hollweg may have been responsible for the hypervigilant coping pattern (*see* Janis and Mann, 1977: 59–62) that he exhibited during the height of the 1914 crisis. At the same time, the Kaiser's "paranoid response" may be explained by a pathological neurosis he had long suffered from, a psychophysiological disorder known as neurasthenia (p. 143, and p. 146, fn. 138). Elsewhere in the book, Lebow examines General Douglas MacArthur's behavior before and during the Korean War, and argues that "it is difficult to avoid the conclusion that MacArthur, by going out of his way so repeatedly to tempt fate both personally and operationally, was acting out of a strong unconscious death wish" (pp. 155–56, fn. 20). These examples are illustrative of the psychopathological approach to the analysis of decision makers' behavior.[11]

A different approach seeks to tie personality structures to their corresponding "belief system" (Holsti, 1962) or "operational codes" (George, 1969, 1970), which are consciously articulated and hence measurable. A recent attempt to do so is Etheredge's (1985) study of government learning. Etheredge argues that the recurring pattern of "blocked learning" discerned in American foreign policy toward Central American revolutions is the result of the workings of a "distinctive and strong system of imagination." This imagination system (or "a personal way of knowing about political power") is typical of the "hard-ball politics decision maker" (HP) and is responsible for blocked learning (pp. 147–48). Etheredge ties the personality traits of the HP with its correspondingly characteristic modes of thought about America's and its own role in world politics. The continuous presence in positions of power of the HP then accounts for the persistence of a foreign policy outlook that, in turn, is responsible for the repeated adoption of defective policies.

Although Etheredge seeks to explain general and long-term patterns in American foreign policy, his conclusions have an interesting bearing on crisis behavior. Specifically, the quality of crisis decision making is related to the "strongly held sensibility concerning power" that typifies the HP (p. 147): "the learning rate, how much people thought and to what effect, was a function of motivation, itself an effect of the issues of power at stake. Against powerful opponents, when the potential damage to America was great, or American troops might be required, latent capacities for extensive, searching analyses of alternatives and reflective discussion were used. But the capacities were not engaged when—as in MONGOOSE—a challenger was perceived weak in power to retaliate" (p. 87). Etheredge thus presents a motivational theory: errors in cognition did not occur "naturally" or autonomously, but were a function of decision makers' motivations (p. 147). (We will return to this point later.)

A variant on the belief-system concept is Brecher's "attitudinal prism" (1972: 11). This term, which comprises societal and personality factors, serves as a mediator between the environment and decision makers' perceptions. However, the perception of crisis, a situational variable, is the independent variable in Brecher's framework (1980: 28), and therefore sets it apart from personality-oriented studies. The argument underlying this conception, which will be discussed next, is the following: "The methodological difficulties concerning the relationship between slowly changing personality variables of belief systems and rapidly changing decision strategies, suggest that personality can best be used as an intervening variable, rather than an independent one, in explanations of decision making processes" (Maoz, 1990b: 59).

Situational Factors

Personality factors, belief systems, and images are important in determining decision makers' detection of, and sensitivity to, the environmental stimuli that give rise to the perception of crisis. According to Brecher (1980), crisis perception is operationalized in terms of three closely related perceptual variables: "threat [to basic values]; time pressure; and high probability of involvement in military hostilities, or high probability of war" (p. 16). The simultaneous increase in the intensity of these three components marks the onset of the crisis period in Brecher's framework (p. 23).[12]

A variable of central importance to the psychological approach is that of stress. Holsti and George (1975) write that "it is customary to regard 'stress' as the anxiety or fear an individual experiences in a situation which he perceives as posing a severe threat to one or more values" (p. 257). Brecher (1980) views stress as the "perception of threat and/or time pressure and/or probability of war" (p. 21). In the precrisis period, perceived threat alone is present, at a low intensity. Therefore, crisis-induced stress is at a low level. With the sharp rise of threat, and its attendant awareness of time pressure and likelihood of war (that is, during the crisis period), the level of crisis-induced stress mounts (pp. 25–26).

Holsti (1972: 36–38), by contrast, opposes the measurement of stress in terms of its effects, because such a measurement precludes the testing of propositions that relate the former to the latter (for example, the effects of stress on perceived time pressure). Stress, argues Holsti, is therefore best indexed by means of perceptions of international hostility. (It is unclear, however, that perceptions of hostility necessarily entail perceptions of threat.)

Having defined the concept of stress, most psychological studies of crisis have proceeded to evaluate its various consequences. The major focus of this line of research has been on the effect of stress on the decisional process, or on the procedural aspects of decision making. Observing this trend, Holsti and George (1975) recommended that research concentrate "not merely on the *process* of decision-making but also on the *content and quality* of the decisions or choices of policy that emerge from that process" (p. 269; emphasis in original).[13]

Research into the effects of stress yielded initially contradictory results. Zinnes, Zinnes, and McClure (1972) drew the following conclusion from their study of the 1914 crisis: "decision makers do not perceive or behave differently in a crisis. In a crisis, as in a noncrisis, they react in proportion to incoming stimuli. They do not perceive hostility when none exists, and they express hostility directly in terms of their perception of hostility" (p. 160).

Holsti (1972), on the other hand, drew the opposite conclusion from his study of the 1914 crisis and the Cuban missile crisis: "The evidence suggests that policy making under circumstances of crisis-induced stress is likely to differ in a number of respects from decision-making processes in other situations. More important, to the extent that such differences exist they are likely to inhibit rather than facilitate the effectiveness of those engaged in the complex tasks of making foreign policy choices" (p. 23).

Subsequent research has tended to support Holsti's general conclusion, though once the decisional process was decomposed into stages—search, revision, evaluation, and choice (*see* Stein and Tanter, 1980)—studies showed less consensus.[14] Still, the pattern that emerges is that of a curvilinear relationship between the level of stress (low, moderate, or high) and the extent and quality of search, revision, evaluation, and choice.

In a recent study, Sergeev et al. (1990) constructed and compared cognitive maps of President John F. Kennedy's speeches before and during the Cuban missile crisis. Following a computer-simulation analysis of these maps, Sergeev et al. discovered that Kennedy's crisis perception resulted from "a serious break in the structure of [the president's] political perception" (p. 197). Specifically, whereas Kennedy's perception prior to the crisis was that the United States could exert control over events in world politics, the Soviet actions in Cuba led to a collapse of that perception. As the analysis of the cognitive maps shows, by October 22 "the interdependence factor makes a powerful breakthrough into the president's world image" (p. 190). Sergeev et al. argue that the restructuring of Kennedy's thinking strongly influenced the resolution of the crisis.

This conclusion is rather exceptional in pointing to a crisis-related change in cognitive structures. Most studies, on the other hand, are concerned with the influence of crisis on the procedural aspects of decision making, a topic we turn to next.

Patterns of Coping

The study of patterns that characterize decision makers' coping with crisis is at the heart of the psychological approach. Researchers have focused primarily on the examination of cognitive processes and modes of information processing, drawing heavily on related studies in the psychology literature. The major mode of inquiry has been the comparison of actual coping patterns with an idealized— "analytic" or "rational"—model of decision making; this Weberian methodology consists primarily of the characterization, categorization, and measurement of departures from an ideal type, which serves as a criterion for evaluating the quality of decision making.[15] The underlying assumption has been that the higher the conformity of an actual decisional process to the analytic model, the better the decisions and outcomes that result. The normative side of this mode of inquiry has consisted of recommendations designed to improve the fit between the ideal type (the analytic model) and actual decisional processes.

Some of the studies examining coping mechanisms and processes have been conducted from the perspective of articulated models of decision making. Findings showing substantial departures from the analytic model have resulted in the development of alternative models, most notably the cybernetic (or bounded rationality) model and the cognitive model.[16] The former derives largely from the work of Simon (1957), Braybrook and Lindblom (1963), Tversky (1972), and Steinbruner (1974). Its main features are sequentiality of the search process; the incremental and conservative nature of revision; the limited evaluation (single-value analysis, and elimination by aspects); and the satisficing principle in choice. The cognitive model derives from the work of such scholars as Holsti (1962), Jervis (1976), and Kahneman and Tversky (whose 1982 volume, written with Paul Slovic, summarizes their findings on judgmental heuristics).[17] The main features of the model are deductive search (that is, within the parameters of the belief system); deductive and categorical revision (evidence compatible with prior beliefs weighted higher than discrepant information); limited evaluation (unidimensional to avoid conflict); and analogizing choice.[18]

Empirical work done on these models has yielded mixed findings, both across studies and within single studies. Allison (1971) has demonstrated the possibility of tailoring different explanations—rational and nonrational—to fit a single event (the Cuban missile crisis). Maoz (1981) found that the Israeli decision to raid Entebbe was characterized by an essentially analytic process; however, cybernetic and cognitive factors were present as well. Shlaim and Tanter's (1978) study of the Israeli deep-penetration bombing in Egypt yielded support for the cybernetic model, as did Steinbruner's (1974) study of the Multi-Lateral Force decision and Mintz's (1992) analysis of the American decision to use force against Iraq. Studies by Janis (1972), De Rivera (1968), Jervis (1976), Lebow (1981), and Vertzberger (1990) provided many examples of cognitive processes.

Snyder and Diesing (1977) were divided in their interpretation of their findings. Whereas Diesing concluded that "the maximization of utility is quite beside the point in crisis bargaining" and that bounded rationality provided the better fit (pp. 405–6), Snyder argued that "either theory would apply with equal validity." This is because "when choosing among two or more imperfect alternatives, whether decision makers choose the one with the best benefit-cost ratio or the one that least violates the constraints becomes pretty much an issue of semantics" (p. 408).

A possible resolution of these conflicting findings was provided by Stein and Tanter (1980), who argued for a model of "multiple paths to choice"—rather than conform consistently with one model or another, decision makers actually use different types of processes to cope with the crisis situation (p. 63). Cohen's (1979) comparative case study of threat perception in crises also indicated that elements from different models could be found both across and within cases.

Finally, Herek, Janis, and Huth (1987) compiled data on presidential decision making in nineteen post-WWII crises, and tested the relationship between the quality of the decisional process and the quality of crisis outcomes. They discovered that there was a direct relationship between the two variables: The more analytic the process, the better the crisis outcome. This result was supported even when the "seriousness" and "difficulty" of the crisis were taken into account. However, because the data were correlational, causation could not be inferred.[19]

A few additional works of importance to the study of cognitive coping should be mentioned. Jervis, in an extensive study (1976) of the sources of misperception in international politics, argued that cognitive consistency is a central organizing principle of cognition (p. 118). He then illustrated the implications of irrational consistency (the avoidance of value tradeoffs) for information processing and inference drawing (for example, the tendency to excessive and premature closure; the tendency to assimilate incoming information to preexisting images; the tendency to be overconfident about the success of a favored policy).

Whereas Jervis centered on the autonomous sources of error, Janis and Mann (1977) argued that decisional pathologies stemmed from motivational sources, or the need "to avoid anticipatory fear, shame, and guilt" (p. 85).[20] Their "conflict-theory model" specifies three forms of defensive avoidance: procrastinating, shifting responsibility, and bolstering. The pervasiveness of these mechanisms "may be due to the frequent occurrence of the antecedent conditions of high conflict with little hope for a satisfactory solution" (p. 81). The implications of these forms of defensive avoidance to decisional processes are detrimental in that they impair search, appraisal, and contingency planning.

Janis (1972) also studied the consequences of these mechanisms for group decision making, and argued that a pattern of defensive avoidance could manifest itself at this level as well. This pattern—"groupthink"—is characterized by concurrence seeking on the part of decision makers of a cohesive group who "use their collective cognitive resources to develop rationalizations supporting shared illusions about the invulnerability of their organization or nation" (Janis and Mann, 1977: 129). As stress mounts, the need for group affiliation increases and with it, the pressures toward conformity. These pressures, in turn, give rise to the defensive avoidance pattern. Hence, the incentives toward uniformity reduce group members' motivation to dissent by voicing objections to or reservations about the group's favored policy. Critical scrutiny is thereby impaired with dire consequences for the quality of decisions.

Finally, a recent study by McCalla (1992) investigated the effects of misperception on American decision making in five Cold War crises. Taking a differentiated view of misperceptions according to their source, McCalla discovered, among other things, that some misperceptions are more likely to change during the course of a crisis than others. Specifically, new information is more likely to correct misperceptions that are "situational" in nature, that is, "involve situations where an actor's perception of the situation is plausible based on the information available, yet that perception turns out to be incorrect" (p. 142); on the other hand, new information is less likely to affect misperceptions that are "dispositional" in nature, that is "come from an actor's internal predisposition to see the world in a certain way or process certain types of information in a particular way" (ibid.). This conclusion, which requires further testing on a larger sample, is at odds with the rather pessimistic conclusions about coping that emanate from most of the studies previously mentioned. However, McCalla's study also indicates that, even in the absence of misperceptions, crises may still occur as a result of conflicts of interest (p. 189). This point, too often overlooked by psychological studies, will be addressed below.

The Psychological Approach: Summary

The single most important conclusion to emerge from the studies reviewed above is that deviations from an analytic (rational) decision-making process are pervasive—particularly in crisis situations—and that these deviations may be attributed to psychological factors. From this follows the corollary that decision makers, at a minimum, are not consistently rational; more likely, according to one formulation, the appropriate conceptualization is the following: "we see man not as a cold fish but as a warm-blooded mammal, not as a rational calculator always ready to work out the best solution but as a reluctant decision maker—beset by conflict, doubts, and worry, struggling with incongruous longings, antipathies, and loyalties" (Janis and Mann, 1977: 15).

The implications of this view for a rational-choice approach to the study of crisis were spelled out by Kirkpatrick (1975): "Crisis situations pose particular difficulty for classical rational choice models since the maximization of expected utility is generally limited, and there is evidence that fewer consequences will be considered while the role of psychological variables takes on added importance" (p. 57).

To evaluate these arguments and their implications for a framework that seeks to combine psychological and rational-choice elements, a review of the rational-choice literature on crisis is in order.

THE RATIONAL-CHOICE APPROACH TO CRISIS RESEARCH

Studies employing the rational-choice approach share the common assumption that decision makers are rational[21]—the principle of rationality is what directs and lends consistency to the theoretical expectations in these studies (as it does in much of economic theory). Explanations consist of demonstrating that the following general pattern holds for a particular actor's behavior: "If a nation performed a particular action, that nation must have had ends toward which the action constituted a maximizing means... The puzzle is solved by finding the purposive pattern within which the occurrence can be located as a value-maximizing means" (Allison, 1971: 33).

Although decision makers are conceptualized as maximizers (or optimizers), what and how they maximize depends on the assumptions of the researcher—the principle of rationality is flexible enough to encompass diverse value structures and risk propensities. Thus, an actor may have strictly egoistic or strictly altruistic values, or some combination of both. It may seek to maximize its expected utility or maximum gain, or act conservatively and maximize its minimum gain or minimize its maximum risk (or regret) (*see* Luce and Raiffa, 1957: 278–86, for a discussion of decision criteria).

Though sharing this fundamental assumption of rational behavior, rational-choice studies of crisis are conducted from several different theoretical perspectives. These may be divided into two broad groups: (1) models based on expected-utility theory or decision theory; and (2) game-theoretic models, which may be further subdivided (with some overlap) as follows: (a) prescriptive game models; (b) game models applied to explain particular empirical cases; and (c) game models designed to introduce and test new theoretical concepts. (Studies of the latter kind often contain case study applications and prescriptive recommendations as well.)

A comprehensive application of expected-utility theory to the study of interstate conflict and war is Bueno de Mesquita's *The War Trap* (1981; *see* also 1985). This study was designed to address four central issues: conflict initiation, conflict outcome, escalation in conflict, and the cost of war (p. 68). Expected-utility equations were used to deduce testable propositions related to these issues. Several counterintuitive propositions were derived from the broad generalization that "wars (or other conflicts) will be initiated only when the initiator believes the war will yield positive expected utility" (p. 127). Thus, for example, Bueno de Mesquita found strong empirical support for the proposition that allies are substantially more likely to engage in conflict with each other than are enemies (pp. 159–64). Another proposition to receive strong empirical support concerns crisis escalation: "the targets of an initiator's demands have a strong incentive to negotiate rather than fight if they expect to lose more in a war than they believe the initiator expects to gain" (p. 167). Under such circumstances, a crisis is unlikely to end in war.

A case study application of expected-utility theory, framed as a problem of decision under uncertainty, is Wagner's (1974) study of Israeli decision making in the 1967 Middle East crisis. Wagner derived cardinal utility values for the various positive and negative outcomes associated with Israel's basic alternative strategies, and ranges of subjective probability estimates for the logical consequences (or "paths") of each alternative. He then showed that the preemptive strike alternative had the highest expected value.

Expected-utility studies, of which Bueno de Mesquita's and Wagner's are good examples, conceptualize crisis as an *action*, rather than an *interaction*, process. The latter viewpoint is inherent in game-theoretic analyses, where the interdependent setting of the decision problem is primary. Prescriptive game-theoretic studies have been concerned with deriving optimal strategies for actors in such settings. Schelling's (1960, 1966) work epitomized this approach with respect to deterrence situations. Drawing attention to the particular characteristics of mixed-motive games (in contrast to zero-sum games), Schelling sought to examine the nature of threats, promises, commitments, and communication in such games, and derive optimal strategies for effective deterrence. Though rich in insights, Schelling's work did not involve testing against reality, and historical examples were used "as illustration, not evidence" (1966: vii; *see* also George and Smoke, 1974: 61–71, and Jervis, 1979).

Other game-theoretic studies undertook the analysis and explanation of specific historical crises. Applications of game models in these studies often had the additional purpose of demonstrating the usefulness of certain game-theoretic concepts. Brams (1985a, 1985b) analyzed the Cuban missile crisis by means of the theory of moves (*see* below), and its attendant nonmyopic equilibria and power concepts. The implications of lack of complete information were investigated in terms of deception strategies (*see* Brams, 1977). Zagare (1987) used the theory of moves to analyze the strategic relationship between the United States and the Soviet Union, with particular emphasis on the 1967 Middle East crisis and the 1973 cease-fire alert (*see* also Zagare, 1983, 1981). Snyder and Diesing (1977) analyzed sixteen historical crises by means of game models that were reinterpreted in an attempt to improve their applicability. Misperceptions and strategic surprise in crisis and war were studied by Shupe et al. (1980), Wright et al. (1980), and Hipel, Wang, and Fraser (1988), who applied hypergame theory to the 1956 Suez crisis, the 1956 Suez War, and the Falkland/Malvinas War, respectively. Finally, Welsh (1971) studied the U.S.-Soviet conflict during the 1956 Hungarian revolt. By including in the game matrix submatrices specifying the outcomes of sequential moves, Welsh attempted to examine the effects of preplay communication on the preferences of the players.

Some game-theoretic models focused on the development of new and empirically applicable game-theoretic concepts, as well as on the derivation, from abstract models, of optimal strategies to stabilize crisis escalation. This approach has been exemplified particularly in the work of Brams: The development of the theory of moves (1983) was designed to improve the applicability of game models to the study of crisis and deterrence by means of articulating dynamic rules of play, and to "uncover stability in certain games that classical game theory hides or places elsewhere" (1985a: 134).[22] The dynamics of crisis escalation were modeled by means of a "Threat Game" based on Chicken and defined on the unit square. The model enabled the derivation of guidelines for optimal threats (that is, threats that maintain deterrence and stabilize the status quo), refining the conclusion reached by Axelrod (1984) with respect to the tit-for-tat strategy (Brams and Kilgour, 1987a, 1987b; *see* also Langlois, 1989).[23]

Two additional attempts at a broad conceptualization of crisis bargaining should be mentioned. Morgan (1984) developed a model of crisis bargaining based on a spatial representation of the theory of games. Each dimension of an *m*-dimensional space represents an issue in dispute, and actors' preferences are represented as (constrained) ideal points in this space. The bargaining process is then conceived as consisting of moves (concessions) designed to narrow the distance between opponents' ideal points. The parameters of the model, which include resolve and relative power, can be manipulated to examine their effects on the outcome. By specifying the probability distribution over the possible outcomes, the model can be used to determine the probability of particular negotiated settlements and the probability of war.

Another broad model of crisis bargaining is Morrow's (1989) limited information model. Seeking to move beyond models that assume simultaneous choice and complete information, Morrow suggested a sequential bargaining model of incomplete information. In the model, each player discloses its private information (or part of it) through its bargaining moves, which are also designed to manipulate the other side's beliefs or the probabilities each side thinks the opponent assigns to the crisis outcome. Beliefs change as a result of Bayesian updating and may lead to changes in what players consider to be optimal moves. Such changes, in turn, communicate new information to the opponent, and so on. The solution of the bargaining game (the sequential equilibrium) yields four distinct cases of crisis, each distinguished by a set of players' moves and beliefs. Based on these, the crisis outcome for each case is specified.

Morrow's work reflects a general trend in game-theoretic studies of deterrence and crisis—the modeling and analysis of strategic situations characterized by informational asymmetries. Thus, for example, Powell (1990, 1989a, 1989b, 1987) studied resolve, retaliation, and stability in nuclear crises by means of games of sequential bargaining with incomplete information; Kilgour and Zagare (1991) analyzed the relationship between threats and deterrence stability; Fearon (1990) examined the tradeoff between the credibility of threats and the risk of unwanted war; and Banks (1990) investigated the effect on crisis outcomes of asymmetric information concerning the expected benefits from war. In an empirical application, Mishal, Schmeidler, and Sened (1987) used a game with differential information to predict the probable outcome of the Israeli-Palestinian conflict. Wagner (1989) developed a game model of the Cuban missile crisis that explicity incorporated uncertainty and rational (Bayesian) learning. The analysis of the model enabled Wagner to suggest that, contrary to common contentions, "bargaining during the crisis was not a competition in risk taking, but a means by which information about Kennedy's preferences was transferred to Khrushchev" (p. 204).[24]

THE PSYCHOLOGICAL AND RATIONAL-CHOICE APPROACHES: A CRITICAL APPRAISAL

The purpose of this section is to make the argument that neither the psychological approach nor the game-theoretic approach in its present formulation, captures the essential dynamics of crisis. Although it is true that both approaches focus on important (but different) aspects of the same phenomenon, they do so at the expense of other, equally important aspects, which remain neglected.

From the perspective of one seeking integration, it is fortunately the case that what one approach neglects, the other emphasizes. Ignoring for the moment areas of incompatibility, it may be said that each approach theorizes about different parts, or aspects, of the same "elephant" (yet suggests it is investigating the reality of crisis). If this latter description is accurate, and if the incompatibilities could be bridged or sufficiently narrowed, then the case for an integrative approach could be convincingly made.

With this in mind, the present section seeks to: (1) identify the major drawbacks of each approach that pertain to the study of crisis. In fact, it will be argued, the weaknesses of one approach are often the strengths of the other (and vice versa); (2) discuss the most significant area of incompatibility—the rationality assumption—and assess its implications for integration.

The Psychological Approach: The Neglect of Interdependence

The first section presented the psychological approach as one that focuses on the analysis of disruptions in normal (noncrisis) cognitive processes as a result of crisis-induced stress. The changes in these processes, measured relative to an idealized rational mode of decision making (the analytic model), are thought to impinge directly on the quality of crisis decisions. Different modes of decision making are perceived to operate under crisis (and, some argue, under noncrisis) conditions—these constitute the elements of alternative decision-making models, including the cybernetic and cognitive.

However important this theoretical focus is to understanding the antecedents of strategy choice, it defines a very limited conception of crisis. Specifically, the psychological approach promotes a view of decision makers as secluded within the "shell" of their respective decision making groups, responding, in various forms, to incoming cues from the environment. At best, the picture is one of isolated centers or systems of decision-making, tied only by the flow of bidirectional stimuli; within this picture, attention is then directed primarily to the processing of incoming stimuli, from reception to decision.

This conception omits a key element of the crisis phenomenon—the *strategic interaction* that takes place at the interstate level and that defines crisis bargaining. In other words, what is missing from the picture is a sense of structure—a notion of the interdependence of states locked in severe conflict.

To argue that an important perspective is not addressed does not *ipso facto* suggest that its omission is theoretically crippling. After all, theory building is a selective process, and even a good theory cannot be expected to account for every aspect of a studied phenomenon. Therefore, the incorporation of the strategic dimension into crisis theory can be justified only if its exclusion impairs our understanding in some critical sense. It can be argued, in fact, that there are at least five serious consequences to the neglect of strategic interaction in psychological studies of crisis.[25]

First, if the perceptions of threat, time pressure, and the probability of war are the defining characteristics of crisis, and, further, if such perceptions are the determinants of stress, then the psychological approach does not provide for a sufficient discrimination among types of crisis. It concentrates on what is common to all crises—in fact on what defines them—but in so doing, it fails to identify the parameters that change from crisis to crisis.

This monolithic view of the subject matter is evident in the Hermann (1972b) typology of "ideal types of situations with respect to threat, time, and awareness" (p. 15): Once a situation ranks high on all three dimensions, it qualifies as a crisis, and more discriminating observations cannot be made.[26] It is also revealing that Lebow's (1981) typology of crises is based on "their political-historical geneses" (p. 23) rather than on the behavioral characteristics of decision makers under stress. In fact, Lebow distinguishes among crises in terms of their bargaining aspects, such as "interest," "accommodation," "commitment," "compellence," and so forth.[27] To the extent that a good theory requires a good typology, the psychological approach has not much to offer.

Second, the focus of the psychological approach precludes serious attempts at theorizing about the causes of crisis. At its best, the approach provides for the identification of "environmental cues" that are perceived by decision makers as threatening to their goals or basic values. Such cues are, however, peripheral to the approach, which primarily seeks to catalogue and analyze their effects on decision making. In a sense, then, the approach is apolitical: It is not concerned with the sources of threat, the intentions of actors, and the impact of power and interests as such, but instead with their (mediated) effects.

Third (and related to the previous point), the neglect of political intent has serious consequences for crisis anticipation. As Tanter (1978: 353) notes, the applicability of a stimulus-response model is limited in cases involving deception. This is so because threat perception may be irrelevant to the incentives of an actor contemplating deception.

The neglect of the initiation factor has already been mentioned: Whether deception is used as a strategy or not, threat perception may be irrelevant. To the extent, then, that one is interested in predicting behavior, the psychological approach becomes relevant once a crisis has erupted, but it is limited in its ability to predict the circumstances under which a crisis is likely to occur.

Fourth, the neglect of interdependence in the psychological approach results in a lack of sensitivity toward the external and objective constraints that operate on decision makers. What is possible for decision makers to achieve is not just a function of their cognitive abilities. It is also a function of their opponent's interests, preferences, power, and choices, in themselves and relative to one's own.[28] In fact, as the findings of Sergeev et al. (1990) indicate, a crisis situation may involve precisely such a realization on the part of decision makers. Also, the fact of interdependence may imply dilemmas, paradoxes, and entrapments that even superb cognitive abilities and information processing may not help overcome.[29]

The psychological approach does highlight the effects of decisional conflicts on decision makers' coping patterns; such conflicts often stem from the perception of certain situations as "no win situations." However, the operational implications of such situations, in terms of what is objectively possible for decision-makers to achieve, are mostly overlooked. This emphasis on subjective constraints in the psychological approach results in the argument that the procedural/formal quality of the decision-making process impinges directly on the substantive quality of outcomes. This argument, however, may not necessarily be true. As Maoz (1990b: 6) notes, "there is no empirical guarantee that high-quality choice procedures would yield adaptive or successful outcomes." (This point will be further discussed in connection with the rationality assumption.)

Fifth, the current focus of the psychological approach is too self-contained, in the sense that the theory it generates cannot be readily related to other research on international conflict. Snyder and Diesing (1977: 4) addressed this difficulty by implication: "The case for using crisis as a data source for the empirical development of general theory rests also on the generality of the primary form of interaction between states in a crisis—that of *bargaining*, broadly defined to include coercion and deterrence as well as mutual accommodation" (emphasis in original). By focusing on stress and cognitive processes to the exclusion of bargaining elements, the psychological approach not only ignores an essential aspect of crisis—the interactive process—but does so at the potential cost of severing its ties with a wider body of international relations theory (*see* Mandel, 1986: 253).

The argument concerning the importance of the interactive aspect of crisis would be misleading if interpreted simply as a call for expanding even further the already long list of potential hazards to decision making that the psychological approach has compiled. In fact, the interdependent setting of crisis may provide decision-makers with the opportunity to use threats, commitments, and deception effectively to further their crisis-related goals (*see* Brams, 1977; Brams and Hessel, 1984; and Brams and Kilgour, 1987b). The psychological approach neglects this aspect of crisis because of its focus on decisional failures. Such failures, however, are not necessarily the rule in international relations—decision making can also be successful and innovative. Yet "the reduction of individuals and collectives into units trapped by fears, desires, and other cognitive limitations fails to account for innovations in foreign policy making" (Maoz, 1990b: 213).

In contrast to the psychological approach, the strength of the game-theoretic approach lies precisely in its concern with interdependent decision making.[30] Thus, (1) whereas the psychological approach neglects the structure of the crisis situation and hence its implications for choice flexibility (or strategic maneuverability), game theory permits a conceptualization of "crisis structure" in terms of the configuration of actors' preferences over outcomes;[31] and (2) whereas the psychological approach neglects political intent (and hence cannot account for crisis initiation where threat perception is absent), game-theoretic models can be constructed on the basis of assumptions about actors' goals (*see* Brams, 1983:

17-19). Such models are therefore capable of explaining why crises are initiated despite the absence of perceived threat.

Although game theory avoids some of the major problems inherent in the psychological approach, its present formulation is in other respects inadequate for the study of crisis. It is important to distinguish between two types of criticism: (1) criticism of the theory itself—its assumptions, solution concepts, and utility in empirical research in general—and (2) criticism of the theory's applicability to crisis research, including the evaluation of extant game-theoretic studies of crisis.

The first type of criticism is, of course, directly related to the second: To the extent that the empirical utility of game theory is found wanting, so is its applicability to crisis research. Still, it is useful to distinguish between these two types of criticism, because there is often a tendency to judge game theory as theory by its extant empirical applications.[32] Lack of knowledge of the mathematical theory, however, cannot be compensated for by finding fault with its applications, whose quality varies with the expertise of the practitioner. The main purpose of the following discussion is to identify problems in the present formulation of game theory that detract from its usefulness to crisis research.

The Game-Theoretic Approach: The Restrictive Notion of Dynamics

The major difficulty in applying game theory to the study of crisis lies in its limited ability to deal with dynamic processes. According to Snidal (1985: 44), the term "dynamic" refers to: "(1) the impact of states making multiple decisions through time, and (2) [the] mutual adjustment among states through time." It is with respect to the latter process that game theory runs into problems: "mutual adjustment" subsumes several types of possible changes—most notably of preferences—that the theory precludes via its assumptions.

Specifically, the game-theoretic representation of crisis dynamics can take the form of actors' moves within *fixed* games, or across *variable* games. The theory's ability to cope with dynamics of the latter type—that is, with *game transformations*—is severely limited because of the assumption of fixed alternatives and preferences. There is no reason to assume, however, that either alternatives or preferences are invariant throughout the duration of a crisis. In fact, various events that transpire over the course of a crisis are likely to modify players' perception of the *strategic structure* of the situation (*see* below). It is this type of change that game theory assumes to be exogenous.[33]

Before we discuss the implications of these problems, let us see in what ways game theory can address dynamic processes in crises.[34] One approach may be to construct fixed games corresponding to distinct points in time throughout the temporal development of a crisis. This, however, would not qualify as truly dynamic analysis, since all one would be showing is that each set of alternatives and preferences would remain fixed until, by some unspecified and obscure process, a new set would materialize. Yet it is precisely these transition points between and among games, and the underlying processes that produce them, that are essential to a model of crisis dynamics.

Another approach is the supergame model (recursive and stochastic games), in which "a normalized game is played at each stage, and the player's strategies control not only the (monetary) payoff but also the transition probabilities which govern the game to be played at the next stage" (Luce and Raiffa, 1957: 457). This model assumes that actors know in advance all the component games that are contained in the supergame. Their calculations, therefore, concern not only the initial game, but its implications for the play of all subsequent games (*see* Mor, 1990, for an empirical application). The problem with such models, however, is that the component games themselves (as well as the transition probabilities) are fixed, and players cannot change their perceptions of subsequent games once the play of the initial game is under way.

Still another approach, concerned with the analysis of dynamic processes within (fixed) games, was suggested by Brams (1983) in his theory of moves. The theory is based on an extension of the rules of play that are assumed for matrix games in classical game theory. The new rules, which define a sequential game, provide for dynamic play by means of three kinds of powers that can be attributed to players (and are exogenous to the game): moving power, staying power, and threat power. The attribution of such powers to players, and the concept of nonmyopic equilibria, enable one to go beyond the Nash equilibrium concept in explaining why actors at times depart from initial outcomes (that is, change strategies) and why, at other times, they choose not to do so.

The theory of moves demonstrates that classical game theory can be extended to incorporate dynamic elements without being emasculated in the process. However, a further extension of the theory to cover variant games would require a different approach from the one consisting of the *a priori* specification of exogenous actors' powers. Still, the end result is likely to consist of the specification of exogenous psychological factors that govern the (dynamic) process by which one game is transformed into another.

A different approach to analyzing dynamics in cardinal games is to provide for the revision of probability estimates by means of Bayesian inference. The assumption of incomplete information represents a significant departure from the restrictive framework of classical game theory, and recent applications (discussed earlier) of Bayesian analysis to the study of deterrence and crisis have produced some of the most dynamic game-theoretic models of crisis behavior.

It should be noted that this approach focuses on the probability component of expected utility. There is no reason to assume, however, that the utilities associated with outcomes may not themselves change during the course of a crisis. For example, the utility of an intermediate crisis outcome may decline once it has occurred, because it entails unexpected costs or fails to bring anticipated benefits. Thus, Bayesian analysis is useful in understanding how players revise their perceptions of the opponent, but it cannot explain preference change (*see* fn. 33).

There is also some doubt as to the usefulness of assuming Bayesian revision when empirical studies indicate that decision makers revise conservatively. Neither is there a consensus on the desirability of Bayes as a procedure that weights tactical indicators more than strategic assumptions (*see* Stein and Tanter, 1980: 262-263). Finally, the need to derive cardinal utilities invites further complications.

It is doubtful that new mathematical concepts and solutions would overcome the theory's difficulty in dealing with dynamics that involve game transformations. Rather, the limitations of the theory in this respect are intrinsic and stem from its exclusion of psychological factors.[35] In order to understand how games change, it is first necessary to understand how preferences change, but one cannot know that in the absence of any information concerning who the actors are and how they respond to changes in their environment. When preferences are taken as given, analysis is simplified, "but at the cost of drawing attention away from areas that may contain much of the explanatory 'action' in which we are interested" (Jervis, 1988: 325).

To the extent that preference change is a *reactive* process triggered by crisis events that alter decision makers' perceptions, it is a form of *learning* that signifies adaptation to changing circumstances. Learning processes cannot be understood apart from the psychological characteristics of actors. In the absence of such characteristics in game models, there is nothing in the theory (apart from Bayesian learning) that can tell us how actors respond when confronted with a discrepancy between their expectations and actual (intermediate) crisis outcomes. It appears, then, that rules of preference change cannot be deduced directly from the game matrix; rather, they must be derived inductively.[36] There is a body of research in the psychological literature that can guide theoretical expectations with respect to crisis learning.

The question concerning the appropriate approach to render game-theoretic models more amenable to dynamic analysis can now be answered in general terms. Given the multitude of factors that may affect decision makers' payoffs in a crisis, the modeling of crisis dynamics cannot make satisfactory progress without a prior systematic attempt at deriving a set of empirical generalizations regarding preference change. Once regularities concerning actors' responses to the consequences of their choices are established, games corresponding to discrete points in time can be meaningfully tied and related. As Welsh (1971: 430) notes, "inductive logic must be introduced if game theory is to develop into a basis for an empirical theory of crisis." (For a more general argument, *see* Simon, 1985.)

This approach is not without its costs, for the introduction of exogenous psychological factors reduces the parsimony of the theory.[37] The tradeoff should therefore be carefully considered: Models that place excessive emphasis on the decision-making process itself are unlikely to supplement game models but rather to compete with them. On the other hand, "less extreme versions which leave a role for intentional behavior will suggest relevant empirical factors that affect strategic behavior" (Snidal, 1985: 42). Thus, one of Snidal's suggestions is that preferences be theoretically specified in advance of the game model. Such an approach is employed in Chapter 2 for the specification of players' crisis preferences.

It is appropriate to conclude this section with a brief mention of Leng's (1988) work, which aptly demonstrates the possibility of linking game-theoretic models of crisis with data-based findings, in this case related to intercrisis learning. In an earlier (1983) study of bargaining behavior in recurrent crises, Leng discovered that winners of past confrontations tend to attribute their victory to effective management strategies, hence repeating their past behavior. Losers, on the other hand, tend to reason that their loss was due to an insufficient demonstration of resolve; therefore, in a subsequent dispute with the same opponent, they tend to employ a more coercive bargaining strategy.

Leng (1988) applied these findings to the analysis of four crisis-learning games. Specifically, he assumed that players choose their initial strategy in accordance with the outcome of a preceding crisis, as noted above; thereafter, the players proceed in a strictly rational manner, following the logic of the theory of moves. The games were solved first under these conditions and then under the assumption that opening moves were not fixed by past experience. The result was that the players fared better in the latter case, with the most effective initial strategy being a cooperative opening move, followed by tit-for-tat bargaining.

Leng's study provides an interesting and innovative example of how factors that are exogenous to the game matrix can be brought to bear on traditional game-theoretic analysis. Of particular importance is the implication that strategic rationality—such as the nonmyopic calculation posited by the theory of moves—can be associated with rationality that concerns belief formation (in this case, learning from previous crises). Although Leng does not state the connection explicitly, this could be done in future research. First, however, one must examine the common belief that the two conceptions of rationality are incompatible. This is done in the next section.

The Rationality Assumption

A major bone of contention between the psychological and rational-choice approaches concerns the rationality assumption. The psychological approach argues that the assumption is largely unrealistic and thus of limited value: Decision making more often than not involves significant departures from rationality. The rational-choice approach, by contrast, argues that political behavior is intentional and goal-seeking, and can therefore be profitably studied by means of rational models. The purpose of this section is to raise some general points with respect to this debate, which impinges on the prospects for a model that incorporates elements from both approaches.[38]

First, the controversy concerning the empirical justification for the rationality assumption often obscures an important point—the two approaches differ in their conception of rationality and its requirements. It is important, therefore, that the meaning of the term be stated precisely.

Although the extant literature on rationality abounds with definitions, a distinction is often made between *substantive rationality* and *procedural rationality*. Simon (1976) argues that "behavior is substantively rational when it is appropriate to the achievement of given goals within the limits imposed by given conditions and constraints" (p. 130). On the other hand, "behavior is procedurally rational when it is the outcome of appropriate deliberation" (p. 131).[39]

Substantive rationality is typical of most models of rational choice, which drop the condition of rationality in belief (Benn and Mortimore, 1976b: 158). Psychological theories of decision-making, on the other hand, are concerned primarily with procedural rationality: They concentrate on the process by which an actor forms its beliefs about the relationship between its goals and its choices. Hence, these theories emphasize misperception and cognitive deficiencies.

This difference between the two approaches has often resulted in unjustified criticism of the rationality assumption in rational-choice models. Whereas the empirical findings of the psychological approach may cast doubt on the theoretical usefulness of procedural rationality,[40] they do not as yet undermine the utility of substantive rationality, which takes the beliefs of actors as given.[41] In other words, it is possible to conceive of a situation in which nonrational or nonanalytic decisional procedures yield an optimal decision in the game-theoretic sense. As Abelson (1976: 60) has noted, practical (substantive) rationality "is consistent with the intrusion into belief-formation of epistemically irrelevant factors or with the omission of epistemically relevant factors, according to the practical decision context of the individual" (*see* also Mandel, 1986: 252–53).[42]

This argument is of critical importance: It says, in effect, that the two conceptions of rationality are not necessarily incompatible. The implication is that it is possible, within a single model or theory, to combine both substantive and procedural rationality. This possibility is now being raised in discussions of deterrence (Zagare, 1990) and peace research (Maoz, 1990a).

The second point to be made concerns the tendency of the psychological approach to discount the degree to which it, too, relies on the rationality assumption. Harsanyi (1977: 8) argues that "in most cases we cannot really understand and explain a person's behavior... unless we can interpret it *either as rational behavior* in this particular situation *or* as an *understandable deviation* from rational behavior" (emphasis in original).[43] Bueno de Mesquita (1981: 33) makes a similar point by commenting that "those who question the rationality assumption might do well to ask themselves whether the alternative is more helpful." In other words, whether one argues from rationality or uses it as a benchmark to measure and characterize deviations (in which case it is necessary to argue from rationality to define the ideal type), the rationality assumption is theoretically useful.

The third and final point concerns Simon's (1957) notion of "bounded rationality," which consists of the argument that in complex decision situations, actors do not optimize, but rather satisfice with respect to some predetermined (but adjustable) "level of aspiration." Though this argument merits more attention than can possibly be devoted to it here, it should at least be pointed out that it is not immediately clear that this view is at odds with game-theoretic rationality. Riker and Ordeshook (1973: 21–23), for example, argue that it is entirely consistent with it because "the principle of satisficing is distinguishable from the principle of maximizing only if, under the latter, perfect information is assumed" (p. 22), and if perfect information is required for rationality, "then only God is or can be rational" (ibid.). Furthermore, when the cost of searching for information about additional alternatives is part of the calculus, an optimal strategy may be to satisfice. Similar points are made by others (for example, Benn and Mortimore, 1976b; Tisdell, 1976).

The three points raised here certainly do not exhaust the arguments that may be made in favor of or against the rationality assumption. However, in evaluating the prospects for a model that combines psychological and game-theoretic elements, they at least convey the general message that criticism of the assumption is not insurmountable and need not thwart the effort.

THE OBJECTIVES AND SCOPE OF THE BOOK

The thesis of this chapter can be summarized as follows: Although the psychological and rational-choice approaches provide indispensable perspectives on crisis behavior, neither is adequate in itself—the study of crisis requires a theoretical framework that combines both approaches.

This thesis defines a research agenda that is too broad to be addressed in a single study. A reorientation of the field—which is what the agenda calls for—will require the attention and efforts of more that one researcher, over a long period of time. It will be a while before the new theoretical framework is sufficiently specified to generate the type of theory for which this chapter has argued.

Still, this book takes a significant step in the proposed direction: It suggests one possible solution to the problem of integrating the psychological and rational-choice perspectives, and develops a model of crisis behavior that is based on this conception. Although the model is essentially game-theoretic, it does incorporate psychological variables. Moreover, the model is conceived and specified as a component of a broader theoretical framework that includes several possibilities for combining psychological and game-theoretic elements.

Several points should be noted about the crisis model developed in this book. First, the model is based on a theoretical—rather than empirical—specification of players' preferences. As Chapter 2 explains, this method defines five typical crisis actors, whose interaction produces a game-theoretic typology of crises. This typology, in turn, differentiates among crisis situations, thus providing for the variability that is lacking in the crisis conception of the psychological approach. Moreover, because the typology is game-theoretic, this variability is expressed in terms of the "structure of the situation," which captures the interactive aspect of crisis that stimulus-response models neglect.

Second, the derivation of crisis preferences is based on *psychological variables*, both situational and personality-related. Although these variables appear as independent variables in the model, in a larger framework, they could be cast as dependent or intervening variables. In this way, psychological theories that specify the antecedent conditions of these variables could be brought to bear on the model (for example, the determinants of attitudes toward the opponent, or the factors that influence decision makers' perception of their opponent).

Third, the specification of parameters—attitudes and perceptions—that determine crisis preferences enables observations about the consequences of preference change. As noted above, the incorporation into an enlarged framework of variables that influence attitudes and perceptions can help predict midcrisis changes in preferences and, hence, the conditions under which transformations over games can be expected to occur.

Fourth, the classification of crises developed in this book is based, as noted above, on the interaction of different decision-maker types: hard-liners, middle-liners, and soft-liners. These types have "equivalents" in the psychological literature, where they are defined in terms of "belief systems," or "operational codes". It is possible, then, to relate the game-theoretic types to their "psychological counterparts." In addition, the differentiation of crisis actors into types allows us to study each type's behavior with respect to crisis initiation, choice of crisis strategy, misperception, and deception (*see* Chapter 3).

Similarly, the specification of multiple sets of preferences (types) opens up the possibility of group and coalition analysis (*see* Chapter 5). In this way, the behavior expected to occur in a group setting—which is of much concern to the psychological approach—can be compared to the behavior expected of unitary actors and to actual crisis behavior.

Finally, the game-theoretic model introduces initiation into the picture, an aspect of crisis that is neglected in the largely defender-oriented psychological literature. The model enables the prediction of the conditions under which different player types are expected to initiate crises (*see* Chapter 3). Moreover, these conditions are expressed in terms of variables that have equivalents in the psychological literature (for example, threat perception and frustration).

Having described the objectives of this study, we conclude with a brief discussion of its scope. A *crisis* is conceived in this book to be a process in which the demand (voluntary or coerced) by one state to change or preserve the status quo forces a policy choice on another state, and generates for the parties involved the perception of a high probability of war.

Note that this definition: (1) identifies the source of a crisis to be a demand for a change in or preservation of the status quo;[44] (2) posits a bilateral interaction; and (3) specifies a high probability of war as characterizing the perception of the parties. Hence, this definition limits the scope of the book to crises that are deliberately initiated, bilateral, security-related, and adversarial. It excludes unintended crises, multilateral crises, economic crises, and crises between and among allies.

The research agenda that this book supports is certainly meant to apply to a broader class of crises. However, given the complexity of the task that this agenda calls for, it is logical initially to confine attention to one category of crises, provided it is not too narrow. In our case, in fact, the definition of crisis and the scope it implies are not as restrictive as they might appear.

First, if unintended crises are crises in which the initiator is unaware that its behavior is perceived as threatening by another party (Maoz, 1982a), then the coerced demand made by the threatened party to preserve the status quo (that is, terminate the threatening behavior) transforms the situation into a crisis by our definition. Thus, the unintended behavior can be considered the *precipitant* of the crisis rather than its initiation (*see* Snyder and Diesing, 1977, Chapter 1).[45]

Second, although this study is limited to bilateral crises (and employs two-person game theory), multilateral crises can sometimes be presented as bilateral crises between *coalitions* of actors. This, in fact, is the approach taken in the case study of Chapter 5.

Finally, security-related crises between adversarial states constitute the category of crises that has been accorded the greatest attention in the literature. This is not surprising, given the momentous implications that such crises have had for world politics. Thus, even if we focus on these crises alone, the phenomena we study are guaranteed to be central and significant.

NOTES

1. For a recent, comprehensive review of the psychological literature on crisis decision making, *see* Holsti (1989); for a general, multilevel treatment of information processing in foreign policy decision making, *see* Vertzberger (1990); and for an in-depth survey of the game-theoretic literature on interstate conflict, *see* Gates and Humes (1989).

2. For comparison, systemic definitions employ objective, interunit characteristics as criteria for the existence of crisis. Thus, for example, "a crisis is, in some way, a 'change of state' in the flow of international political actions. It must be some kind of identifiable departure from a pre-existing and temporary status quo in the stream of events of international relations" (McClelland, 1968: 160).

3. In Holsti's words, a crisis is "a situation of unanticipated threat to important values and restricted decision time" (p. 9).

4. The complete definition is the following: "An international crisis is a sequence of interactions between the governments of two or more sovereign states in severe conflict, short of actual war, but involving the perception of a dangerously high probability of war"

(p. 6). On p. 7, they state that this perception is by the governments involved, implying that a crisis exists only when both (or all) parties perceive the probability of war as high.

5. Contrary to Snyder and Diesing's definition, however, Lebow's definition only requires one actor to perceive the probability of war as significant, providing for situations in which one state perceives itself to be in a crisis, whereas the other does not.

6. These modifications are the following: (a) "surprise" as a necessary condition was excluded; (b) "short" time was replaced by "finite" time for response; (c) a crisis could be induced by the external or the internal environment; (d) the perceived threat was to "basic values" rather than to "high-priority goals"; and (e) the condition of "high probability of involvement in military hostilities" was added (p. 3). Brecher then defined crisis as a "situation with three necessary and sufficient conditions, deriving from a change in its external or internal environment. All three conditions are perceptions held by the highest-level decision-makers: (1) *threat to basic values*, with a simultaneous or subsequent (2) *high probability of involvement in military hostilities*, and the awareness of (3) *finite time for response to the external value threat*" (p. 1; emphasis in original).

7. "An international crisis is a process in which the national actors involved are willing or forced to make a trade-off between highly valued but mutually incompatible objectives. This trade-off situation involves a rapid and acute change in the perceptions of threats and promises for each of the individual participants, thus generating acute and rapid changes in the systemic balance (status quo) and in the relations among states" (p. 219). Note that this definition also takes the perceptions of decision makers, whether initiators or defenders, as the starting point of a crisis. These perceptions are a requirement for the systemic-level changes that follow, and since the latter are implied as a criterion in the definition, all situations characterized as crisis are also those involving "acute and rapid changes" in systemic variables. Maoz's definition, then, is broader in one sense and more restrictive in another: It allows for initiated crises, but requires that they involve significant systemic changes.

8. Note that Lebow's defender-oriented definition of a crisis still allows for the inclusion of initiated crises in his typology. However, because his definition assumes the defender's viewpoint, cases falling in this category (of initiated crises) qualify as a crisis only once they are perceived as such by the defending party. The implication for initiated crises, then, is that both sides perceive themselves to be in a crisis.

9. For a good discussion of the advantages and disadvantages of systemic and perceptual definitions of crisis, *see* Maoz (1982a, 1982b).

10. The discussion omits studies that are not concerned specifically with crisis behavior. For a critical review of work on the effects of personality on political behavior in general, *see* Maoz (1985).

11. The psychopathological approach does not characterize Lebow's study as a whole; however, analyses in this mode are employed in some instances.

12. Creary (1984) has noted that there may be cultural differences in the perception of crisis (as a result, for example, of differences in the perception of time). This possibility has not been sufficiently explored in the crisis literature, even though its implications could be momentous for a theory that predicts behavior from actors' perception of the situation (*see* below).

13. Following this recommendation, Brecher (1980: 29–30), for example, examined the relationship between stress and coping processes and mechanisms, and between stress levels and choice patterns. The effects of stress on choice were decomposed into eight

components: core input(s), cost, importance, complexity, systemic domain, process (rational, effective, or routine), activity, and novelty of the choice.

It should be noted that in this major effort to evaluate the consequences of stress, the initiation factor was again largely neglected. Yet if threat is not a necessary ingredient in the perceptions of crisis initiators (as was mentioned before), it follows that stress, conceived as a function of threat, does not necessarily characterize the decisional process of crisis initiators (Maoz, 1982a: 219). However, the perception of opportunities or promises, especially when combined with perceived time pressure, could result in crisis-induced stress for crisis initiators as well.

14. There is contrasting evidence as to the quality, in the decisional process, of the search activity (that is, whether the search for alternative courses of action is increased or decreased); contrasting evidence as to the evaluation stage (whether fewer or more alternatives are evaluated relative to noncrisis situations, and the quality of the evaluation in terms of values engaged and the consequences considered); mixed views with respect to the choice stage itself (to what extent optimization criteria are employed); and some consensus as to the revision stage (how new incoming information is treated) (Tanter, 1978).

15. There is no general consensus on the characteristics and requirements of the analytic model. Variants may be found in Allison (1971); Holsti (1972); George (1972); Stein and Tanter (1980); Maoz (1985; 1990a); and Janis (1989).

16. A third model, the bureaucratic politics model, has been suggested by Allison (1971) and Allison and Halperin (1972). This model emphasizes group decisional processes; such processes, however, are not at odds with the analytic mode of decision making, as Snyder and Diesing (1977) have argued. Their findings, too, indicate that bureaucratic role does not have the predicted effect on decision makers' attitudes (p. 408).

17. Kahneman and Tversky's work in psychology has spurred much interest in the applicability of prospect theory to the study of international relations, including crises. For an excellent summary and evaluation of this literature, *see* Levy (1992a, 1992b).

18. These characteristics are conveniently summarized in Stein and Tanter (1980: 65) and in Maoz (1985: 42).

19. For a critique of this study, and a rebuttal, *see* Welch (1989) and Herek, Janis, and Huth (1989), respectively.

20. Janis and Mann argue that cognitive consistency "may be a weak end in many individuals" (p. 86), thus downplaying the significance of this principle, which is central for Jervis. *See* Lebow (1981: 111–15) for a comparison of Jervis's theory with that of Janis and Mann. Etheredge (1985) also argues that defects in decisional processes stem from motivational sources (*see* The Basic Elements of the Psychological Approach).

21. The issue of rationality and its different definitions are examined in The Rationality Assumption.

22. For recent applications and extensions of the theory of moves, *see* Kilgour and Zagare (1987), Aaftink (1989), Zagare (1987, 1989), Leng (1988), and Brams and Mor (forthcoming). Zagare (1984b) and Kilgour (1984) examine the implications for nonmyopic equilibrium of varying the number of moves and countermoves that players can make. Brams (forthcoming) offers the most comprehensive and up-to-date version of the theory of moves.

23. James and Harvey (1989) have tested a modified version of the Brams and Kilgour model by means of aggregate empirical data.

24. Thus Wagner (1989: 204) writes that "the risk of conflict entailed by the blockade seems most plausibly understood, not as something that the American used to put pressure on the Soviets so that they would back down, but as something that allowed the Soviets to put pressure on the Americans so that Kennedy's threat of subsequent military action would seem more credible. And since the Soviets had good reason to want to know how seriously to take Kennedy's threats, this was something they were not averse to doing."

25. For a more general argument concerning the treatment of strategic problems as decision theory problems—the so-called Robinson Crusoe fallacy—*see* Tsebelis (1989). Bendor and Hammond (1992) show how such a fallacy in Allison's rational actor model affects his analysis of the Cuban missile crisis.

26. The game-theoretic approach, by contrast, introduces diversity via the game structure. *See* Snidal (1985) and Snyder and Diesing (1977) on this point.

27. *See* Lebow's definitions of justification of hostility crises (p. 25); spinoff crises (p. 41); and brinkmanship crises (p. 57).

28. Wagner (1989) demonstrates that one consequence of studying crisis decision-making in a strategic context is a greater sensitivity to the complexity of the task facing actors in crisis bargaining: "In the best of circumstances rational learning is more difficult than much of the psychological literature on crisis suggests, and thus 'misperception' may not be so easily attributed to faulty reasoning as at least some of this literature implies" (p. 203).

29. Rosenau (1967: 209) eloquently argues for the need to tie the decisional phenomena with which decision-making theory is concerned with the political environment that exists outside the minds of decision makers.

30. The concept of "game" refers to "any social situation involving two or more actors (players) in which the interests of the players are interconnected and interdependent" (Zagare, 1984a: 7). Also, as Davis (1983: xiv) remarks, "It is this blending of players' mutual and conflicting interests that makes game theory fascinating."

31. Preference structure is a highly compact form of representing the "distribution of interests" in a crisis. This is done by means of the simultaneous "mapping" of payoffs over outcomes. The notion of interdependence, without which the structure concept would be meaningless, is represented in terms of the joint nature of outcomes, which are the result of intersecting strategies. In other words, what actually transpires in a crisis is the product of the implemented choices of states, none of which totally controls the outcomes of their unilateral acts—these are jointly determined. Snidal (1985: 40) has expressed this particular conception as follows: "game theory allows for an autonomy in state choice even as it predicts and explains those choices deterministically through an understanding of the overall strategic interaction."

32. *See*, for example, the exchange between Zinnes and Robinson (cited in Hermann, 1972a: 18–19), following the latter's criticism of game theory as a theory that "does not include the concept [of crisis]" (p. 27).

33. To be precise, it is the determinants of preference change that are exogenous to the theory. As Ferreira, Gilboa, and Maschler (1992) show, game theory can cope with situations in which utilities change during play. However, even if we imagine a Bayesian player with a probability distribution over various possible utility functions, the nature of the probability distribution and its determinants must still be derived exogenously.

34. At an elementary level, the theory defines a (pure) strategy as "a detailed description of what a player should do in each eventuality" (Luce and Raiffa, 1957: 55). In that sense, there is a built-in element of dynamics in the theory. Axelrod (1984) provides an interesting application of this conception of strategy: To the extent that an actor would in fact follow a contingent plan from beginning to end (as the participants in Axelrod's tournament of Prisoners' Dilemma did), an observer would detect changes of strategy over iterated plays of the same game.

Although we cannot discuss here the view of international processes that this conception of strategy implies (for a detailed discussion, *see* Maoz, 1990a), it should be noted that the assumption of fixed games, which is implicit in this view, may be reasonable when the processes one is analyzing are relatively invariant over the long run. Thus, the Prisoners' Dilemma and Stag Hunt games have been invoked in studies concerned with such issues as state behavior under anarchy, international cooperation, and regimes (for example, Jervis, 1978; Keohane, 1984; Oye, 1986). This assumption, however, is not very realistic in the context of crisis, where the circumstances facing decision makers change rapidly, and influence their perception of constraints and opportunities.

35. One should qualify this statement somewhat since the psychological characteristics of players are implicitly reflected in their payoffs (*see* Luce and Raiffa, 1957: 48, 104). However, in order to theorize about crisis dynamics in terms of game transformations, these characteristics need to be featured in the model as distinct variables. This, in turn, requires that they be explicitly stated.

36. Leng's (1988) study is an example of such an approach (*see* below).

37. Rapoport (1966: 206) has argued that the incorporation of psychological elements into the theory would render it a behavioral one.

38. Comprehensive discussions are readily available in the literature. Two good collections of essays on rationality are Benn and Mortimore (1976a) and Elster (1986).

39. Gibson (1976: 117) likewise distinguishes between *practical rationality*—"the rationality of the action which consists simply in the recognition of the correctness of the action, given the belief"—and *epistemic rationality*, or "rationality of the belief about means to an end, which consists of the recognition of the correctness of the belief, given the available evidence for it."

40. These findings are by no means conclusive or noncontroversial. As noted before, the evidence is mixed, and certain studies do provide empirical support for the rational/analytic mode of decision making.

41. There are nevertheless empirical concerns that impinge directly on the game matrix itself. George and Smoke (1974: 74–75) mention four: (1) values, which decision makers may find difficult to order consistently and unambiguously; (2) outcomes, which decision makers may have problems defining; (3) courses of action, which decision makers may not be able to relate to outcomes; and (4) information, which decision makers may not have enough of to assess values, outcomes, and courses of action. These difficulties are best dealt with when they arise in the context of specific empirical cases. For now, it is sufficient to note that although actors in game-theoretic models are assumed to know all the information contained in the game matrix, ordinal preferences are not so demanding, and the theory admits games of imperfect and incomplete information.

42. A different issue concerns the nature of explanations one may derive on the basis of substantive rationality. Gibson (1976: 127) makes the argument that "a proper explanation requires that there be some reason for accepting the explaining facts which is

independent of the fact to be explained." In other words, in trying to explain why a particular course of action was adopted by an actor, it is unsatisfactory simply to argue that the actor believed such course would promote its goal when the belief itself is inferred from the actor's goals and known choice. Gibson's conclusion is that some epistemic (procedural) rationality must be attributed to the actor (p. 129).

Explanation in game-theoretic models consists of showing that a particular strategy was chosen because, given the preferences of the actor, it was the optimal strategy to choose (by whatever standard of optimality is used). "Belief in optimality" is inferred from the actor's preferences and known action, and then proposed as explanation. It is possible, however, to conceive of a situation in which an actor decides on its strategy by tossing a coin (not in the mixed-strategy sense). A model that incorporates psychological elements avoids this problem, because it does not take the formation of beliefs as given.

43. This is evident even in attempts to formulate a distinct psychological paradigm of decision making (*see* Kinder and Weiss, 1978).

44. The definition thus identifies the crisis initiator as the party that demands a change in, or a preservation of, the existing state of affairs, and the defender as the target of initiation—the party in the position to grant the demands of the initiator.

45. It should be noted that the empirical distinction between initiators and defenders is not always clear-cut, even when rigorous definitions are supplied. Consider the Cuban missile crisis. Were the Soviets the initiators (in installing the missiles), as Lebow (1981: Chapter 4) argues, or were they the defenders (against the American challenge of the blockade), as Snyder and Diesing (1977: 568–69) claim?

The distinction is complicated further by the fact that the terms initiator and defender carry a normative connotation that, at least in the Western world, is related to the legitimacy accorded to the status quo. As Maoz (1982a: 215) writes: "The status quo orientation of western strategic thought has led to a predisposition to view international crises as generically 'bad' and disruptive processes." Logically, then, crisis initiation is perceived to be a foreign policy tool employed by actors intent on undermining the status quo. It becomes important, therefore, that one's own role in a crisis be seen as defense, and the opponent's as initiation.

In addition, what appears to be initiation may be a defense against an earlier initiation, which in itself is a defense against an earlier initiation, and so on. Finally, actors do not always agree on the arrangements and norms that define the status quo. Therefore, whether a particular demand or behavior is a departure from the status quo or not depends on the observer.

2

The Crisis Model I: Player Types and the Composite Matrix

The basic argument of the previous chapter was that a general theory of international crisis must address both the strategic and psychological aspects of this type of conflict. Unfortunately, the development of such a theory has been obstructed by the continuing breach between the psychological and rational-choice approaches: Whereas the former has concentrated on decisional processes to the neglect of strategic interaction, the latter has focused on the strategic aspect of crisis while ignoring intra-unit processes. The omissions in both approaches have resulted in two competing but equally deficient conceptions of crisis.

The purpose of this and the next chapter is to develop a model of crisis that addresses some of the theoretical concerns raised in the previous chapter. To this end, two related tasks will be undertaken. The first task is to develop a preliminary theoretical framework that can serve as a future bridge between the psychological and game-theoretic approaches. This framework will require much additional development and elaboration before it can give rise to a general theory of crisis, but the specification of such a framework—however rudimentary—is an essential first step on the road to a comprehensive theory.

The second task is to strengthen the empirical foundations of game-theoretic models of crisis. This will be done in two ways: first, by developing a game-based typology of crises that is representative of the empirical population of cases—such a typology is needed if an empirically based game theory of crisis is to emerge; second, by providing a theoretical basis for understanding the formation and transformation of players' preferences. This component is necessary for a game-based theory of crisis to be truly dynamic, namely capable of explaining why decision makers sometimes change their crisis preferences and move from one game situation to another. It is here that the link with the psychological approach will be forged, because the sources of players' preferences will be specified in terms of psychological variables.

In other words, the model to be developed in this and the next chapter is conceived to be the focal point of a theoretical framework within which a general theory of crisis can one day be constructed. Because such a general theory will have to integrate strategic and psychological variables (as argued in the previous chapter), the framework and model presented in this book are specified in accordance with this requirement: They provide a bridge to the psychological approach and actually incorporate some attitude- and perception-related variables.

The crisis framework and model will be introduced in two stages. The present chapter discusses the source of actors' preferences, and shows how attitudes and perceptions interact to produce typical preference structures, or "types." This is done in the first section, which also looks at some of the consequences of attitude and perception change, and presents the rationale for making preferences the focus of a general theory of crisis. In the second section, the different types of players are combined in a large matrix—the *composite matrix*—consisting of the set of crisis games. Several empirical interpretations of this matrix are suggested.

Whereas the present chapter looks at attitudes, perceptions, and preferences, the next chapter examines their consequences in terms of crisis strategy and crisis outcome. Specifically, the chapter explores the conditions under which different types of players initiate crises, traces the effects of players' misperceptions on the crisis outcome, and establishes the conditions in which players choose to engage in deception.

THE DERIVATION OF CRISIS PREFERENCES

Introduction

In order to develop a game-based theory of international crisis, it is necessary to advance beyond the study and *ad hoc* modeling of individual crises. This latter approach has resulted in numerous analyses of single games, whose interrelationships have not been specified. A theoretical approach to crisis, on the other hand, must rest on the description of the population of cases to be studied. Specifically, one needs to specify a set of games that can be considered representative of the empirical population of international crises.

There are basically two methods of deriving the set of "crisis games." The first has been employed by Snyder and Diesing (1977), and it consists of "fitting" games to a preselected sample of empirical cases. This inductive approach yields a set of games that may or may not be representative of past crises; in either case, however, it cannot anticipate new patterns of crisis interaction (or "future crisis games"). In addition, this approach does not hypothesize about the source of players' preferences; hence the reason for the applicability of one game situation rather than another remains an accident of history.

A second approach consists of: (1) imposing a few substantively based restrictions on preferences (to prevent nonsensical rankings and to reduce the number of games in the resulting set); (2) working out all the logically possible combinations of preference rankings for an individual player, subject to the restrictions imposed earlier; and (3) listing all the possible combinations of individual preferences to define the set of two-person crisis games.

This second approach is based on an *a priori* specification of players' preferences and, therefore, is not restricted by the representativeness of any empirical sample of cases. If the restrictions on preferences reflect realistic assumptions, the resulting set of crisis games should be representative of past crises and suggestive of future ones. This statement is valid, however, to the extent that additional simplifying assumptions—beyond those that justify restrictions on preferences—produce games that capture the essence of empirical crises. Thus, for example, if a 2 x 2 game is used to model single crises, then the assumptions of two players, two strategies, and (possibly) strict preferences will have to be made as well.[1]

Still, this second approach, like the first one, does not provide a theoretical basis for the source of preferences, and it is not clear why a particular game should be applicable to a particular situation. The players, too, remain anonymous, in the sense that their preferences are not explicitly tied to their beliefs and attitudes, or to the objective features of the situation. Yet any theory of crisis that aims to be dynamic requires that the source of preferences be considered, or else changes in preferences cannot be explained.

A third possible approach to the derivation of the set of crisis games, then, consists of specifying the parameters that determine players' preferences in crisis.[2] These parameters should be able to relate the characteristics of decision makers and their environment to their crisis preferences. In the remainder of this section, we will present a set of parameters that can be used to derive the set of crisis games. First, though, the crisis game itself needs to be defined.

The Crisis Game

The crisis game is essentially the "Generalized Bargaining Game" suggested by Snyder and Diesing (1977: 40). In this generalized game—presented in Figure 2.1—each player has two broadly defined strategies: *accommodation* ("C" in the Figure), which consists of making concessions or intentionally signaling one's willingness to make them if the opponent does likewise; and *coercion* ("D" in the Figure), which consists of an effort to use coercive means—threats, displays of force, and use of force short of war—to force the opponent's hand.

It is clearly a simplification to present as dichotomous the strategic choices facing decision makers in crisis. In fact, strategies often consist of a mix of coercive and accommodating tactics.[3] Still, the 2 x 2 game model "brings out the basic structure of crises" (Snyder and Diesing, 1977: 40). It captures well the fundamental dilemma of cooperation versus noncooperation confronted by crisis decision makers: how to make concessions without appearing to be weak and thereby inviting exploitation.[4] In addition, the simplicity of the 2 x 2 game is

Figure 2.1
The Crisis Game

	COOPERATE (C)	DEFECT (D)
COOPERATE (C)	CC Mutual compromise	CD Victory by Column
DEFECT (D)	DC Victory by Row	DD Mutual escalation, possibly to war

desirable in a model whose variability derives from the specification of multiple preferences sets.

The four outcomes in the crisis game are defined as follows:

1. *Outcome 1 (CC)*: Both players are willing to make concessions. This results in a compromise agreement, which defines a new status quo acceptable to both parties.[5]
2. *Outcome 2 (CD)*: One player is willing to make concessions, but the other stands firm. This results in a new status quo favoring the party standing firm. The latter party is then the "winner" in the crisis.
3. *Outcome 3 (DC)*: Same as outcome 2, with the roles of the parties reversed.
4. *Outcome 4 (DD)*: Neither party is willing to make concessions. This results in deadlock, with subsequent escalation leading possibly to war.

Having defined the crisis game, we can now turn to the parameters that determine players' preferences in this game.

The Parameters of Crisis Preferences

There are two types of demands that can be put forth by actors in a crisis situation: a demand to change the status quo (the initiator) and a demand to preserve the status quo (the defender) (*see* Snyder and Diesing, 1977: 12). We begin the discussion with the specification of an assumption about the basic goal (BG) of all crisis actors, whether initiators or defenders: Crisis actors prefer that all or some of their crisis demands be acknowledged rather than none of their demands be acknowledged.

The outcomes of the crisis game can be redefined in those terms, as follows:

1. *The DC or CD outcome*: an acknowledgment of one side's demands.
2. *The CC outcome*: a partial acknowledgment of each side's demands.
3. *The DD outcome*: an acknowledgment of one side's demands, based on the expectations of the players concerning a victory or a defeat at this outcome (*see* below).

In terms of the outcomes of the crisis game, then, the basic-goal assumption (stated for the row player) says that all crisis actors prefer DC and CC to CD: As defined above, at DC and CC all or some of their demands are acknowledged, whereas at CD none of their demands are acknowledged.[6]

We turn now to three parameters that can be seen as interacting to determine individual players' crisis preferences:

1. *Attitudes Toward the Opponent*—attitudes that reflect views and beliefs about the relationship between conflict outcomes and national security. These attitudes may stem from fundamental beliefs about international conflict (belief systems), or they may be context-dependent and therefore subject to change even in the short run.
2. *Attitudes Toward Loss*—attitudes that reflect dispositions toward defeat.
3. *Capabilities*—decision makers' perceptions of relative capabilities in conflict situations.

Let us examine each parameter in turn.

Attitudes Toward the Opponent. Decision makers in an interactive (conflict) environment realize that control over situations is not unilateral, and that peace and security can be maintained only as long as they are preserved by both sides to a relationship. What can, however, induce the opponent to abstain from challenges to the status quo in the future?

There are two basic beliefs about the relationship between conflict outcomes and national security. The first states that in order to prevent the opponent from threatening the security of the player in the future, the principle that should be adhered to is that: It is better that the opponent have none of its demands acknowledged ("lose") than some of its demands acknowledged ("win something") (A1).

This principle reflects the attitude of "peace through victory," or "peace by empire" as it was termed by Aron (1966). It is generally characteristic of a hard-line view of international politics, according to which power, firmness, and resolve are the means of protecting national security. Only an opponent who is proven weak can be expected to observe the peace. This attitude is reflected, for example, in the demand for an unconditional surrender of the opponent (for example, World Wars I and II) and in security doctrines that emphasize superiority over parity.

The second principle reflects the opposite basic belief, according to which: It is better that the opponent have some of its demands acknowledged ("win something") than none of its demands acknowledged ("lose") (A2). Thus, the way to ensure peace is through a willingness to consider the security concerns and interests of the opponent, and to attempt a compromise that will satisfy both sides to the conflict. An opponent who has a stake in preserving the new (postconflict) status quo becomes a partner in maintaining the peace. This is the "peace without victory" principle.[7] It was advocated, for example, by President Woodrow Wilson prior to the American entry into World War I, and by Henry Kissinger during the 1973 Middle East war.

The two incompatible attitudes toward the opponent imply alternative rules of preference ranking. Thus, A1 implies that $DC > CC$ (for Row), because at DC, none of the opponent's demands are acknowledged, whereas at CC some of its demands are acknowledged. A2, on the other hand, implies that $CC > DC$.

Attitudes Toward Loss. There are two basic attitudes to the prospect of defeat. The first is reflected in the principle: Make opponent pay (L1). This principle states that when a player is faced with the prospect of defeat, it should make the opponent pay the highest cost possible for "victory." The biblical hero Samson revealed such an attitude in action when, upon crying "let me die with the Philistines," he pushed the columns of the Philistine temple, killing many of his captors as well as himself. When such a principle is incorporated into or underlies a strategic doctrine, its purpose is to deter the opponent by letting it know that victory is going to be costly.

A different attitude to defeat is reflected in the principle: Cut costs (L2). This principle states that, in the face of defeat, it is better to lose less than lose more through useless resistance. That is, if loss is unavoidable, an actor should minimize its costs by terminating resistance.

Prior to discussing the implications of the attitude-toward-loss parameter for the ranking of crisis outcomes, we present the third parameter, upon which this ranking depends.

Capabilities. Beyond attitudes and beliefs, there are the "hard facts," or at least their perception by the actors. Attitudes toward victory and defeat, of oneself or of the opponent, become operative when a victory or a loss situation develops. The actors' *expectations* concerning a win or a loss depend on their perceptions of the balance of capabilities, most important of which is military capability.[8] Thus, an actor may perceive itself to be: stronger (C1) than the opponent, or weaker (C2) than the opponent.[9]

By itself, the capabilities parameter does not imply any rules of preference ranking. However, it defines the DD outcome (in perceptual terms) as an expected victory or an expected defeat for a player, and therefore interacts with the other parameters to imply a preference ranking for that player.

Thus, the capabilities parameter affects both the attitude-toward-the-opponent parameter and the attitude-toward-loss parameter. Specifically, it affects them as follows:

1. When DD is defined by the capabilities parameter as an expected victory for a player (that is, the player expects to win at DD), A1 implies DD > CC, as well as DC > CC: at both outcomes—DD and DC—the player is in a position to refuse to acknowledge the demands of the opponent, which, by A1, it prefers to the acknowledgment of some of the demands of the opponent (that is, CC). On the other hand, if the player expects to win at DD and has an A2 attitude, then CC > DD, as well as CC > DC.
2. When DD is defined by the capabilities parameter as an expected defeat for a player (that is, the player expects to lose at DD), L1 implies DD > CD: both outcomes—DD and CD—are defined by the player as a loss, but at the DD outcome the opponent will incur a much higher cost for its victory, which is what the L1 player prefers. On the other hand, if the player expects to lose at DD and has an L2 attitude, then CD > DD.

Deriving Players' Preferences

Whereas the basic-goal assumption applied to all players, the other three parameters consist of pairs of alternative attitudes and perceptions. These three parameters, then, define six alternative situations, as follows:

1. A1-C1
2. A1-C2-L1
3. A1-C2-L2
4. A2-C1
5. A2-C2-L1
6. A2-C2-L2

Note that the L parameter—attitude toward loss—is applicable only to players who expect to lose: These are players who perceive themselves to be weaker, that is, have capability perception C2.

Figure 2.2
The Derivation of Crisis Preferences

C1	C2	
	L1	L2
A1 DC,DD > CC (A1) CC > CD (BG) DC > DD (AA) DC > DD > CC > CD **HL**	DC > CC (A1) DD > CD (L1) CC > CD,DD (BG) DC > CC > DD > CD **ML1**	DC > CC (A1) CD > DD (L2) CC > CD,DD (BG) DC > CC > CD > DD **SL1**
A2 CC > DC (A2) DC,DD > CD (BG) DC > DD (AA) CC > DC > DD > CD **ML2**	CC > DC (A2) DD > CD (L1) DC > CD,DD (BG) CC > DC > DD > CD **ML2**	CC > DC (A2) CD > DD (L2) DC > CD,DD (BG) CC > DC > CD > DD **SL2**

Figure 2.2 shows the crisis preferences that derive from each of the six situations listed above. As an example, consider the derivation of preferences for the situation characterized as A1-C2-L1 (that is, the middle cell in the first row of the Figure; all preferences are given for the row player in the crisis game):

1. The player has the attitude A1. This attitude, as we saw above, implies the ranking DC > CC.
2. The player perceives itself to be the weaker party (C2). Therefore, in addition to the possibility of losing by surrendering (CD), the player also expects to lose if the crisis becomes a trial of strength (DD). C2, then, defines DD as an expected loss, in addition to CD.
3. The player has the attitude (L1). This implies, as we saw above, that DD > CD.
4. All players are assumed, by the basic-goal assumption, to prefer that all or some of their demands be acknowledged rather than none of their demands

be acknowledged. This implies that CC > CD, but since the player expects that none of its demands will be acknowledged at DD as well (step 2), CC > CD,DD.

From steps 1–4, we can conclude that, since DC > CC (step 1), CC > CD,DD (step 4), and DD > CD (step 3), the preference ranking of the player has to be DC > CC > DD > CD.

As a second example, consider the derivation of preferences in the A2-C1 situation (that is, the left-hand cell in the second row of the Figure):

1. The player perceives itself to be the stronger party (C1). Therefore, in addition to the possibility of having all of its demands acknowledged as a result of the opponent's capitulation (DC), the player also expects all its demands to be acknowledged if the crisis becomes a trial of strength (DD). C1, then, defines DD as an expected "victory," in addition to DC.
2. The player has the attitude A2. This implies CC > DC, as we saw above, but since at DD the opponent will have none of its demands acknowledged (step 1), CC > DD as well for this A2 player.
3. By the basic-goal assumption, DC,CC > CD, but since at DD the player expects to have all of its demands acknowledged (step 1), DD > CD as well.

Thus, from steps 1–3, we can conclude that CC > DC,DD (step 2) and DC,DD > CD (step 3), but the preference between DC and DD cannot be established. This same problem occurs in the A1-C1 situation, but in none of the C2 situations.

In order to obtain strict preferences, we add the assumption that DC > DD.[10] The reasoning behind this assumption is as follows. In the A2-C1 situation just examined, the player prefers compromise most; it is reasonable to assume, therefore, that it also prefers the opponent's capitulation to war. In the A1-C1 situation (*see* Figure 2.2), if the ranking of DC and DD is switched, a preference set in which DD is ranked highest will be produced. A player with such preferences will initiate war, which is excluded from our definition of crisis.

Turning to Figure 2.2, note that one duplication is produced: The A2-C1 situation results in the same preference set as that derived for the A2-C2-L1 situation. Because the difference between the two situations is the perception of relative capabilities, the conclusion is that the player's preferences are unaffected by how strong it thinks it is: It is magnanimous in victory—hence ranks CC above DC—and defiant in defeat, ranking DD above CD. Thus, irrespective of its capabilities, it prefers compromise if the opponent cooperates, and prefers resistance if the opponent coerces. The result is a tit-for-tat preference structure, typical of a middle-liner.

Figure 2.2 contains five preference sets:

1. $DC > DD > CC > CD$: A preference set typical of a hard-liner (henceforth, HL). This type is highly conflictual because compromise is valued less than war. Such an actor has a dominant strategy of coercion.[11]
2. $DC > CC > DD > CD$: A "hard" middle-liner (ML1). Compromise is ranked higher than war, but coercion is still a dominant strategy.
3. $CC > DC > DD > CD$: A middle-liner (ML2). Mutual accommodation is ranked highest, but war is preferred to capitulation. Such a decision-maker has a strategy of conditional cooperation (tit for tat): It will cooperate with an opponent who is willing to accommodate, but it will resist—even at the cost of war—an opponent who is unwilling to make any concessions.
4. $DC > CC > CD > DD$: A "hard" soft-liner type, or an "opportunist" (SL1). Such a decision maker has a conditional tat-for-tit strategy, which is the reverse of the ML2 strategy: It coerces if the opponent is willing to accommodate and accommodates if the opponent stands firm.
5. $CC > DC > CD > DD$: A soft-liner (SL2). Such a decision maker would like to avoid war at all costs: Although it prefers mutual accommodation most, it would rather capitulate than risk war. This decision maker has a dominant strategy of accommodation.

A Note on Preference Change

Although the development of a theory of preference change is a task left for the future, it is interesting to examine some of the implications of changes in attitudes and perceptions that can be derived from Figure 2.2.

Among the determinants of crisis preferences, the most likely variable to change in the short run is the perception of relative capabilities, expressed as a shift from C1 ("stronger") to C2 ("weaker"), and vice versa. Such a change in perception produces a change in crisis preferences, but the continuing effect of stable attitudes is easily discerned. Thus, a change from C1 to C2 by an HL player results in a shift either to an ML1 or an SL1 preference set, depending on the player's attitude toward loss (L1 or L2). In either case, the hard-line element produced by the stable A1 attitude remains intact: Whether the HL player becomes an ML1 or an SL1, it still prefers that the crisis end in the opponent's capitulation rather than in mutual compromise. The effect of the shift in the perception of relative capabilities is in terms of the relative ranking of the DD outcome, which declines as one moves from HL to ML1 and SL1 (that is, along the A1 row in the Figure).

As an empirical example of an opposite shift in the perception of capabilities, consider Gamal Abdoul Nasser in the 1967 Middle East crisis.[12] According to one historical version (to be critically examined later in the study), Nasser was a hard-liner who nevertheless believed that he could not defeat the Israelis on the battlefield until three conditions were met: (1) the concentration of a superior military force; (2) Israel's diplomatic isolation; and (3) Arab unity. At the outset of the crisis and in its initial stages, these conditions were not present. Thus, in terms of Figure 2.2, Nasser had an A1 attitude and a C2 perception of capabilities. Assuming (for the sake of argument) that Nasser also had an L1 attitude, his preference type was initially ML1. As such, he preferred an Israeli capitulation more than any other outcome, but in its absence, he preferred to reach some compromise settlement with Israel—say, a restoration of the *status quo ante* in return for an Israeli pledge not to attack Syria—over a war with an opponent who would defeat him. (In the ML1 preference set, CC is ranked above DD.)

As the crisis progressed, however, Nasser began to believe that his three conditions for confronting Israel successfully were beginning to materialize. At some point, then, his perception shifted from C2 to C1, and his crisis preferences from ML1 to HL. This shift would explain Nasser's growing audacity and confidence—according to this version of the events—toward the end of the crisis: He would now accept nothing less than Israeli capitulation; in its absence, he was ready to fight a war. (In the HL preference set, DD is ranked above CC.)

The effects of a shift in the C perception for players with an A2 attitude (second row in Figure 2.2) have been noted above. The ML2 preference type is unaffected by a change in C perception: A player of such type is magnanimous in victory and defiant in defeat, whether it perceives itself to be stronger or weaker. The SL2 preference set, on the other hand, undergoes a change by a shift from C2 to C1: The ranking of the DD outcome is now above CD, making the new preference set an ML2 type.

Attitudes are more stable than perceptions of capabilities and are unlikely to change during the course of a crisis, particularly if it is a short one.[13] Assuming that such a change does occur in the relations between and among states, however, we find that shifts in the attitude toward the opponent (the A parameter) have dramatic effects. If we consider the recent transformation in the relationship between the superpowers, we can characterize it as a shift from an A1 attitude—which sees the denial of any gains for the opponent as a foreign policy objective (that is, the Cold War)—to an A2 attitude, which recognizes the legitimacy of at least some of the opponent's claims and concerns. Assuming a C1 perception, such an attitude change is translated into a shift from an HL to an ML2 type. Whereas the former type is conflictual and ranks confrontation above accommodation, the latter type prefers accommodation to any other type of settlement.

An empirical illustration of an opposite shift in attitudes—from A2 to A1—may be found in Woodrow Wilson's perception of World War I. Prior to the American entry into that war, Wilson advocated mutual accommodation in Europe, expressing the attitude of "peace without victory." However, two developments in early 1917—unrestricted German submarine warfare and the Zimmermann Telegram—led Wilson to change his attitude toward Germany.[14] If Wilson was initially an ML2 player (assuming a C1 perception), then his attitude shift resulted in a preference change from ML2 to HL: Wilson now no longer advocated accommodation but German capitulation, consistent with the ranking of DC (and DD) above CC in the HL preference set.

Figure 2.2 does not answer the most intriguing question: Why and how do attitudes and perceptions change? It does, however, show how and when such change is translated into new preferences, and, in conjunction with another variable—the perception of the opponent's preferences (to be introduced in the next section)—the Figure can predict how changes in attitudes and perceptions will affect the behavior of players.

Thus, we have here the beginning of an empirical theory of preference change. The advantage of the scheme presented above for the derivation of decision makers' preferences is that it is based on psychological variables, and therefore can be related to psychological theories that deal with attitude and perception change (for example, personality, cognitive, social, and learning theories).

The model developed in this study looks at the other "end" of the process—the effect of attitudes and perceptions on rational action. Thus, as far as a general theory of crisis is concerned, preferences may serve as the central organizing concept that ties attitudes and perceptions on the one hand to actions and outcomes on the other. In this way, the psychology of decision makers can be related to strategic interaction, and the psychological approach to crisis can be integrated with the game-theoretic approach.

A TYPOLOGY OF CRISIS GAMES: THE COMPOSITE MATRIX

It is possible to construct a 5 x 5 *composite matrix* (*see* Figure 2.3), in which the types described above are arranged along the horizontal and vertical axes. The composite matrix consists of twenty-five games, which correspond to the possible combinations of pairs of types.

The matrix is symmetrical along its main diagonal; thus, only fifteen games are distinct:[15] the five games along the diagonal (in which players have symmetrical preferences) and the ten games lying above (or below) it. The twenty-five games are numbered both consecutively and in terms of the typological number—given in parentheses—assigned to them by Rapoport and Guyer (1966). Both numbers appear under each game in Figure 2.3.[16]

The composite matrix may be interpreted in several different ways. First, it may represent the set of "objective" crisis games.[17] Such a set may be used to evaluate foreign policy decisions, by determining—for any pair of players—the behavior and outcome that would have occurred had the players perceived each other accurately. The deduced and actual outcomes can then be compared to determine whether the players could have obtained a better outcome than the one they actually obtained.[18] This method is also a way by which the impact of misperceptions—the incorrect assessment of the opponent's preferences—can be established (*see* Chapter 3 for further discussion).

Figure 2.3
The Composite Matrix

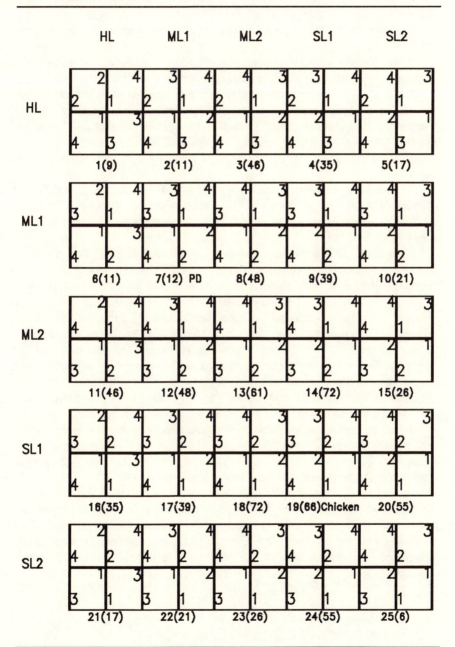

The matrix may also be interpreted in perceptual terms. That is, the games in each row (column) of the matrix may be seen as representing alternative perceptions of the opponent's type for that row (column) player. For example, game 6(11) represents (for Row) the ML1 player's perception of the opponent as HL, whereas game 7(12) represents that player's perception of the opponent as ML1.

If we assume unitary actors, then the crisis perception of states—and ultimately their behavior—can be analyzed in terms of their perception of the opponent. Since this perception determines which game situation is perceived by the state at any given moment, changes in the perception of the opponent produce changes in the game perception. Once the crisis games are solved—that is, the optimal (rational) choice of strategy is specified for each player—the crisis behavior of states can be studied as a function of their perceptions of the opponent.

Another interpretation of the composite matrix follows the assumption of nonunitary actors. Disagreements on crisis strategy among internal coalitions and factions can then be shown to arise from differences in the perceptions of the crisis game.

Competing game perceptions can be the result of differences in preferences, in the assessment of the opponent's type, or both.[19] The composite matrix can be used to represent each of these cases (assume "the player" is Row and "the opponent" is Column): (1) When internal players share the same preferences but disagree over the opponent's type, then their competing game perceptions are represented in terms of different games in the same row of the matrix; (2) when internal players differ in their preferences but share the perception of the opponent, their competing game perceptions are represented by different games in the same column of the matrix; and (3) when players differ in both their preferences and their perceptions of the opponent, their competing game perceptions are represented by games in different rows and columns.

When differences in game perceptions are translated into disagreements on strategy, the composite matrix can be used to display the configuration of policy positions. Thereby, coalitions that will be represented in, and compete for dominance of, the decision-making unit become perspicuous.

In Chapter 5, a coalition configuration will be specified in this manner for Israeli decision making in the 1967 Middle East crisis. In the next chapter, the composite matrix will be used to examine the crisis strategies of players and the outcomes effected by these strategies. In this way, the matrix will tie the preferences and perceptions of the players to their behavior and the crisis outcome.

NOTES

1. Snyder and Diesing (1977), who suggest that nine 2 x 2 games characterize all the empirical cases they examined, argue that this nine-game set is representative of the universe of crisis situations. Stein (1982) has conducted an analysis of misperception based on the assumption that players are aware that these nine games constitute a representative set.

2. The discussion of preference formation in this section draws on prior work by Aggarwal and Allan (1988) in the area of International Political Economy and by Kavka (1987) in the area of deterrence. The third approach to the derivation of preferences is discussed at some length by Snidal (1985), who also evaluates the inductive method of preference derivation.

3. This is the idea underlying game-theoretic models that allow players to choose levels of coercion and accommodation. *See* Brams and Kilgour (1987a, 1988) for such an approach. For a recent criticism of matrix games, *see* Gates and Humes (1989).

4. *See* Podell and Knapp (1969), and Pruitt (1981).

5. The CC outcome does not represent the *status quo ante*. That is, it is not assumed that the players are at CC when the crisis begins.

6. Ignore for now the DD outcome, which is discussed below.

7. Oren (1982) discussed this principle, which he called "prudence in victory," with respect to postwar settlements. For an empirical test of the two hypotheses ("peace by empire" and "prudence in victory"), *see* Maoz (1984). A game-theoretic analysis of the two hypotheses is provided in Brams and Mor (forthcoming).

8. In effect, this parameter may be interpreted as applying to that balance of capabilities that the players consider most relevant to the determination of the crisis outcome.

9. We assume that actors perceive their capabilities in such dichotomous terms. This assumption is admittedly a strong one: Sometimes capabilities may be perceived as equal, and at other times, actors may not be able to form a clear assessment of them. Yet the incorporation of such possibilities either inflates the set of crisis games or admits nonstrict preferences. The restrictive assumption does rule out some preference structures, but as we shall see, it yields a sufficiently varied set of player types to be theoretically and empirically useful.

10. This assumption is denoted in Figure 2.2 by the abbreviation "AA" (additional assumption).

11. A strategy is *dominant* if it provides outcomes at least as good, and better in one or more contingencies, than any other strategy.

12. The 1967 crisis will be analyzed in detail in Chapter 5. The present discussion is meant for illustrative purposes only.

13. An empirical theory of preference change would have to specify the determinants of attitude change. Here we are concerned only with the consequences of such a change.

It is also important to note that Figure 2.2 may apply to other conflict relations between and among states: There is nothing in the specification of the attitude and perception parameters that relates them necessarily to crises, although we have interpreted them in terms of the crisis game.

14. It would be more accurate to say that Wilson changed his image of Germany, which in turn affected his attitude toward it. As we shall see later, another variable in the crisis model is the perception of the opponent (image). Together with attitudes and the perception of capabilities, this variable is seen to determine decision makers' perceptions of the crisis game. Although attitudes and images are both treated as independent variables in the model, the relationship between them could be specified in subsequent developments of the model.

15. They are distinct in the sense that no interchange of players, strategies, or both will transform them into one of the other seventy-eight 2 x 2 ordinal games with strict preferences that are given in Rapoport and Guyer (1966).

16. Note that nondistinct games differ in terms of their consecutive numbers but have identical typological numbers (for example, games 2[11] and 6[11]; the latter can be derived from the former by interchanging the players).

17. First defined by Maoz (1990b), an "objective game" is based on the actual, rather than the perceived, preferences of the players.

18. For such an approach to the evaluation of foreign policy decisions, *see* Maoz (1990b).

19. Because preferences and the perception of the opponent are often related, it is very likely that differences in preferences be accompanied by competing images of the opponent. Thus, for example, during the 1938 Munich crisis, the British cabinet was divided internally between hard-liners and soft-liners, who also differed in terms of their images of Hitler.

Earlier, we pointed out that there is a relationship, which is unspecified in the model, between the image of the opponent and the attitude toward it. Since attitudes are a determinant of crisis preferences, it is not surprising that preferences and the perception of the opponent are related.

3

The Crisis Model II:
Crisis Behavior and Outcome

The previous chapter focused on the formation of crisis preferences and the derivation of the set of crisis games (the composite matrix). We saw that players' preferences are determined by their attitudes toward the opponent and toward loss, and by their perceptions of relative capabilities. These parameters yielded five typical preference sets, or player types. We then combined the crisis preferences of players with their perception of the opponent's type to obtain the game perception of players. All the possible game perceptions for all five types of players are contained in the composite matrix.

In this chapter, we proceed from the game perception to the analysis of crisis behavior and outcome. This transition requires that the games in the composite matrix be solved—that is, that the optimal (rational) strategy choice in each game of the matrix be specified. This is done in the first section, which starts off with a brief introduction of a crisis-initiation model, and then proceeds to discuss the game-theoretic solution concept that is applied to solve the games. The section ends with the incorporation of the game solutions into the composite matrix. The second section examines crisis initiation and derives the conditions under which different types of players initiate crises. The third section examines the impact of misperceptions on crisis behavior and the crisis outcome. Finally, the fourth section establishes the conditions in which players attempt to induce misperceptions through image projection, or deception, and traces the consequences of deception strategies.

GAME SOLUTIONS

The Initiation Game

Prior to presenting the solution concept to the crisis games, a model of crisis initiation is introduced. Although a detailed analysis of the conditions for initiation is reserved for second section, the initiation model is briefly discussed at this point for two reasons. First, crises do not emerge out of nowhere, and therefore, a discussion of crisis initiation must precede the examination of crisis behavior (strategy choice). Second, and consistent with the first point, the initiation game and the crisis game are closely linked. Specifically, the initial outcome in the crisis game is directly related to the choices that the players make in the initiation game. Therefore, this latter game will be introduced next, followed by the presentation of the solution concept.

The model of crisis initiation is based on the conception of a two-stage game (*see* Figure 3.1). The second stage (Game 2) consists of the crisis game. In the first stage—Game 1—the players face a choice between noninitiation (NI) and initiation (I). These two strategies for each player yield a 2 x 2 game—the *initiation game*—in which there are four outcomes. These outcomes are defined as follows:

1. *NI-NI*: Noninitiation. Status quo persists.
2. *I-NI*:   Unilateral initiation: Row unilaterally departs from the status quo. The players move to the DC outcome in the crisis game (Game 2).

Figure 3.1
The Crisis Initiation Model

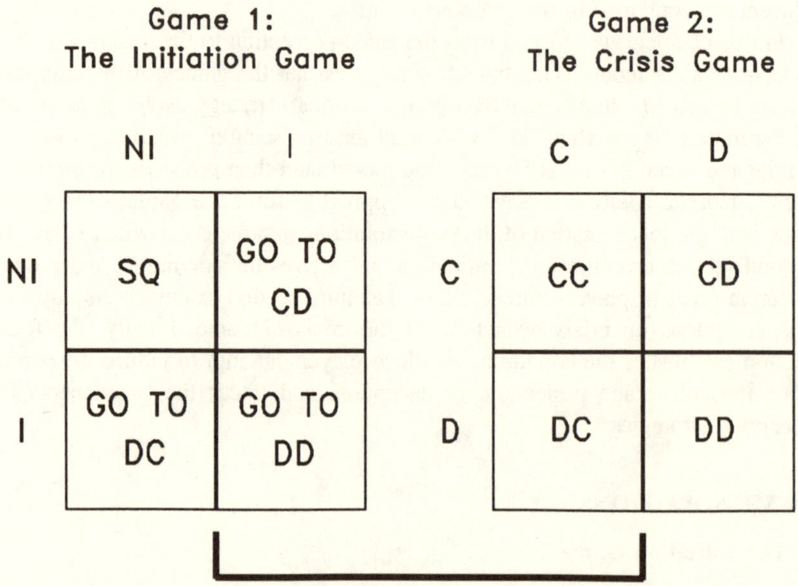

3. *NI-I*: Unilateral initiation: Column unilaterally departs from the status quo. The players move to the CD outcome in the crisis game.
4. *I-I*: Mutual initiation. The players move to the DD outcome in the crisis game.

The two-stage game is played as follows. If both players choose their noninitiation strategies, the status quo persists, and the game is terminated prior to the second stage. If at least one player decides to initiate, both players move to the second stage, as is indicated by the instructions contained in each of the three non–status quo outcomes in Game 1 (that is, NI-I, I-NI, and I-I).

The rules of play for Game 2 are discussed below. Once the play of Game 2 is terminated, the final outcome is fed back to Game 1. This is done as follows:

1. The final outcome of the game with initial outcome CD is substituted for the NI-I outcome in Game 1.
2. The final outcome of the game with initial outcome DC is substituted for the I-NI outcome in Game 1.
3. The final outcome of the game with initial outcome DD is substituted for the I-I outcome in Game 1.

Game 1 now consists of final outcomes only.

The inclusion of the crisis game in a model of crisis initiation reflects the conception of decision makers as *nonmyopic* players. The idea here is that, in considering whether or not to initiate a crisis, decision makers look ahead and take into account the possible consequences of such a conflict. That is, the decision to initiate depends on the outcome a player believes it can obtain if it initiates. This outcome, in turn, is compared to the status quo: If it is ranked higher in the preference ranking of the player, then that player will initiate; if lower, then the player will not initiate. The two stages described by the model, then, are clearly linked in the minds of decision makers when they consider initiation.

Since the decision on initiation depends on the crisis outcome the player believes it can obtain, the derivation of these outcomes—the final outcomes in the crisis games—must precede the analysis of initiation. Therefore, we turn now to the discussion of the solution to the crisis games. (Players' choices with respect to initiation will be discussed in the second section.)

The Nonmyopic Solution Concept

The Rules of Play and the Nonmyopic Calculation

The conception of nonmyopic calculation (which defines nonmyopic rationality) is derived from the *theory of moves*, initially developed in Brams and Wittman (1981).[1] This theory extends the rules of play that characterize classical game theory to allow for sequential moves and countermoves within a fixed game.

Since players are assumed to have complete information about the game matrix, they can anticipate the choices of the opponent in response to their own possible moves and, thereby, determine the end result of an alternating sequence of moves. Depending on the results of this calculation, they then decide whether or not to depart from an initial outcome.

The rules that govern the play of the crisis game (and determine the final outcomes to represent the I-I, I-NI, and NI-I outcomes in the initiation game) are the following:

I.   Both players simultaneously choose strategies, thereby defining an *initial outcome*.
II.   Once at an initial outcome, either player can unilaterally switch his strategy and change that outcome to a subsequent outcome in the row or column in which the initial outcome lies.
III. The second player can respond by unilaterally switching his strategy, thereby moving the game to a new outcome.
IV.   The alternating responses continue until the player whose turn it is to move next chooses not to switch his strategy. When this happens, the game terminates, and the outcome reached is the *final outcome* (Brams, 1983: 75; emphasis in original).

In the initiation game, the players are assumed to be initially at the status quo outcome. A departure from this outcome (that is, through the choice of the initiation strategy) by either or both of the players sends them to one of three outcomes in the crisis game: CD, DC, or DD. The nonmyopic calculations of the players apply to these outcomes, which are taken to be the initial outcomes in the crisis game. Once the players determine the result of the sequence of moves triggered by a departure from each of these initial outcomes, they compare this result to the status quo outcome in the initiation game. They can then decide whether a departure from the status quo (that is, crisis initiation) would be rational for them.[2]

How does a player determine the result of the move-countermove process triggered by a departure from the initial outcome, or, in our case, how does a player determine which outcome it can expect to obtain in the crisis, should it initiate one? The answer provided by the theory of moves is that a player "performs a backward induction analysis, based on the *game tree* of possible moves that could be set off if he departed from the initial outcome" (Brams, 1983: 75; original emphasis). Then, for an outcome to be final, two conditions need to obtain:

1. *That specific outcome survives*: the backward comparisons of the game-tree analysis eliminate all other outcomes.
2. *There is termination*: there exists a node in the game tree such that the player with the next move can ensure his best outcome by staying at it (Brams and Wittman, 1981: 45; emphasis in original).

The second condition comes to guarantee that the move-countermove process is not intransitive (that is, cycles back to the initial outcome):[3] A player has no incentive to continue moving once it gets to its best outcome, and therefore, the existence of such an outcome at a point where this player moves next effectively terminates the process.

In a later development of the theory of moves,[4] Brams incorporated the termination condition directly into the players' calculations by stipulating a different rationality criterion, which he called "Rational Termination." This criterion states that a player "will move from an initial outcome if and only if he can ensure a better outcome for himself before the process returns to the initial outcome and a new cycle commences" (Brams, 1983: 106–107). This rationality criterion, then, includes conditions 1 and 2 above. It has the additional advantage that "no arbitrary stopping rule [that is, condition 2] is required because all cases—with or without possible cycling—are covered by [it]" (ibid., p. 108). Thus, we shall use Rational Termination to determine the strategy choices of the players in the crisis game.[5]

It is useful at this point to mention two considerations (in addition to the problem of intransitivity) that favor a guarantee against cycling. First, as Brams argues (1983: 107), cycling may be rational, but it requires assumptions about cardinal utilities and the probability of being at each outcome. In an ordinal framework, such information is lacking, and players cannot perform the necessary averaging calculations. Second, cycling in the crisis game presents problems of empirical interpretation, in part because players in real crises are unlikely to engage in it.[6] The aversion-to-cycling assumption, then, may be interpreted as the reluctance of players to waste precious resources by implementing strategies that do not improve their situations.

Two additional points should be noted before we turn to the solution of the crisis games. First, because Rational Termination states that, unless a player can obtain a better outcome before cycling is completed, it will not depart from an initial outcome only to return to it, the game tree analyzed by the players covers the complete cycle of moves and countermoves.[7] Second, I assume that players engage in a two-sided analysis of the game tree:[8] Such an analysis does not require more information than the players are already assumed to possess when they perform a one-sided calculation. (As we shall see, a two-sided analysis may help players extricate themselves from Pareto-inferior outcomes, which they would have no incentive to leave on the basis of a one-sided analysis.)

The rationality criterion of Rational Termination and the principle of two-sided analysis were applied to the twenty-five crisis games in the composite matrix.[9] For each of the twenty-five games, the backward induction process was applied three times, in accordance with the three initial outcomes possible in each game: CD, DC, and DD. This procedure is illustrated in the next section by means of an example.

Figure 3.2
Solution to the ML1-ML2 Game (8[48])

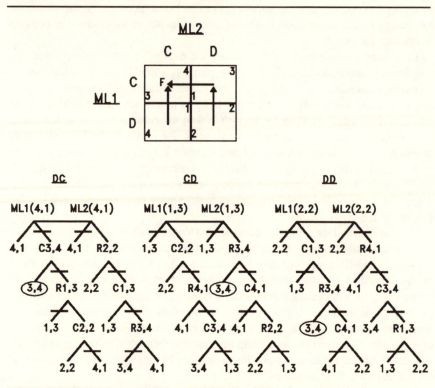

Two-Sided Nonmyopic Calculation: An Example

Consider Figure 3.2, where the crisis game is game 8(48) of the composite matrix,[10] and the players are ML1 (as Row) and ML2 (as Column). The players consider the moves and countermoves that would be triggered by their departure from each of the three initial outcomes possible in this game (CD, DC, and DD). Hence, Figure 3.2 contains three pairs of game trees: Each pair starts at one of the three initial outcomes and consists of a game tree for each of the two players as the first-moving player.

Consider first outcome DC, which is best for ML1 and worst for ML2. The calculations of the players at this outcome are based on the pair of game trees beginning with (4,1). ML1 is the first-moving player in the first game tree, and ML2 is the first-moving player in the second. It is obvious that ML1, who gets its best outcome at DC, has no incentive to move. ML2's calculation is as follows. Working backward up its game tree, it can see that, at the bottom of the tree, ML1 (Row) has a choice between staying at the (3,4) outcome or moving back to the initial (4,1) outcome. Since the latter is better for ML1, it will move. Now ML2 (Column) has to decide between staying at (1,3) or moving to (3,4), from which it already knows that ML1 will move to (4,1). Since ML2 prefers (1,3) to (4,1), it will stay. Next up the tree is a choice for ML1 between staying at (2,2) and moving to (1,3), where it knows ML2 will stay. Since ML1 prefers the former, it will choose to stay. Outcome (2,2) now moves up to a final comparison with the initial outcome, where ML2, as first-moving player, has to decide whether to stay at (4,1) or move to (2,2), where ML1 will stay. Preferring (2,2), ML2 chooses to move. Thus, if DC is the initial outcome, ML2 would move the game to DD, where the move-countermove process would come to an end.

We see, then, that if each player consults its game tree only, the result is that ML1 decides to stay at (4,1), but ML2 moves the game to (2,2), where the process ends. Outcome (2,2), however, is a Pareto-inferior outcome: Both players would prefer to be at (3,4), the CC outcome. We demonstrate next that if the players consult each other's game tree in addition to their own—that is, engage in two-sided analysis—the game terminates at the (3,4) outcome.

If ML1 consults its game tree only, it cannot foresee ML2's move to the (2,2) outcome and, therefore, concludes wrongly that (4,1) would be the final outcome. However, by examining also the game tree of ML2, it can see that ML2 will move the game from (4,1) to (2,2). Still, ML1 need not settle for this outcome, its next worst: A second look at its own game tree reveals that, although it cannot stop the game at its best outcome, it can obtain its next-best outcome by moving the game to CC (where ML2 will stay) before ML2 moves the game to DD. Similarly, a two-sided analysis by ML2 should tell that player that if it holds at DC, ML1 will move the game to CC, which is better for ML2 than DD. In this way, the players—through individually rational calculations—can avoid the Pareto-inferior outcome DD, which is the outcome indicated by one-sided analysis.

Next, consider outcome CD and the pair of game trees beginning with (1,3). At this outcome, a one-sided analysis indicates to each player that it should depart: ML1 to DD and ML2 to CC. A two-sided analysis, however, should tell ML1 that it is in its interest to hold at CD and await ML2's departure—ML2 as first-moving player would bring the game to CC, an outcome better for ML1 than DD (and better, of course, for ML2 than CD).

Finally, consider outcome DD and the pair of game trees beginning with (2,2). ML2 has no incentive to depart to DC—its worst outcome—because ML1, obtaining its best outcome, would stop the game there. ML1's analysis, on the other hand, shows that were it to move the game to CD, ML2 would move it to CC, which is better for both players than DD.[11]

We see, then, that no matter where the game begins—at DC, DD, or CD—the players converge on the CC outcome. (This is indicated in Figure 3.2 by the arrows emanating from the DC, CD, and DD outcomes and pointing to the CC outcome.) Once at CC, neither player has an incentive to depart: ML2 obtains its best outcome, and a departure by ML1 would lead to cycling, to which the players are assumed to be averse. CC, then, is an equilibrium outcome in the nonmyopic sense. (It is not, however, a nonmyopic equilibrium according to the Brams and Wittman definition, because there is no termination when ML1 [Row] departs from it.)[12]

The Crisis Game Solutions

The solution procedure outlined above for Figure 3.2 was performed for each of the crisis games in the composite matrix. The results are given in Figure 3.3. In each game, the moves of the players are indicated by means of incoming and outgoing arrows. In each game, then, outcomes are characterized by one of the following:[13]

1. A *single outgoing arrow* (for example, outcome CD in game 1[9]). This indicates a move (that is, a change of strategy) by either the row player (vertical arrows) or the column player (horizontal arrows). The players move to an adjacent outcome, either in the same row (if Column is the moving player) or in the same column (if Row is the moving player).
2. *Two outgoing arrows* (for example, outcome DD in game 13[61]). This indicates that both players move away from an outcome simultaneously. As a result, they arrive at an outcome lying diagonally to the original outcome.
3. A *single or two incoming arrows* (and no outgoing arrows; for example, outcome DC in game 4[35]). This indicates that once the players arrive at such an outcome—either from one of the initial outcomes or from the initiation game directly—they will stay at it (that is, the outcome is a final one). Final outcomes are denoted by "F."
4. *One incoming arrow and one outgoing arrow* (for example, outcome DD in game 4[35]). This indicates that the players pass through such an outcome on their way from one outcome to another.
5. *No arrows* (for example, outcome CC in game 1[9]). This indicates that the players neither arrive at nor pass through such an outcome.

All games have unique solutions (that is, a single final outcome), with the following exceptions:

1. *Game 7(12)* (Prisoners' Dilemma): In this game—played by a pair of ML1 players—the initial outcomes DC and CD lead to final outcome CC. However, the initial outcome DD is also a final outcome, since neither player has an incentive to depart from it. (Hence, in this game, mutual initiation ends in war.)
2. *Game 19(66)* (Chicken): In this game—played by a pair of SL1 players—the initial outcome DD is worst for both players. Since one cannot say *a priori*

Figure 3.3
The Composite Matrix: Solutions

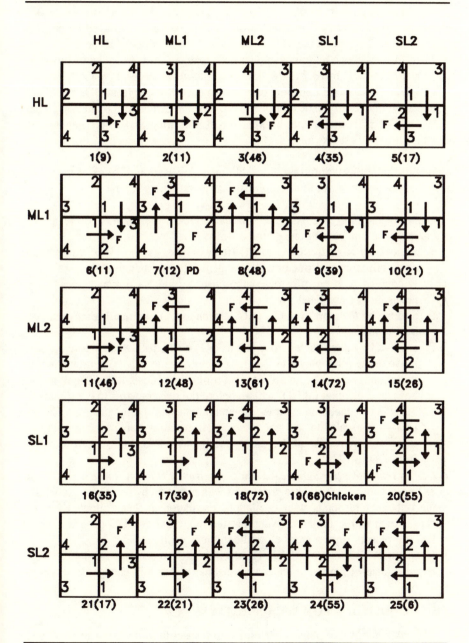

which player will depart first, the final outcome may be either DC or CD. In addition, if either of these latter outcomes is the initial outcome, the player obtaining its next-worst payoff has an incentive to move to DD whence, again, the game may move to either DC or CD (hence the double-headed arrows).[14]

3. *Games 20(55) and 24(55)* (Chicken-like): In these games—played by an SL1 and an SL2 player—the initial outcome DD is worst for both players. Therefore, the same reasoning applies here as in the case of Chicken. However, a "victory" at DD by SL2 allows this player to move the game to CC—its best outcome—because SL1, having been forced once to move from DD, would not depart from CC only to be returned to DD when SL2 retaliates by moving from DC to DD. This means that in order for SL2 to bring SL1 to the negotiation table, it must first prevail at DD.[15]

It is useful at this point to provide additional clarification of some of the game solutions by pointing out their empirical interpretation, as follows:

1. *Games with final outcome CC.*[16] In these crises, the players arrive at the compromise outcome in one of three ways:
   A. a move by Row from DC to CC (for example, game 8[48]): a unilateral crisis initiation by Row, in which its demand for a change of the status quo is coupled with an offer of compromise, to which Column agrees. Such crises do not escalate.
   B. a move by Column from CD to CC: same as (A), with unilateral initiation by Column.
   C. a move by either player from DD to DC or CD, followed by a reciprocal move of the other player to CC (for example, game 13[61]): a mutual crisis initiation followed by an accepted offer of compromise. It is difficult to say how far escalation (at DD) will go before the players agree to compromise, but it is reasonable to assume—given both players' preference for CC over DD—that escalation will not be acute. (It is also possible for both players to offer compromise at the same time, in which case they move directly from DD to CC.)
2. *Games that move through the DD outcome, from CD to DC or vice versa* (for example, game 4[35]). These crises start with initiation by one player, to which the opponent responds with escalation. Escalation is then followed by the capitulation of the initiator. (Note that the move through DD does not mean that the players fight a war before the initiator capitulates.)
3. *Games with final outcome DD.* These crises are expected to escalate to war, because once escalation is under way, neither player will change its strategy.

THE CONDITIONS FOR CRISIS INITIATION

The calculations that players perform with respect to initiation were described

Figure 3.4
The Solution to the ML1-ML2 Initiation Game

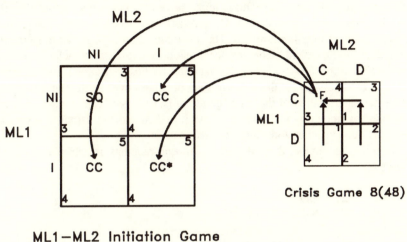

Crisis Game 8(48)

ML1—ML2 Initiation Game

```
               5    4    3    2    1
        ML1: DC > CC > SQ > DD > CD
        ML2: CC > DC > SQ > DD > CD
```

earlier (*see* The Initiation Game). Recall that, for nonmyopic players, the decision on initiation depends on the outcome they expect to obtain in the crisis game. These outcomes have now been determined and can be fed back into the initiation game—that is, we can now substitute the final outcomes of the crisis games for the non–status quo outcomes in their corresponding initiation games.

This procedure is illustrated by means of Figure 3.4, where game 8(48) is given once again.[17] We saw earlier that all three initial outcomes in this crisis game converge on the CC outcome. This final crisis outcome can now be substituted for the non–status quo outcomes in the initiation game. Hence, the I-NI, I-I, and NI-I outcomes in the initiation game are now designated as "CC," whereas the NI-NI outcome remains the status quo outcome ("SQ").[18]

The players' choice of strategy depends now on their relative ranking of the status quo. In the example, assume that the players rank the status quo as follows:

1. *ML1*: DC > CC > SQ > DD > CD
2. *ML2*: CC > DC > SQ > DD > CD

When incorporated into the initiation game,[19] these preferences yield a dominant strategy of initiation for both players. Hence, the outcome of the initiation game is I-I—mutual initiation.

Thus, the initiation model can be used to derive the conditions under which different players initiate crises. This requires, however, assumptions about players' ranking of the status quo outcome. On substantive grounds, a restriction on this ranking can be reasonably imposed. This restriction says that, for all players, the status quo must be ranked higher than capitulation and lower than victory. In other words, DC > SQ > CD (for Row). The rationale for this restriction is that decision makers most likely prefer the existing state of affairs over a situation involving the further deterioration of the status quo (that is, their own capitulation). On the other hand, a victory by the initiator allows it to dictate the revisions it desires in the status quo and, therefore, improves its situation.

Given this restriction, the following status quo rankings are possible for each of the players:

HL: DC > **SQ** > DD > CC > CD
       DC > DD > **SQ** > CC > CD[20]
ML1: DC > **SQ** > CC > DD > CD
       DC > CC > **SQ** > DD > CD
       DC > CC > DD > **SQ** > CD
ML2: CC > DC > **SQ** > DD > CD
       CC > DC > DD > **SQ** > CD
SL1: DC > **SQ** > CC > CD > DD
       DC > CC > **SQ** > CD > DD
SL2: CC > DC > **SQ** > CD > DD

Applying the solution procedure outlined above for game 8(48) to initiation games incorporating these different status quo rankings allows us to derive the conditions for initiation given in Figure 3.5. Two points should be noted before we summarize the findings of the Figure. First, the strategy choice (initiation or noninitiation) of an ML1 player with status quo ranking of 3 cannot be determined when this player perceives an ML1 opponent with status quo ranking 3 or 2 (hence the question marks following these two rankings in the Figure). The reason is that neither of these players has a dominant strategy in the initiation game.

Second, since the outcome of the Chicken and Chicken-like games depends on which player can hold out longer at the DD outcome (that is, has greater resolve), the decision on initiation depends in turn on whether a player perceives its opponent to have more or less resolve in these games. Thus, for example, the SL2 player will initiate against an SL1 player only if it believes that the latter has less resolve than it does. In Figure 3.5, this is indicated by the abbreviation "lr" (less resolve).

Figure 3.5 shows the relationship between different players' levels of satisfaction with the status quo (that is, their ranking of this outcome relative to

Figure 3.5
SQ Ranking and Crisis Initiation

Player	SQ Ranking	Initiation against...
HL	4	SL
	3,2	All
ML1	4	SL
	3	ML1(SQ=4,3?2?), ML2, SL
	2	All
ML2	3	ML, SL
	2	All
SL1	4	SL(Ir)
	3	ML2, SL1(Ir), SL2
SL2	3	ML2, SL1(Ir), SL2

crisis outcomes) and the type of opponents they initiate against. The first point to note is that dissatisfaction with the status quo (i.e., this outcome is ranked lower than at least one crisis outcome) does not automatically lead to crisis initiation. The reason is that although dissatisfaction (as defined here) is a necessary condition for the existence of a motivation to initiate, it is not a sufficient condition for initiation: A player must also perceive an opportunity to do better than the status quo, and that opportunity depends on the opponent the player perceives. Thus, for example, the HL player will initiate only against soft-liners if it is at most somewhat dissatisfied with the status quo (that is, it ranks the status quo next best in its preference ranking).

In general, the relationship between dissatisfaction and crisis initiation is straightforward: the more dissatisfied a player is, the wider the range (from hard-liners to soft-liners) of opponents it will initiate against. If there is an equal likelihood of perceiving any given type of opponent, we can say that the greater the dissatisfaction of a player the more likely this player is to initiate.

Across players, the relationship between dissatisfaction and initiation is the following: the more dovish (hawkish) a player the greater (smaller) the level of dissatisfaction needed to trigger initiation. Specifically, at the extreme ends of the hard-line/soft-line scale, we find the following:

1. In the case of hard-liners (HL), any level of dissatisfaction is sufficient to trigger initiation against at least one type of opponent.
2. In the case of soft-liners (SL1&2), no level of dissatisfaction is sufficient to trigger initiation against hard-liners and "hard" middle-liners (ML1).

So far, we have sought to explain players' decisions on initiation as a function of their valuation of the status quo and their perception of the opponent. The discussion cannot be complete, however, without an examination of the role of misperceptions. After all, if players always assessed each other's preferences correctly, they would never (in our model) make foreign policy mistakes by initiating crises they should not initiate—and, perhaps, not initiating crises that they should. Moreover, if players knew that their assessments of each other's preferences were accurate, crises would become unnecessary: Their outcome could be calculated in advance and the status quo adjusted accordingly. The following section, then, examines the effects of misperceptions on the behavior of crisis actors and on the crisis outcome.[21]

MISPERCEPTIONS

The first point to note with respect to misperceptions is that their study has been biased by an almost exclusive focus on crisis or war initiation. That is, the study of foreign policy failures has been practically defined by an emphasis on crisis and war initiations that should not have taken place. The relationship between misperception and initiation, however, may also be studied in terms of *failures to initiate*, and not only in terms of initiation failures.

That such has not been the focus of the literature is the result of a bias, at least in Western scholarship, in favor of the status quo (*see* Maoz, 1982a).[22] It also stems from methodological considerations that make the study of nonevents more difficult to undertake—in order to argue that noninitiation was a foreign policy failure, one would have to engage in counterfactual hypothesis testing (*see* Fearon, 1991).

Such a bias is unwarranted, however, in a game-theoretic model in which a noninitiation strategy is explicitly modeled as an alternative for players to consider. Moreover, because decisions in such a model are explained as a function of players' preferences, it is certainly reasonable to ask whether and how misperceptions prevent players from initiating, and thus from obtaining, outcomes they might have otherwise obtained.

Figure 3.5 offers two conclusions about the relationship between misperceptions—defined as wrong assessments of the opponent's type—and noninitiation. The first conclusion follows from the earlier observation that the more dissatisfied a player, the greater the range of opponents it will initiate against. If this is so, then the more dissatisfied a player, the smaller the likelihood that misperception will lead it to fail to initiate when it should (that is, when it considers initiation and when its preferences make such a strategy rational). The obverse is that failures to initiate as a result of misperception are more likely to occur when players are moderately or only somewhat dissatisfied with the status quo.

This conclusion has the ironic implication that those actors who view themselves as the guardians of the status quo (that is, are most satisfied with it) are precisely the actors who are most likely to fail to initiate as a result of misperceiving the opponent. Knowledge of this fact can be used by the opponent to induce misperception and, hence, noninitiation. Thus, at the time when Adolf Hitler's military power was still inferior to that of England and France, he managed to project a much tougher image than his capabilities warranted. This deception resulted in a British and French failure to force Hitler's hand while they still had the ability to do so.[23]

The second conclusion from Figure 3.5 is that misperception does not lead to noninitiation by highly dissatisfied hard-liners and middle-liners—a high level of dissatisfaction is a sufficient condition for them to initiate against any opponent type. This result has the interesting implication that deterrence cannot succeed against such players: Even if the opponent manages to deceive them by projecting a tough image, the induced misperception does not affect their decision to initiate.

It is worthwhile at this point, before we turn to the effects of misperception on crisis behavior and outcome, to take a closer look at the relationship between initiation and deterrence and at some of the policy implications that this relationship suggests.

To the extent that initiation is viewed by a state as a threat to the status quo, its prevention becomes a foreign policy objective. The crisis model indicates that there are two crisis-prevention strategies available to the state. First, because motivation is not a sufficient condition for initiation, the state can try to prevent initiation by addressing the second condition for initiation, that is, capabilities. Thus, the state can develop its capabilities to the degree necessary to modify the initiation calculus of the dissatisfied opponent. This strategy of deterrence would be successful to the extent that it would convince the opponent that its initiation could not achieve the desired restructuring of the status quo. In effect, then, a successful strategy would induce noninitiation on the part of the opponent.

This strategy of initiation prevention has at least one critical weakness: Even if it works in the short run, it may backfire in the long run. The reason is that this strategy does not address the underlying causes of the opponent's dissatisfaction. In fact, by repeatedly frustrating the opponent's desires and objectives the state induces an even greater degree of dissatisfaction and, hence, a stronger motivation to initiate.

As we saw above, the model indicates that, in the case of hard-line and middle-line opponents, once dissatisfaction with the status quo reaches a certain level, capabilities cease to become a necessary condition for initiation. At that point, the state's capabilities can no longer induce noninitiation on the part of the opponent. The paradox, then, is that by successfully deterring initiation, the state may achieve precisely the opposite effect—initiation by an opponent who can no longer be deterred.[24]

The second initiation-prevention strategy suggested by the model is that the motivation to initiate, rather than the balance of capabilities, be addressed. This strategy does not consist of granting the opponent all it wishes. Rather, it seeks to lower the dissatisfaction of the opponent to a level at which the motivation to initiate is once again a necessary, but not a sufficient condition for actual initiation. In practical terms, this strategy consists of negotiating with the opponent to restructure the status quo. The crucial issue in such negotiations is to discover the opponent's "reservation price" for initiation—the minimal level of concessions that the opponent would accept "in return" for noninitiation.

The risks of such a strategy are well known: It may not only whet the opponent's appetite for more concessions, but, moreover, it may inadvertently signal weakness and tempt further exploitation. Therefore, an optimal strategy of initiation prevention should seek to influence both the motivation of the opponent and its perception of relative capabilities.

In the long run, the model suggests that such a strategy may modify the relationship itself between the adversaries. Specifically, to the extent that the attitude toward the opponent (as defined in Chapter 2) is determined by how willing the opponent is to acknowledge the demands of the state, a change in this attitude may be induced by a strategy that deals directly with the underlying causes of dissatisfaction. As we saw in Chapter 2, a shift from a peace-through-victory attitude (A1) to a peace-without-victory attitude (A2) results in shift to a less conflictual type.

We turn now to the effects of misperception on crisis behavior and outcome. In the composite matrix, misperception is represented in terms of an incorrect game perception. That is, given the opponent's (Column's) true preferences, there is only one game perception for each row player that represents the accurate crisis situation, that is, the objective game composed of the two players' true preferences. The remaining four games in each row are misperceived crisis games. Therefore, when Row misperceives Column's preferences, the two players necessarily play two different crisis games: Row plays the game based on its true preferences and the misperceived preferences of Column; Column plays the game based on its true preferences and the (mis)perceived preferences of Row.[25]

If players choose simultaneously, then, as Stein (1982) has pointed out, misperception matters (that is, affects the behavior of players) only if they have contingent strategies. Players with dominant strategies, on the other hand, are affected by misperception only in terms of their expectation of the crisis outcome.

If players choose sequentially—as they do in our model—then, argues Stein, misperception matters even less, because a player with a contingent strategy "simply takes its cue from the immediately preceding behavior of the other" (p.

516). He concludes, therefore, that for misperception to matter in a sequential-choice interaction, the misperceiving actor's choice must be dependent on the future choice of its opponent.[26]

Let us examine these conclusions for a world of sequential choice by nonmyopic players. We will look at each player in turn, in the role of both initiator and defender. To simplify the analysis, we will assume that all players know that the composite matrix constitutes the universe of crisis situations[27] and that they are aware of the contents of Figure 3.5. In addition, the discussion will be restricted to unilateral misperceptions.

Hard-Liner (HL). As a defender, the hard-liner always chooses its defection strategy, as the game solutions in Figure 3.3 indicate. Therefore, in the case of a hard-line defender, misperception has an effect on expectations only, but not on behavior.

As an initiator, the choice of the hard-liner (that is, to initiate or not) may be affected by misperception. Specifically, if it ranks the status quo as "4" (*see* Figure 3.5), the hard-liner initiates against soft-liners only, with the expectation that the soft-line opponent will capitulate. If the opponent is misperceived as a soft-liner, misperception leads the hard-liner to initiate a crisis it would not have initiated under accurate perception; moreover, the initiation results in war—against a middle-line or hard-line opponent—that the hard-line initiator would have wished to avoid.

On the other hand, if the hard-line player is highly dissatisfied with the status quo, misperception affects its expectation only, because it prefers initiation to noninitiation against all opponents.

"Hard" Middle-Liner (ML1). As a defender, the ML1 player can assess or form its initial perception of the opponent on the basis of the latter's initiating move. To begin with, since soft-liners do not initiate against ML1 players, as Figure 3.5 shows, the act of initiation itself eliminates these players from consideration. Second, initiation by middle-liners against the ML1 player is coupled with an offer of compromise, as Figure 3.3 indicates. Therefore, if such an offer is not forthcoming, the initiator has to be a hard-liner by elimination, and the ML1 player's response is to defect. If compromise is offered with initiation, the ML1 reciprocates, whether it perceives the initiator as ML1 or ML2.

This case supports Stein's contention that if an actor chooses its strategy on the basis of the preceding behavior of the opponent, misperception does not matter. Either it is corrected before the response is chosen, or the perception itself is formed on the basis of the initiation act.

As an initiator, the choice (to initiate or not) of the ML1 player is affected by misperception as long as it is not highly dissatisfied, in which case misperception affects its expectation only. Specifically, if the ML1 player is only somewhat dissatisfied (a "4" ranking in Figure 3.5), it initiates against soft-liners only.

Therefore, if it misperceives the opponent, the ML1 player has to make compromises (with middle-line opponents) or fight wars (with hard-liners) it would have wished to avoid. If the ML1 player is moderately dissatisfied ("3" ranking), misperception matters only if the opponent is a hard-liner; it does not affect the initiation behavior of the ML1 player if it misperceives a middle-liner as a soft-liner, and vice versa.[28]

Middle-Liner (ML2). As a defender, this player expects initiation by middle- and soft-line players to be coupled with an offer of compromise, which it reciprocates. If such an offer is not made, the ML2 player can conclude that the opponent is a hard-liner and, therefore, choose its defection strategy. Here, too, an initial misperception does not affect the response of the player.

As an initiator, the choice of the ML2 player is affected by misperception as long as it is not highly dissatisfied, in which case only its expectation is affected. Thus, if the ML2 player is somewhat dissatisfied ("3" ranking), misperception matters if a hard-line opponent is misperceived as a middle-liner or soft-liner. In any other case—a misperception of a middle-line opponent as a soft-liner and vice versa—misperception has no effect on the initiation behavior of the ML2 player.

"Hard" Soft-Liner (SL1). In contrast to the hard-line and middle-line defenders, misperception can affect the behavior of an SL1 defender. Specifically, since only the ML2 and SL2 players couple their initiation with an offer of compromise, the absence of such an offer still leaves the SL1 defender with three alternative perceptions of the initiator: HL, ML1, and SL1. Since it prefers to capitulate to the first two players and resist the third, misperception can result either in an avoidable war (or, at a minimum, avoidable escalation) or in an unnecessary capitulation.[29]

Even if an offer of compromise is made at the point of initiation, however—which points to an ML2 or an SL2 initiator—the SL1 defender prefers to reciprocate if it perceives the former and defect if it perceives the latter. Therefore, misperception can affect the behavior of the SL1 player in this case as well.

As an initiator, the behavior of SL1 can be affected by misperception at any level of dissatisfaction. If it is only somewhat dissatisfied (a "4" ranking), misperception matters if the opponent is misperceived as a soft-liner. If the player is highly dissatisfied (a "3" ranking), misperception matters if the opponent is misperceived as an ML2 or SL player.

Soft-Liner (SL2). Like the SL1 defender, the SL2 defender has to contend with three alternative perceptions of the opponent—HL, ML1, and SL1—if initiation is not coupled with an offer of compromise. Also, like the SL1 defender, it prefers to capitulate to the first two and resist the third. The consequences, therefore, are the same. However, the SL2 defender's position when an offer of compromise accompanies initiation is different from that of the SL1 defender: It prefers to reciprocate, regardless of whether it preceives the initiator to be ML2 or SL2. Therefore, misperception does not affect the behavior of the SL2 defender in this case. As an initiator, the behavior of SL2 is affected by misperception if it misperceives the opponent to be an ML2 or SL2 player.

We can summarize the discussion as follows. In a world of sequential choice by nonmyopic players, misperception does not affect the behavior of hard-line and middle-line defenders, as Stein has argued. It does affect, however, the behavior of soft-liners. When these players misperceive the initiator, they either get involved in an otherwise avoidable escalation or war, or they capitulate unnecessarily. The vulnerability to misperception of soft-liners in particular derives from the fact that any dissatisfied player is motivated to initiate against them; the variety of alternative opponents that soft-liners have to contend with—coupled with the contingent nature of their own strategy—makes it more difficult for them than for other players to identify their opponent correctly. (This observation will become very significant in the discussion of deception.)

The effect of misperception on initiation is more equally distributed among the different player types. The initiation behavior of hard-liners and middle-liners is affected by misperception at low and moderate levels of dissatisfaction, because at these levels, the decision to initiate still depends on the perception of the opponent. At high levels of dissatisfaction, on the other hand, initiation is always preferred, and misperception has therefore no effect. Soft-line initiators are always vulnerable to misperception, whether at low or high levels of dissatisfaction. Since they never initiate against hard-liners and "hard" middle-liners, the possibility of misperceiving such an opponent as softer and therefore initiating always exists.

DECEPTION

Introduction

The effects that misperception has on initiation, crisis strategy, and crisis outcome do not escape the attention of players who can use these effects to their own benefit. Thus, players may deliberately attempt to induce misperception—that is, engage in *deception*—so as to modify the opponent's perception of the crisis game and thereby obtain a better outcome.

The objectives of this section are: (1) to identify the players who are motivated to deceive; (2) to specify the opponents against whom they employ deception; (3) to describe the nature of deception strategies; and (4) to trace the consequences of deception.[30]

The Final Outcomes Matrix

We begin the analysis with Figure 3.6, which describes the final outcomes

Figure 3.6
Regions in the Final Outcomes Matrix

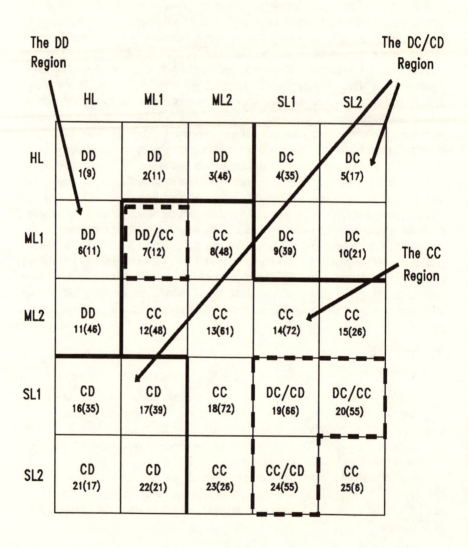

matrix. This matrix is derived directly from the composite matrix (Figure 3.3),[31] but whereas the latter includes moves and countermoves in each game, Figure 3.6 omits them and provides the final outcomes only. Thus, the analysis shifts from the microlevel of individual games to the macro level of the entire composite matrix.

Within this matrix, regions consisting of identical final outcomes have been demarcated and identified. There are three main regions (with exceptions to be noted shortly):

1. *The DD region*, in the upper-left section of the matrix. This region consists of games played between hard-line opponents, and between hard-line and middle-line opponents.
2. *The CC region*, in the center and lower-right sections of the matrix. This region consists of games played between middle-line opponents, between middle-line (ML2) and soft-line opponents, and between soft-line opponents.
3. *The CD or DC region*, in the lower-left and upper-right sections of the matrix. This region consists of games played between hard-line and soft-line opponents, and between hard middle-line (ML1) and soft-line opponents.

In addition, there are three games (or single-game regions)—enclosed in dashed lines—which cannot be classified *a priori* into one of the three groups above: (1) the Prisoners' Dilemma game (7[12]), which may end in DD or CC; (2) the Chicken game (19[66]), which may end in DC or CD; and (3) the Chicken-like game(s) (20[55] and 24[55]), which may end in CC (if SL2 wins), or in DC (in game 20[55]) or CD (in game 24[55]) if SL1 wins.

With respect to the three main regions described above, the following should be noted:

1. At least one hard-line player is associated with (that is, is a player in) each and every game in the DD region.
2. At least one middle-liner (ML2) is associated with every game in the CC region, with the exception of the SL2-SL2 game.
3. At least one soft-liner is associated with each and every game in the DC/CD region (always as the loser).
4. None of the player types is associated exclusively with a single region: As we run across the rows (or columns) of the matrix, we cross at least once from one region to another.

These points will become important when we discuss moves in the final outcomes matrix, which is the topic of the next section.

Image Projection and Deception: Moves in the Final Outcomes Matrix

We have just seen that no player is associated exclusively with a single region in the final outcomes matrix. This implies that, as the opponent's type varies, so does the final crisis outcome a player can obtain. To be precise, the final outcome need not change each and every time the opponent's type varies, but it changes at least once for each player. Thus, for example, in the case of the HL player, the final crisis outcome changes only once—from DD to DC—as we move across the HL row. On the other hand, the crisis outcome changes twice in the case of the ML1 player and three times in the case of the soft-liners.

Since this variability in final crisis outcomes depends on the opponent's type, the players cannot exert control over it. Also, since it exists for all player types, no single player can be said to perform consistently across all opponents. Furthermore, because players are assumed to rank the crisis outcomes in a strict manner (that is, indifference is ruled out), each player necessarily performs better against some opponents than others. In other words, even if a player obtains its best outcome against some opponents, there is at least one opponent against whom it can at best obtain its next-best outcome.

This variability in performance—coupled with the inability to control the opponent's type—is what motivates players to attempt occasionally to "escape" their preferences. That is, the players seek to project a preference ranking that would allow them to perform better against a particular opponent than they could with their true preferences. In effect, then, the players may choose types, in the sense of simulating the preferences of other players.

Several points should be noted about this type of preference simulation, or image projection. First, it is strategic in nature. That is, the players do not experience a sincere preference change as a result of a revision in their valuation of one or more crisis outcomes. Thus, even as they choose to simulate a preference set other than their own, hard-liners remain hard-liners, middle-liners remain middle-liners, and soft-liners remain soft-liners. What the selection of type means is that these players—for strategic reasons—behave *as if* their true preferences have changed.

Second, when players choose types, they are guided by their genuine preference ranking. That is, the players choose to simulate preferences that would allow them to improve their crisis outcome, but what they consider to be an improvement is determined by their true preferences.

Third, because the ability of players to obtain better outcomes by simulating insincere preferences depends on their ability to mislead the opponent, they engage in *deception* when they choose types other than their own. Thus, deception is defined here as the simulation of an insincere type.

We already mentioned that whenever a player fails to obtain its best outcome with its genuine preferences, it is motivated to simulate insincere preferences, or deceive. Note that this condition is equivalent to one of the conditions for initiation, namely that a player ranks the status quo lower than at least one crisis outcome. However, as was mentioned in the discussion of initiation, this is a necessary, but not a sufficient condition; a player also needs to perceive an opportunity to do better than the status quo. Likewise in the case of deception: Its occurrence requires that, in addition to being unable to obtain its best outcome with its true preferences, a player also perceives a preference set that allows it to obtain a better crisis outcome against a given opponent.

In terms of the final outcomes matrix, this latter condition implies that a row (column) player has to scan the column (row) corresponding to its opponent's type in order to determine whether there exists an alternative row (column) type that performs better against this same opponent. This reasoning is best illustrated by means of several examples, given in Figure 3.7. (For the purpose of illustration, the examples provided will be supplemented with *ad hoc* assumptions about the information that the players possess.)

Consider first the SL1 row player, and assume that this player knows the initial game is SL1-SL1, the Chicken game (19[66]). If Row plays this game according to its true preference set, the outcome it can expect to obtain is either DC or CD (as shown in Figure 3.3). However, by scanning its opponent's column (the SL1 column), Row observes that there are two types—HL and ML1—that obtain a better outcome against this player. Whereas Row can get either DC (its best outcome) or CD (its next-worst outcome) by playing its true type, it is assured of getting its best outcome by simulating one of the two other types.[32] In other words, when Row perceives the opponent to be SL1, it chooses to project the HL or ML1 type. This is denoted in Figure 3.7 by the arrow indicating a move from game 19(66) to games 9(39) or 4(35).

Similarly, if the ML1 row player accurately perceives its opponent to be ML1 (and knows it), its game perception is 7(12), and it has an incentive to project an ML2 type. With its own type, Row can expect to obtain either DD or CC; by projecting type ML2, Row can avoid the DD outcome—its next worst—and obtain CC, which it prefers (provided its deception is not detected and Column does not deceive). Again, this move by Row is denoted in Figure 3.7 by the arrow emanating from game 7(12) and pointing to game 12(48).

What the players actually do through this form of deception is induce a misperception on the part of the opponent by manipulating the opponent's perception of the crisis game. To see this, consider once again the move by the SL1 row player from game 19(66) to, say, game 9(39), and assume that Row knows its initial game perception is accurate. If Row's deception attempt is successful, Column will change its perception of Row from SL1 to ML1 and, hence, its game perception from 19(66) to 9(39). This latter game lies in the DC region, that is, it ends in Column's capitulation.

A more benign—and unexpected—use of deception is the one by the ML1 player who, as we saw, simulates an ML2 type. Here the purpose of deception is not to defeat the opponent by pretending to have more conflictual preferences—as is the case with the SL1 player—but rather to avoid a disastrous outcome and

Figure 3.7
Moves in the Final Outcomes Matrix I

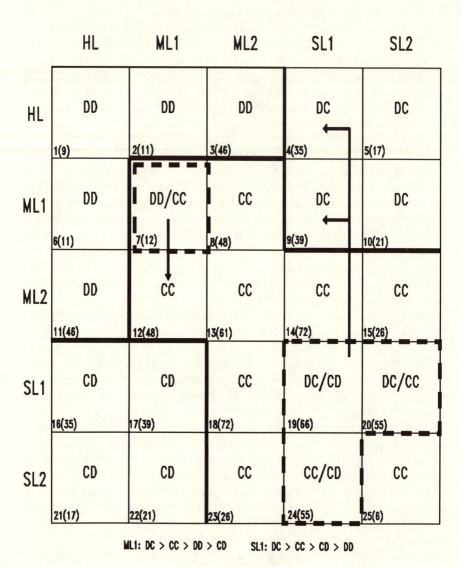

ML1: DC > CC > DD > CD   SL1: DC > CC > CD > DD

forge a compromise agreement. Hence, in this case, the player is interested in simulating a softer type in order to avoid the conflict outcome. In such a case, too, the opponent has an incentive to be deceived: CC is preferred by both players to DD/CC.

As these examples indicate, certain outcomes in the composite matrix become unstable (in the Nash sense) when players are allowed to simulate types, or engage in deception. Stability analysis was carried out for all the row players, and the results are given in Figure 3.8 (note that all arrows are now labeled). They may be summarized as follows:

1. The only players who are motivated to simulate types in the final outcome matrix are the soft-line and "hard" middle-line (ML1) players. The hard-line and middle-line (ML2) players never have an incentive to deceive in this way, no matter what their perception of the opponent's type.
2. Players simulate types in order to (a) avoid capitulation or war and induce compromise (arrows C, D, E, and F), and (b) force the opponent to capitulate (arrows A and B). This latter type of deception is used only by the SL1 player, and only against an opponent who is perceived to be a soft-liner.
3. Deception is never used against hard-line and middle-line (ML2) players.
4. All cases of deception, with a single exception, involve a shift to more conflictual preferences, even when the objective of deception is to induce compromise (arrows A, B, C, E, and F point upwards). The single instance in which a shift to less conflictual preferences occurs involves the ML1 player, when the perceived opponent is also ML1 (arrow D).
5. All cases of deception intended to induce compromise consist of a shift to the ML2 type. (Thus, arrows C, D, E, and F are incoming with respect to the ML2 row in the CC region.)

These propositions pertain to general observations that can be made with respect to deception, such as the types of players that deceive and the objectives and targets of deception. The arrows in Figure 3.8 also point to the consequences of deception. However, the actual occurrence of these consequences presumes several prior conditions.

First, for deception to occur at all, three conditions need to be met. The first two were already mentioned: (1) the player does not obtain its best outcome with its true preferences, and (2) the player identifies an insincere type that would allow it to do better against its perceived opponent. The first condition provides the motivation to deceive, and the second condition provides the means with which deception can be carried out. The third condition is this: (3) the player believes that its true type is not known to the opponent. This condition provides the opportunity to deceive, because if the player believes that the opponent knows its true type, deception is useless.

Once the three conditions are met, the player simulates an insincere type.

Figure 3.8
Moves in the Final Outcomes Matrix II

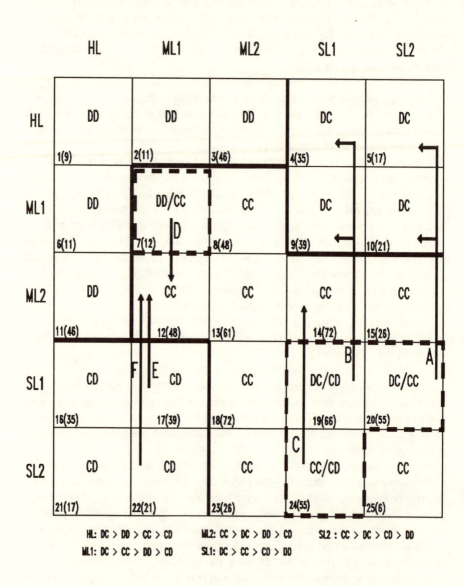

	HL	ML1	ML2	SL1	SL2
HL	DD 1(9)	DD 2(11)	DD 3(46)	DC 4(35)	DC 5(17)
ML1	DD 6(11)	DD/CC D 7(12)	CC 8(48)	DC 9(39)	DC 10(21)
ML2	DD 11(46)	CC 12(48)	CC 13(61)	CC 14(72)	CC 15(26)
SL1	CD 16(35)	F E CD 17(39)	CC 18(72)	DC/CD B 19(66)	DC/CC A 20(55)
SL2	CD 21(17)	CD 22(21)	CC 23(26)	CC/CD C 24(55)	CC 25(6)

HL: DC > DD > CC > CD   ML2: CC > DC > DD > CD   SL2 : CC > DC > CD > DD

ML1: DC > CC > DD > CD   SL1: DC > CC > CD > DD

However, for the consequences of Figure 3.8 to occur, three additional conditions need to obtain: (1) the deceiver perceives the opponent's type correctly at the point of deception; (2) the opponent does not deceive; and (3) the deception is not detected. The first condition is required in order to assure that the deceiver does not misperceive the opponent, in which case the outcome predicted in Figure 3.8 may not be the actual outcome. The second condition is required if deception is to be in fact one-sided, as described in the Figure. The third condition simply defines the deception as successful.

In a strategic situation, the choice to engage in deception is given to both sides. Therefore, we need to examine the consequences of *double deception*, that is, the mutual (rather than unilateral) simulation of types by players.

Figure 3.9 adds the deception moves of the column player to those of the row player (Column's moves are naturally symmetric to Row's and, therefore, do not require additional explanation). Note that double deception occurs in three games only. Specifically, only games 7(12), 19(66), and 20(55)/24(55) have two outgoing arrows. This indicates that the three conditions (specified above) that give rise to deception are met for both players. This is the difference between single-sided deception—where the three conditions are met for only one player (the deceiver)—and double-sided deception.

Figure 3.10 was obtained from Figure 3.9 by deleting all the cases that do not meet the conditions for double deception (these are cases of single-sided deception, whether by Row or by Column). The dashed lines trace the possible consequences of double deception.

Consider, for example, the departures of Row and Column from game 19(66). Assume that both players simulate the preferences of HL. This is denoted by arrows B and B' for Row and Column, respectively. If Row were the only player to simulate the HL type (that is, single-sided deception where Column adheres to its genuine SL1 type), the resulting game would be 4(35), as we saw earlier (in Figure 3.8). Similarly, if Column were the only player to project an HL type, the resulting game would be 16(35). When two-sided deception occurs, the "unilateral" departures of the players intersect in game 1(9), as is indicated by the intersection of the dashed lines emanating from games 4(35) and 16(35). Thus, the (potential) outcome of double deception in this case is game 1(9), denoted by BB'.

The possible consequences of two-sided deception in the remaining cases are likewise indicated by the intersection of arrows denoting departures by Row and Column. As in the case of single-sided deception in Figure 3.8, the consequences predicted by Figure 3.10 for double deception will occur only if: (1) both players perceive each other's type correctly at the point of deception (though each believes the other does not know its own true type); and (2) both players are deceived.

The most striking aspect of Figure 3.10 is the possibility that games played by soft-liners could be transformed—through double deception—into games played

Figure 3.9
Moves in the Final Outcomes Matrix III

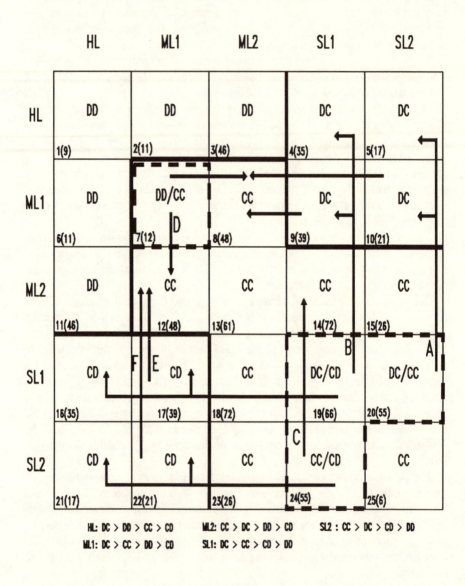

HL: DC > DD > CC > CD   ML2: CC > DC > DD > CD   SL2 : CC > DC > CD > DD
ML1: DC > CC > DD > CD   SL1: DC > CC > CD > DD

Figure 3.10
Double Deception

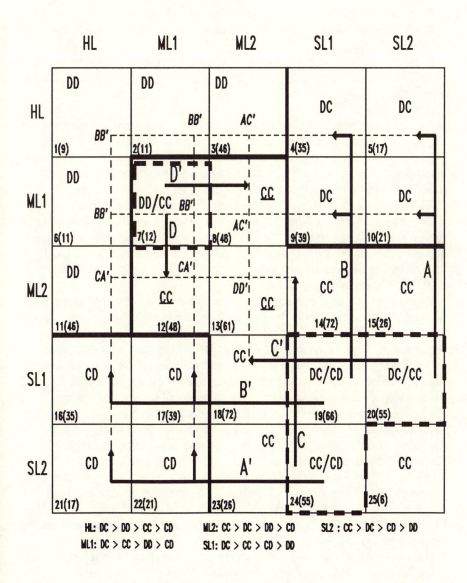

	HL	ML1	ML2	SL1	SL2
HL	DD BB' 1(9)	DD BB' 2(11)	DD AC' 3(46)	DC 4(35)	DC 5(17)
ML1	DD BB' 6(11)	DD/CC BB'| D 7(12)	D' CC AC'| 8(48)	DC 9(39)	DC 10(21)
ML2	DD CA' 11(46)	CC CA'| 12(48)	DD'| CC 13(61)	CC B 14(72)	CC A 15(26)
SL1	CD 16(35)	CD B' 17(39)	CC| C' 18(72)	DC/CD 19(66)	DC/CC 20(55)
SL2	CD 21(17)	CD A' 22(21)	CC 23(26)	CC/CD C 24(55)	CC 25(6)

HL: DC > DD > CC > CD   ML2: CC > DC > DD > CD   SL2 : CC > DC > CD > DD
ML1: DC > CC > DD > CD   SL1: DC > CC > CD > DD

75

by apparent hard-liners.[33] (Compare this result to Figure 3.8, where not a single case of two-sided deception crosses into the DD region.) Note that all games in the DD region are labeled as either BB' or AC' (CA'). This indicates that the players converge on this region in one of two ways:

1. In the case of BB' games, as a result of mutual defection by SL1 players from game 19(66) (Chicken), when at least one of the players simulates a hard-line type.
2. In the case of AC' (or CA') games, as a result of mutual defection by SL1 and SL2 players from games 20(55)/24(55) when the SL1 player simulates a hard-line type.

This result is particularly interesting, because the outcomes of all games in the DD region are ranked lowest by both soft-line players. Thus, the attempt by SL1 players to force their opponent to capitulate by means of projecting an HL type could result in a game in which these players prefer themselves to capitulate rather than fight! (See the game solutions in Figure 3.3.)

The fate of the SL2 player could be even more tragic under double deception (that is, in case 2 above). Note that this player simulates an ML2 type in order to induce compromise, which is the outcome it can obtain under single-sided deception. However, when its opponent simulates a hard-line type, both players may end up in disaster, which could have been avoided had neither of them, or only one of them, engaged in deception.

Despite the potential consequences of double deception by soft-liners, these players' attempts at deception become understandable when we consider a point raised earlier in our discussion, namely that soft-liners are the most likely targets for initiation. Thus, whereas the willingness of middle- and hard-line defenders to wage war in their defense deters all potential initiators except those who are highly dissatisfied, soft-line defenders are expected to offer little or no resistance. Thus, deception becomes for them a logical means of deterring initiators.

It is not surprising, therefore, that soft-liners are the only players who use deception to avoid capitulation, as we saw in Figure 3.8. Moreover, the targets they select for deception are only those opponents who prefer capitulation most, but rank compromise above war: "hard" middle-liners (ML1) and "hard" soft-liners (SL1). By deceiving these opponents, soft-liners can avoid war and capitulation and obtain, at a minimum, a compromise settlement. It is not surprising, too, that soft-liners do not attempt to deceive hard-liners and middle-liners (ML2): The former rank war above compromise, and the latter prefer compromise most.

An empirical case that exemplifies the use of deception by soft-liners is the 1905 Morocco crisis between France and Germany.[34] The crisis erupted following an attempt by the French to extend their control over Morocco and turn it into a French colony. The French sought the approval of England, Spain, and

Italy, but did not consult the Germans, who in response declared their support for Moroccan independence. This German challenge to French colonial interests triggered the crisis.

According to Snyder and Diesing (1977), the crisis preferences of the two countries were as follows: France had Prisoners' Dilemma preferences—that is, ML1 in our typology—and Germany had Chicken preferences, that is, SL1. However, the Germans were misperceived and believed French preferences to be SL1, too. Therefore, they perceived the crisis game to be Chicken.

Given the game perception of the Germans, they sought to coerce the French into making concessions by simulating an ML1 type (a departure from the Chicken game in Figures 3.8 and 3.10).[35] Therefore, despite the fact that "they had no intention of starting an unpopular and costly war over Morocco" (Snyder and Diesing, 1977: 110), the Germans attempted to convey the opposite through threats and demonstrations of firmness. It is interesting that the initial effect of German deception was disbelief on the part of the French foreign minister, Theophile Delcassé, and belief on the part of the premier, Pierre Rouvier. Their responses were consistent with those that can be predicted from Figures 3.8/10: Delcassé, who was not deceived, perceived the crisis game as 9(39)—the ML1-SL1 game—and therefore opposed concessions; Rouvier, on the other hand, was deceived, and hence perceived the game to be 7(12), the ML1-ML1 game. In this latter game, each player seeks to avoid war and induce compromise by projecting an ML2 type. In fact, Rouvier offered the Germans a compromise settlement (which they hastily rejected, demanding instead and obtaining the removal of Delcassé).

Eventually, the German bluff was exposed, with the French insisting on German capitulation, in accordance with the outcome expected in an ML1-SL1 game. The crisis in fact ended with unilateral German concessions at the 1906 Algeciras conference.

Soft-liner deception does not always fail, however, as illustrated by the example mentioned earlier of the May 1938 Czech crisis. It is doubtful that the British intended to fight Hitler over Czechoslovakia, yet Neville Chamberlain issued warnings that seemed to indicate—however ambiguously—that such would be his reaction to Hitler's crossing of the Czech border.

To conclude this discussion of deception, it is important to emphasize its more benign effects. Thus, we see in Figure 3.10 that although successful double deception may lead to consequences that are diametrically opposed from those intended by the players, successful deception may also induce cooperation. Specifically, pairs of SL1 and SL2 opponents can reach a compromise agreement by successfully simulating ML1 and ML2 types, respectively, and "hard" middle-liners (ML1) can achieve the same by projecting ML2 types.[36]

There is an interesting lesson in conflict resolution to be derived from the ability of ML1 opponents to secure agreement through deception. Although these actors' first preference is a coercive outcome—their opponent's capitulation—their concomitant realization that such a strategy can lead to war brings them to seek compromise. However, in the absence of trust, they cannot be certain that their offer of concessions will be reciprocated. By deceiving their opponent into thinking that even though they cannot be coerced, they still prefer a compromise agreement most (that is, ML2), they are able to induce the necessary trust. Once trust is present, deception is no longer necessary—the relationship between the players has been transformed.

NOTES

1. The following discussion of the theory also relies on its presentation in Brams (1983).

2. In the theory of moves, (1) the initial outcome is a real outcome, not a hypothesized situation, and (2) hypothesized moves and countermoves are translated automatically into action if a departure from the initial outcome is deemed rational by at least one of the players. The interpretation of the rules of nonmyopic play in the case of the initiation model are somewhat different. First, the "mental replication" (or imaginary reasoning) process applies to the entire game, so that the initial outcome (CD, DC, or DD) is also a hypothesized situation. Second, although a departure from the initial outcome may be rational for one or both of the players, it does not follow automatically that such a departure would take place. The decision to do so depends on the ranking of the final outcome in the crisis game relative to the status quo outcome in the initiation game.

3. Thus, Brams and Wittman (1981: 46) write that "only if the process can in fact reach an outcome best for a player with the next move—before cycling—will the surviving outcome be indisputably final."

4. *See* the discussion of "staying power" in Brams, 1983, pp. 104–108. For the most recent version of the theory of moves and its applications, *see* Brams, forthcoming. The solution concept discussed in this section is generally consistent with the revised theory.

5. It should be noted that Rational Termination is defined in conjunction with rules of play that are somewhat different from rules 1–4 specified above, which govern the play of the crisis game. (*See* the rules distinguishing players with staying power from those without it in Brams, 1983: 104–108.)

6. In protracted conflict, however, cycling may be interpreted as a form of attrition, wherein one party forces another to return to the battlefield repeatedly. For such an interpretation of the Israeli-Egyptian conflict, *see* Brams and Mor (forthcoming).

7. This is the reason why the algorithm for determining staying-power outcomes is applied to game trees with four nodes (*see* Brams, 1983: 108–114). The derivation of nonmyopic equilibria, on the other hand, is based on game trees with three nodes, because the stopping rule to prevent cycling is a constraint exogenous to the players' calculations. It is expected, therefore, that the final outcomes in the crisis games—which are based on four-node game trees—will coincide with staying-power outcomes rather than with nonmyopic equilibria.

8. The concept of *two-sided analysis* has been developed by Brams, who writes: "a rational choice is dictated not only by one player's own game-tree analysis but by that of the other player as well, which may cause a player to override his or her own (one-sided) rational choice" (1985a: 131). The notion of nonmyopic equilibria takes into consideration

departures from the initial outcome by both players, but does not assume that the players themselves perform a two-sided analysis when making their choices.

9. Recall also that there are in effect only fifteen distinct games in the composite matrix. The remaining games are obtained by interchanging the Row and Column players in the ten games in which the players have different preference rankings.

10. This is also game 12(48) in the same matrix.

11. For comparison, the DD outcome in this game meets the first condition specified by Brams and Wittman for nonmyopic equilibria: The backward induction process—performed on the three-node game tree!—indicates that this outcome survives the elimination process of both players. Hence, if DD were the initial outcome, neither player would depart from it. However, this outcome does not meet the second condition for nonmyopic equilibria, because there is no termination when Row is the first-moving player.

12. The CC outcome is a staying-power outcome, which is to be expected given the use of Rational Termination as the rationality criterion for the game solution.

13. Ignore for now games 7(12), 19(66), and 20(55)/24(55), which are discussed separately below.

14. A game-tree analysis of Chicken indicates that the player who initially obtains its next-worst outcome can obtain its best by departing to DD, whence the other player would be forced to move first. A two-sided game-tree analysis, moreover, indicates that the player who initially obtains its best outcome has an incentive to depart to CC, before the second player reduces it to 2 by departing first to DD (*see* Brams, 1985a: 128–133). This analysis is based on strict sequentiality, which makes the player who obtains initially its best outcome necessarily the next-moving player at DD. Because such an analysis leads to difficulties in the empirical interpretation of the game, I assume that the inability to predict who will move first from initial outcome DD remains in effect also when DD is not an initial outcome. This assumption implies the possibility of backtracking in this game, and in games 20(55) and 24(55), where the DD outcome is also ranked worst by both players.

15. Note that this game solution is closely linked with the attitudes toward the opponent that underlie the preference types of the two players. SL2 has the attitude of "peace without victory" and, therefore, prefers to reach the CC outcome without going through the DD outcome first. However, SL1's attitude of "peace through victory" forces SL2 to escalate (go through DD) so as to convince SL1 that it cannot obtain unilateral concessions.

16. The following discussion excludes game 20(55)/24(55), which was discussed above.

17. This game was discussed in Two-Sided Nonmyopic Calculation: An Example.

18. There is an implicit assumption here that the cost involved in the path leading from the initial crisis outcome to the final outcome does not affect the ordinal ranking of the final outcome in relation to the status quo.

19. Note that in the initiation game, the players now rank five, rather than four outcomes. The status quo outcome is ranked third by both players—hence, the number 3 in the NI-NI cell.

20. Logically, it is also possible that the status quo will be ranked below the CC outcome for the HL player. This ranking is not shown, however, because, as we shall see, the ranking of the status quo below the DD outcome is already a sufficient condition for this player to initiate against any type of opponent.

21. For an earlier analysis of misperceptions using 2 x 2 games, *see* Stein (1982). The following section addresses several issues not included in Stein's analysis, but it also examines some of his conclusions in light of the game solutions for nonmyopic players.

(Stein's article deals primarily with simultaneous choice by myopic players.)

22. The failure to study nonevents is even more puzzling if we consider that the purpose of deterrence is to induce nonevents: noninitiation of crises and wars. Moreover, even if we assume, for the sake of argument, that all initiation is detrimental to the international system, the study of failures to initiate is still important if the "guardians of the status quo" are not to fail to initiate preventive strikes against potential challengers of the existing order.

23. British and French warnings to Hitler during the May 1938 crisis over Czechoslovakia forced the German leader to withdraw his troops from the Czech border. That these warnings succeeded in deterring Hitler indicates that he was not unaware of his still inferior military power. That the warnings were feeble and devoid of a commitment to Czech security did not go unnoticed by the Germans. Shirer (1960: 364) has written that by failing to deal with Hitler more firmly at that time, Chamberlain probably missed the last opportunity to prevent World War II.

24. Maoz (1990b) discusses this paradox, which he calls "the paradox of successful deterrence," with respect to war initiation, and offers the Egyptian attack on Israel in October 1973 as illustration of the frustration factor at work. Specifically, Israel's credible deterrent allowed her to reject negotiations, which worked to increase the frustration of the Egyptians even further.

25. Since each player knows its own preferences, it follows that it is sufficient for one player to misperceive its opponent for the two players to play different games. If only Row is misperceived, it plays one of the four games in its own row that do not contain Column's true preferences, and Column plays the "true" game. If both players are misperceived, then, in addition to the four possible misperceived games for Row, there are also four possible misperceived games for Column (that is, those that lie in its own column and do not contain Row's true preferences). Thus, there are sixteen (4 x 4) combinations of pairs of game perceptions possible under mutual misperception.

26. To this condition, Stein adds a second one: that the opponent's future preferences be in fact different from the preferences that can be inferred from its past behavior.

27. Stein makes a similar assumption in his analysis of the Snyder and Diesing set of crisis games.

28. From the perspective of soft-line defenders, an initiation by an ML1 player who misperceives them as middle-liners will involve an offer of compromise, which the soft-liners prefer to the capitulation forced upon them by an ML1 initiator who perceives them correctly.

29. The perception of relative resolve in the case of the perceived SL1 initiator—and in the case of the SL2 initiator discussed below—is left out of this analysis.

30. For an analysis of deception by myopic players in 2 x 2 games, *see* Brams (1977).

31. The lower-left numbers in each cell of Figure 3.6 indicate the corresponding game numbers in Figure 3.3.

32. This is true provided it does not misperceive Column's type, its deception is not detected, and Column does not shift its type.

33. Note that this result is consistent with recommended bargaining tactics in Chicken and Chicken-like games. In these games (from which soft-liners "depart" when they deceive), players can prevail by convincing the opponent that they would rather fight than capitulate. The soft-liner attempt to simulate a more conflictual type is designed precisely to achieve such an effect on the opponent.

34. The following discussion relies on the account of the crisis in Snyder and Diesing (1977). The interpretation, however, is in terms of our analysis of deception.

35. It appears that the Germans attempted to project an ML1 type (in contrast to HL), because they sought to obtain concessions (that is, compromise) rather than a French capitulation.

36. Brams (1977) suggests that in the Cuban missile crisis, the Soviets misrepresented their preferences in order to induce the cooperative outcome. Specifically, the Soviets shifted from a tat-for-tit to a C-dominant preference structure. Brams writes that "from a normative perspective, the fact that the compromise outcome in this [Cuban missile crisis] game was a salutory—if not optimal—outcome for both players indicates that deception, on occasion, may be socially desirable. At least its effects, desirable or undesirable, deserve to be more carefully analyzed instead of being cast aside as simply cynical machinations of amoral actors" (pp. 196–97).

4

The 1967 Middle East Crisis:
Designing a Single-Case Study

This chapter and the next are concerned with the application of the crisis model to an empirical case—the 1967 Middle East crisis. The present chapter will discuss the research design of the case, examining issues of operationalization, measurement, units and levels of analysis, data, rules of inference, and validity. The next chapter will focus on the case itself.

The function of the case study with respect to the crisis model developed earlier is twofold: (1) confirmatory—to test the model by comparing its predictions with the actual crisis behavior of the states involved in the 1967 crisis; and (2) exploratory—to amend and refine the model in light of the empirical application.[1]

A single-case study—such as will be undertaken here—presents several methodological obstacles to a rigorous testing of the model's predictions. One notable problem is that of external validity, or the ability to generalize the conclusions of the study beyond the case under examination. However, even in terms of the single case itself—where control over competing explanations is weak or non-existent, and where variability in the monitored variables may be absent—the validity of inferences concerning causality (that is, internal validity) is difficult to guarantee.[2]

These problems and others require that careful attention be paid to the research design of the case. Thus, the present chapter prepares the ground for the empirical application in the next chapter. The discussion of research design and the methodology of single-case studies is organized as follows. The first section explains the focus of the case, namely the parameters and the relationships that will be studied empirically. The second section discusses operationalization, measurement, and data sources. The third section examines the issue of units and levels of analysis, and the fourth section discusses problems of inference and validity. (The reasons for the selection of the 1967 case are addressed at various points in the discussion and at the end of the chapter.)

WHAT IS TO BE EXPLAINED

A Brief Note on Causation and Game Theory[3]

The methodological discussion in the following sections will be cast in terms of causal relationships, or the process by which a change in one or more independent variables produces a change in one or more dependent variables. This notion of cause and effect, however, is not self-evident when it comes to a model based on rational choice. It is important, therefore, to specify what we mean by causal explanation in this context.

Beginning with a simple formulation, explanation in rational-choice models consists of establishing a relationship between the goal of an actor and its behavior. This relationship is one of maximization: An actor chose to behave in a particular way because that behavior maximized the actor's (realization of its) goal. Thus, if we can show that a certain observed behavior maximizes the hypothesized goals of an actor, then we have successfully explained that actor's behavior. (For further discussion, *see* Allison [1971] and Niou, Ordeshook, and Rose [1989].)

This formulation can be stated in causal terms as follows: The cause of a rational actor's choice of a particular behavior is its perception that the chosen behavior will maximize its goals. In a game-theoretic model, the cause of an actor's choice of a particular strategy is its perception that the selected strategy will yield the highest-ranking outcome possible against a given opponent.

The relevant variables in this formulation are the player's preferences among outcomes and (its perception of) the opponent's preferences. Together, these parameters produce the player's perception of the strategic situation—the game perception. Thus, we can say that the rational player chose a particular strategy because it perceived the game in a certain way. The game perception is the cause of a rational actor's choice of a particular strategy.

What causes a player to perceive the game in a particular way? We saw earlier (in Chapter 2) that the crisis-game perception depends on: (1) the player's attitudes toward the opponent and toward defeat (loss); (2) the player's perception of relative capabilities; and (3) the player's perception of the opponent's preferences (or type). Each of these factors may vary over players, and from one situation to another for a given player. Therefore, variability in the perception of the crisis game is caused by variations in one or more of the above factors.

So far, then, we have argued that a player's attitudes and perceptions are the cause of a particular game perception, which in turn causes the player to choose a particular course of action. Along these lines, we can continue to say that the behavior of the players (that is, their strategy choices) causes the occurrence of a particular outcome.

The Focus of the Case Study

The case study is designed to provide answers to two research questions: (1) What explains the behavior of the actors involved in the 1967 crisis?; and (2) What explains the outcome of that crisis?

Behavior and outcome, then, are the *dependent* variables in the case study. The crisis behavior of the actors is defined in terms of their choice of crisis strategy,[4] which was broken down into two broad categories—cooperation and defection. In addition, the possibility of deception—through image projection—implied the existence of four categories of crisis behavior: (1) sincere cooperation; (2) insincere cooperation (when deception occurs); (3) defection; and (4) insincere defection (when deception occurs). A fifth and distinct category is crisis initiation, which consists of sincere defection from the status quo.

The (final) outcome of the crisis can be one of the four outcomes defined in the crisis game (*see* Chapter 2): mutual cooperation; mutual defection (or escalation); and victory by one or the other player (the initiator or the defender). Intermediate crisis outcomes are defined somewhat differently (*see* discussion below).

Figure 4.1
The Crisis Model

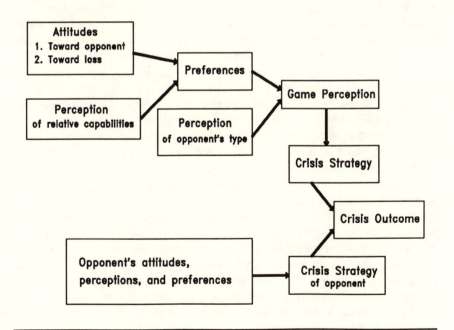

Figure 4.1 specifies the variables that produce behavior and outcome, and the process by which they do so. Thus:

1. The process begins with the player's attitudes toward the opponent and toward loss, and its perception of relative capabilities. These two variables produce the player's preferences among crisis outcomes, that is, the player's type. The preferences of the player and its perception of the opponent's type produce the player's game perception, and the game perception of the player produces its crisis strategy.[5]
2. The strategy choices of the player and the opponent produce the crisis outcome.[6]

In order to specify the testing procedure that will be used in the next chapter, it is important to identify and label the variables involved in the model. In the process described above (Figure 4.1), we can identify three *independent* variables: the player's attitudes; its perception of relative capabilities; and its perception of the opponent's type. There are two intervening steps between these variables and crisis behavior. The first is crisis preferences, produced by attitudes and the preception of relative capabilities. The second is game perception, produced by preferences and the perception of the opponent's type. We will refer to the player's preferences and its game perception as *intervening* variables (between the independent variables and the crisis strategy). Finally, in explaining the crisis outcome, the strategy choices of the players are the independent variables.[7]

Next, consider the explanation for crisis initiation, given in Figure 4.2. (Note that this figure is in effect an extension of Figure 4.1, with the game perception as the starting point.) Thus, the player's game perception produces its crisis strategy, as well as its expectation of the opponent's strategy.[8] These two variables in turn produce the player's expectation with respect to the crisis outcome. (The actual crisis outcome is produced by the player's crisis strategy and the actual crisis strategy of the opponent.) The expected crisis outcome and the player's valuation of the status quo determine its perception of the initiation game (not shown), which in turn produces the decision on initiation.

Viewing this process in conjunction with Figure 4.1, the decision on initiation is produced by (1) the independent variable of status quo valuation, and (2) the intervening variable of expected crisis outcome.

Having identified and labeled the variables involved in the model, we can proceed to outline the procedure to be followed in the case itself. In general, this procedure consists of measuring or assessing some of the variables empirically, then tracing their effects theoretically through the model. The resulting theoretical predictions (but not the intervening steps) are then compared with the empirical data in order to evaluate the utility of the process specified by the model. In other words, the "contact points" between the model and the empirical case are at the beginning of the process hypothesized by the model and at its end.

Specifically, the variables that will be measured empirically are the independent variables identified above: (1) the player's attitudes; (2) the player's perception of relative capabilities; (3) the player's perception of the opponent's type; and (4) the player's valuation of the status quo. These variables will serve as inputs to the model, which will then be used to generate predictions with respect to the dependent variables, namely (1) crisis behavior (including initiation), and (2) crisis outcome. These theoretical predictions will then be tested against the empirical evidence, that is, the actual behavior of the players and the actual outcome of the crisis.

To the extent that the data will permit it, and in the case of inconsistencies between predictions and actual events, the intervening variables will serve as access points to the process hypothesized by the model. This is one way in which the case can serve its exploratory function—by indicating how the model can be refined and modified.

Figure 4.2
The Crisis Initiation Model

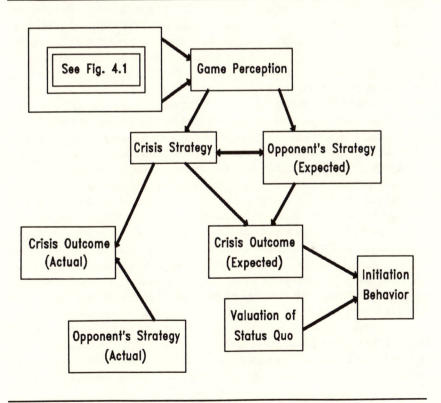

OPERATIONALIZATION, MEASUREMENT, AND HISTORICAL SOURCES

This section addresses the operationalization and measurement (or assessment) of the independent and dependent variables that will be monitored empirically. Each variable will be discussed in turn.

Attitudes

Prior to discussing the assessment of attitudes, we need to identify the actors whose attitudes will be examined. Broadly speaking, we will consider Egypt and Israel to be the two actors in the 1967 crisis. Empirically, this choice is justified, because these two countries were certainly the key participants in the crisis. Theoretically, the choice is guided by the bilateral nature of the crisis model.[9]

Since attitudes (as well as perceptions, preferences, and so forth) have been defined with respect to individual decision makers, no attempt will be made to aggregate them into group or state attitudes. This variable, then, will be assessed at the individual level of analysis (*see* Levels of Analysis for more details).

The model hypothesizes that two types of attitudes are crucial to the explanation of an actor's strategy choice.[10] The first is the attitude toward the opponent, defined in terms of the actor's belief about the relationship between conflict outcomes and national security. Thus, an actor may either believe in the "peace through victory" (or "peace by empire") argument, or it may believe in the "peace without victory" (or "magnanimity in victory") argument. (*See* Chapter 2 for a discussion of these terms.)

The second type of attitude is the actor's attitude toward loss (defeat). Thus, in the face of defeat, an actor may believe that the opponent should be made to pay the highest price that can be imposed on it, or the actor may believe that unavoidable defeat should not be resisted and that costs should be cut.

As argued in Chapter 2, these attitudes are basic enough to be assumed stable in the short run, so we would expect decision makers to have them in the period preceding the crisis itself. Furthermore, the content of these attitudes (especially the first) is such that if they were to change, the change would most likely be induced by an acute interstate conflict in which the decision maker would be a participant or to which he or she would be a witness. Therefore, the reasonable historical time frame for the establishment of an actor's attitudes is the period beginning with the most recent serious conflict in which the actor's state was involved and ending with the onset of the crisis. For most Egyptian and Israeli decision makers, this period lies between the 1956 war and the 1967 crisis.

The attitudes we wish to establish can be derived by reviewing the historical record of each individual, in search of statements and policy positions that indicate that individual's attitudes toward the issues we have specified. Public speeches at home and abroad; written statements, official and private (memoirs, diaries);

interviews; previous policy behavior; advocacy and support—these are some of the sources that have been traditionally used to establish attitudes. Prior academic research and the accounts and reminiscences of other participants are an additional source.

With respect to previous policy behavior, the security issue-area is particularly relevant. As argued in Chapter 2, the attitudes in question appear to underlie, and are therefore revealed by, security doctrines and defense policies. Evidence that a decision-maker was responsible for the formulation of a major security policy, or expressed support or opposition to it, can be very useful in inferring that decision maker's attitudes.

Although the use of multiple sources increases the reliability of attitude assessment, inconsistencies may be encountered in the process, both across sources and for a given source over time. Inconsistencies may be due to assessment error, or to reversals and changes in the attitudes themselves.

To begin with the latter, unless the decision maker is unable to formulate definite beliefs and/or shifts constantly from one position to another (*see* below), inconsistencies over time will be resolved in favor of recent, rather than earlier attitudes, because the former are the ones that impinge on crisis behavior.

Inconsistencies across sources will require certain criteria for evaluating the quality and reliability of evidence. Thus, for example, statements intended for internal consumption are generally (though not always) more indicative of a decision maker's attitudes than statements made abroad to a foreign audience; statements and arguments made to a restricted and high-level (internal) audience (for example, in governmental and committee debates) are generally more reliable than statements intended for the ears of the public and the media, and actual policy formulation is generally a more reliable source than mere support. In addition, the cumulative effect of the evidence should be considered: How significant is the inconsistency in relation to the evidence as a whole?

The possibility of political expediency is one of the major threats to the assessment of sincere attitudes. Wherever possible—though this requires in-depth study—the context in which a particular statement was made, or a policy position taken, should be examined closely. Was the decision maker under strong pressure to support one side or another? What were the incentives and costs associated with each position the decision maker could take on the issue? Clearly, the more politically courageous the policy position taken, or statement made, the more reliable an indication it is of the policy maker's attitudes.[11]

When inconsistencies cannot be resolved, or when the data are restricted or ambiguous, it may be impossible to derive a complete and strict preference ranking for the decision maker. In such as case, two or more types may have to be associated with the same individual. For testing purposes, that individual may have to be characterized in "negative" terms, that is, by specifying which types are inconsistent with the evidence available on his or her attitudes, and can therefore be ruled out. As a minimal test, then, we would expect that the decision maker's crisis behavior would be inconsistent with the (theoretical) behavior predictions made for the excluded types.

Turning to the 1967 case and to the Egyptian side, the single key decision maker whose attitudes we will establish is Gamal Abdoul Nasser, who, by nearly all accounts, dominated Egyptian decision making. Analyses of Nasser's attitudes toward the Arab-Israeli conflict and Egypt's role in it have been provided by his biographers, by several key Egyptian policy makers and confidants of the president, and by students of Egyptian and Middle East politics. Most of these sources cite extensively or reproduce primary sources, such as speeches and public statements made by Nasser prior to the crisis. An especially useful source is Harkabi's (1972) in-depth study of Arab attitudes toward Israel. In addition, for reasons already mentioned, Nasser's security policy with respect to Israel—as it developed in the period since 1956—will be the focus of particular attention.

On the Israeli side, the attitudes of several decision makers need to be established, since most of Israel's crisis decisions were group decisions (the Cabinet forum). Of particular importance were the attitudes and resulting policy positions of Prime Minister Levi Eshkol, Foreign Minister Abba Eban, Defense Minister (from June 1) Moshe Dayan, and Minister of Labor Yigal Allon. Some of the most useful analyses of elite images and beliefs, as well as extensive data on the internal debates during the crisis itself, are found in Brecher (1980; 1972) and Stein and Tanter (1980). These studies draw on a large variety of primary sources and will therefore serve as the basis for the analysis of Israeli decision making. As in the case of Nasser, works that discuss Israel's security policy during the 1956–1967 period are an important source for attitudes.

Perception of Relative Capabilities

The "perception of relative capabilities" refers to decision makers' *subjective* and *context-dependent* assessment of their state's capabilites in comparison with those of the opponent. The assessment is subjective in the sense that decision makers may differ in terms of the criteria they employ in forming their judgments. The assessment is context-dependent in the sense that it applies to a very specific situation—it is an answer to the question, "Should this particular crisis escalate to an armed conflict, which side is expected to be stronger?"

Given the context dependence of this variable, situational factors that perhaps would not figure into an objective estimate of relative capabilities can nevertheless enter into the assessment of individuals. Thus, for example, policy makers may decide that their state would be stronger only if it had the benefit of surprise or only if it initiated war.[12] Alternatively, if decision makers conditioned their assessment of relative capabilities on the support of outside parties, then their judgment would depend on what they expected the position of these parties to be.[13]

This definition of the relative capabilities variable introduces a potential instability into the preferences of decision makers, but given the perceptual nature of the model, it would not be very reasonable to operationalize the variable in terms of objective and uniform criteria for estimating capabilities. The problem, then, is not conceptual, but one of measurement: how to treat conditional assessments of capabilities in an empirical context, specifically in the determination of preferences.

The solution is dictated by the model itself. To the extent that different assessments result in different crisis preferences for a given player, then the preferences themselves should be stated in conditional terms. That is, if a player determines that the state will be stronger under condition x and weaker under condition y, then at any point in time the player's preferences depend on whether it perceives condition x or y to apply. It follows, then, that predictions of *policy recommendations* for such players should be specified in conditional terms too.

Empirically, it is very likely that players' assessments of relative capabilities will be available and apparent at the beginning of the crisis, if not before, because the issues and stakes involved are crucial enough to justify long-term consideration by top policy makers. During the crisis itself, then, the problem confronting decision makers with conditional assessments will be to determine which set of conditions applies at any given time. With respect to such players, the test of the model's (conditional) predictions will consist not only of demonstrating a congruence between the predicted and actual policy recommendations of the players, but also of showing that the conditions associated with each prediction were in fact the conditions perceived by the players to apply at the time they made their policy recommendations.

Data on perceptions of relative capabilities will be gathered in a manner similar to that indicated above for attitudes. However, more extensive data will be required on the crisis decision-making process itself in order to determine the perceptions of players with conditional assessments of capabilities.

Perception of the Opponent

"Perception of the opponent" refers to how a decision maker perceives the opponent's preferences during a crisis. Together with attitudes and the perception of relative capabilities, this variable determines the game perception of individuals.

In the model, the perception of the opponent is featured as an independent variable. Therefore, we do not offer propositions about the conditions under which such perceptions undergo change. Prior empirical research (for example, Snyder and Diesing, 1977; Jervis, 1976; and Hoslti, 1967), however, indicates that the perception of the opponent can change in midcrisis, in response to discrepant incoming information. More specifically, the types (that is, structure of beliefs) of some individuals predispose them to process current information that is inconsistent with initial beliefs, whereas the types of other individuals predispose them to resist such information.[14]

Thus, we would expect that the crisis perception of the opponent would be stable for some decision makers; for others, however, this variable may acquire different values during the course of the crisis. To the extent then that players' attitudes and their perceptions of relative capabilites are stable, midcrisis changes in game perceptions will be induced by changes in the perception-of-the-opponent variable.

As in the case of the perception of relative capabilities, data on the crisis decision-making process will be required in order to determine whether changes occur in individuals' perceptions of the opponent. As to the perceptions themselves, the opponent's perceived type will not be derived in the same manner as players' types (that is, from the attitudes and perception of relative capabilities attributed to the opponent), because such extensive data are unlikely to be available for each player examined.

Instead, we will assume that the five typical preference sets derived in the model (Chapter 2) in fact capture most decision makers' definitions of hard-, middle-, and soft-liners. Thus, for example, when the data will be found to indicate that a certain policy maker perceived the opponent as a "hard-liner," we will assume that the meaning of this description is adequately conveyed by the preference ranking attributed to hard-liners in the model. Since the data are likely to provide more than mere labels—as discussions of the opponent's crisis intentions often do—validation of this assumption will be possible to some extent through the construction of partial rankings for the opponent from the opinions expressed by individual decision makers.

Valuation of the Status Quo

In a strict sense, the internal and external environments of states change constantly and are thus never stable. In terms of the concerns of foreign policy decision makers, however, only changes in certain key factors—those that can or do impinge on the security and welfare of the state—are monitored and responded to. With the exception of periods of constant upheaval, the "relevant world" of such policy makers is stable in the short run: It consists of the existing configuration of territorial, political, and military factors that are perceived to affect the security of the state.

The "valuation of the status quo" variable refers to the utility that decision makers associate with the existing (precrisis) configuration of factors. In the ordinal framework of the model, this variable is defined in relative terms, that is, by how the status quo outcome is ranked in relation to the four possible crisis outcomes. Thus, if the SQ outcome is ranked above any crisis outcome, the player is considered satisfied; if it is ranked below at least one crisis outcome, the player is considered dissatisfied.

In the empirical application of the model, two points should be noted with respect to the valuation of the status quo:

1. It is not the case that whenever decision makers express their dissatisfaction with the status quo, we can immediately infer that they rank the status quo lower than at least one crisis outcome: Their dissatisfaction may be such that they prefer a noncoercive resolution of the conflict over the status quo, but still prefer the status quo to any crisis outcome. However, in the context of the adversarial relationships we are dealing with, we will consider such decision makers to be satisfied with the status quo. Dissatisfied players, on the other hand, will be those for whom only coercive diplomacy, or war at the extreme, may forestall or induce a change in the current configuration of territorial, political, and military factors.[15]

2. One reason for a player to rank the status quo below at least one crisis outcome is that it is dissatisfied with the existing state of affairs. Dissatisfaction, however, may also arise when a player considers the status quo satisfactory, but perceives it to be threatened. Such a player may initiate a crisis in order to preserve the status quo, by issuing a demand that the opponent stop the threatening behavior (*see* Chapter 1 for further discussion). If we treat such a player as satisfied—ranking the SQ outcome above any crisis outcome—then we exclude from the model empirical cases in which initiation is designed to preserve, rather than change, the status quo. Therefore, we will broaden the meaning of the term "status quo" (and the variable "valuation of the status quo") to include perceived threats to the existing configuration of territorial, political, and military factors. A dissatisfied player could then be either a player who opposes the existing state of affairs, or a player who favors it but perceives it to be threatened. (In either case, and consistent with point 1 above, such players would be considered dissatisfied only if they believed the situation to be resistant to noncoercive change.)

The two points raised above provide criteria for the distinction between satisfied and dissatisfied players, namely between those players who rank the status quo above any crisis outcome and those who rank it below at least one crisis outcome. These criteria can be stated in terms of questions that are to be answered in the empirical case: (1) Do decision makers want to change the status quo or preserve it? If the latter, do they perceive the status quo to be threatened? (2) If decision makers wish to forestall or induce a change in the status quo, do they believe their objective can be accomplished through peaceful means, or does it require the use of coercion?

Such questions can be answered by scrutinizing the foreign policy agendas of decision makers, as revealed by word and deed. In particular, *casi belli* and their interpretation by decision makers provide a good indication of how individuals view the status quo.

Casi belli delineate the borders of the status quo by specifying thresholds that distinguish between acceptable and unacceptable behavior. These thresholds guide the state in responding to high external threats, and can serve as a deterrent by signaling to the opponent what behavior would be considered a serious challenge to the status quo. In addition, because *casi belli* are threshold levels specified for certain aspects of relations between adversarial states, they also identify, in substantive terms, the dimensions of the relationship—the territorial and political arrangements, and the military balances—that the state deems to be critical to its security and welfare.[16]

In the empirical case, the *casi belli* of Egypt and Israel—or, rather, their interpretation by decision makers—will be noted or inferred. These thresholds will serve as indicators of what decision makers perceived to be the critical substantive dimensions of their country's relations with the opponent prior to the 1967 crisis. In particular, we will have to establish whether in the actual circumstances they confronted, individuals believed that their country's *casi belli* were threatened or violated.

So far, we discussed the ranking of the status quo relative to crisis outcomes in general, and relative to the war outcome in particular. However, for some types of players (ML1 and SL1; *see* Chapter 3), an above-war ranking of the status quo still leaves open the question of whether the status quo is valued more or less than the *compromise outcome*. For these players, the question is this: Although the acts of the opponent are acute enough to generate dissatisfaction but not acute enough to warrant war, is compromise with an opponent who is not expected to capitulate better than tolerating the situation for the time being? The answer depends on the issue at stake—whether or not it is perceived as divisible and whether the state can afford to wait. Therefore, the determination of the status quo ranking relative to the compromise outcome will be made on the basis of a substantive, *ad hoc* judgment, guided by the question posed above.

Another point with respect to the status quo has to do with shifts in its relative ranking that are not induced by changes in its valuation. That is, the relative ranking of the status quo can also be affected by changes in the valuation of crisis outcomes. In the model, such changes can occur only as a result of transformations in attitudes and in the perception of relative capabilities (*see* Figure 4.1). As argued earlier, however, the crisis preferences of each individual will be established on the basis of that individual's most recent precrisis attitudes and perceptions. The valuation of the status quo will be determined in relation to this preference set, thus in effect ruling out changes in the relative ranking of the status quo that result from changes in the valuation of crisis outcomes.

Finally, for some players, the decision on initiation depends also on their perception of the opponent's relative ranking of the status quo (*see* Chapter 3). Should such players be identified in the empirical case, their perception of the opponent as satisfied or not—and if not, to what extent—would have to be established.

Data on such perceptions should not be hard to obtain. Because the opponent's relative ranking of the status quo affects its motivation to initiate, we can expect decision makers to be highly sensitive to such information. It is possible, however, that their estimates be conveyed in operational terms, that is, by what they expect the opponent to do (for example, "the opponent is desperate enough to try this or that," or "the opponent knows his limitations and will not provoke us"). Data of these sort are particularly desirable because they eliminate the need to establish players' perceptions of the opponent's status quo ranking.

Crisis Behavior

Crisis Initiation

Crisis initiation occurs when a party issues a demand—coupled with some compellent threat for noncompliance—requesting a revision (or restoration) of the status quo. A game model of crisis initiation was developed in Chapter 2. In the empirical case, the test of the model is to predict the initiation of the crisis for the initiator, in terms of a defection from the status quo outcome in the initiation game.

Specifically, crisis initiation has to be predicted from the initiator's type, perception of the opponent, and valuation of the status quo outcome (*see* The Focus of the Case Study and Figure 4.2 above). The conditions under which initiation is expected to occur were specified in these terms in Chapter 2. Methodological issues that relate to initiation will be discussed later.

Crisis Strategy

The two broad strategies available to players in the crisis game are coercion and accommodation, or cooperation and defection. In Chapter 2, accommodation was described as a strategy that consists of making concessions or intentionally signaling one's willingness to make them if the opponent does likewise; coercion, on the other hand, consists of an effort to use coercive means—threats, displays of force, and use of force short of war—to force the opponent's hand. Thus, a strategy that uses coercive means in order to force an opponent to come to the negotiation table is nevertheless coercive, despite its ultimate objective of cooperation.[17] In general, then, the cooperative or coercive nature of a strategy will be determined by the means used, not by the objectives pursued.

This general criterion, however, is not always helpful, because it is context-free. In an ongoing crisis, the reference point for accommodation and coercion changes with the moves of the actors. Thus, an actor may not make concessions explicitly, but if it reverses an established pattern of, say, escalatory moves, then that reversal may be seen as a cooperative move, especially if the actor had the means and the opportunity to engage in further escalation. In other words, what an actor does not do at a particular point in a crisis may be as important as what the actor does, given a history of prior moves or an established pattern of strategy choices.

Therefore, in determining whether a particular move is coercive or not, both the means used and the context in which the move was made should be taken into account. With respect to context, particular attention should be paid to reversals of trends and patterns: A move that extends, and is consistent with, a pattern of coercive moves is coercive, and vice versa.

In a model that conceives of strategy choices as dichotomous, another issue is the interpretation and classification of moves that appear to combine coercive and accommodating elements. It is difficult to lay down *a priori* guidelines for classification in such cases, because much depends on the context in which they occur. In fact, the particular circumstances of the crisis, and their reasoned and explicit interpretation by the researcher, are often sufficient to make a determination on the essential nature of a particular strategy. One guideline that can be applied to the classification of such "mixed" strategies has to do with the substantive characteristics of the coercive elements they contain. Specifically, it is important to determine whether the coercive aspect of the strategy raises the ante, or is a response to a prior, truly escalatory move by the opponent. If the latter, then the coercive element is essentially a defensive move (though it may not appear as such to the opponent); when such a move is undertaken in conjunction with the sincere offering of concessions or the indication of a willingness to compromise, the strategy itself is essentially accommodating.

A second issue that needs to be addressed is that of deception. Specifically, how can deception be detected in the empirical case? There are two types of inconsistencies that suggest the possibility of deception: (1) an inconsistency between the crisis preferences implied by official statements on the one hand and the crisis game perception (as derived by the researcher from attitudes, the perception of relative capabilities, and the perception of the opponent) on the other hand; and (2) an inconsistency between actual strategy choices on the one hand and the crisis strategy deduced from the game perception on the other hand.

The problem lies in the interpretation of these inconsistencies, because they can be attributed to several factors besides deception, such as an error in the derivation of the game perception (as a result of the researcher's misinterpretation of players' attitudes and perceptions), or the inapplicability of assumptions underlying the game solutions (for example, nonmyopic calculation when decision makers actually think myopically). In other words, inconsistencies may be the result of deception, but they may also be the outcome of a faulty or misapplied model.

A possible method of confirming the occurrence of deception is "process tracing" (to be discussed later). Briefly, this procedure involves the tracing of the process leading to the decision to engage in deception. In applying this method to the empirical case, particular attention should be paid to the justification provided by decision makers for their policy recommendations.

Even if the model successfully predicts an inconsistency that is observed in reality, there is still the question of whether the model predicts an inconsistency (that is, deception) that does not occur in reality. It is important, therefore, to examine the model's predictions with respect to deception once the game perception of each actor has been established. The model performs well to the extent that inconsistencies are not observed when the model does not predict them (or predicts that they should not occur), and that inconsistencies do occur when the model says that they should.

In addition, when inconsistencies occur, they should be in the direction specified by the model. As noted earlier, deception strategies are divided into insincere cooperation and insincere deception. Insincere cooperation occurs when the projected type signals a willingness to compromise; insincere defection occurs when the projected type signals an intention to use coercion in order to force the opponent to comply. Specifically:

1. A shift in type from a dominant-coercive type (that is, HL and ML1) to a dominant-cooperative (SL2) or a tit-for-tat type (ML2) constitutes insincere cooperation.
2. A shift in type from a dominant-cooperative type to a dominant-coercive or tat-for-tit type (SL1) constitutes insincere defection.
3. A shift in type from a dominant-cooperative type to a tit-for-tat type constitutes insincere cooperation.[18]

Crisis Outcome

There are four crisis outcomes defined by the intersection of strategies in the crisis game: (1) mutual cooperation (CC); (2) mutual defection (DD); (3) capitulation by the row player (CD); and (4) capitulation by the column player (DC).

These are final outcomes. The players may pass, however, through one or more of these outcomes on their way to the final outcome, where the game terminates (that is, the crisis ends). In this case, the outcomes through which the players pass are *intermediate outcomes*. It is important to note that when the players pass through the DC/CD outcomes—that is, when these outcomes are intermediate outcomes—they are not interpreted as capitulation by one or the other players, but rather as the making of concessions with the expectation that the opponent will reciprocate.

In addition, it is possible that the players do not share the same game perception. In this case, their subjective interpretations of the crisis outcome at which they are located at any given moment in the crisis may differ. The outcome of the 1967 crisis was unambiguous: an Israeli initiation of war. As I shall argue in the next chapter, however, whereas the Israelis perceived the crisis outcome to be DD at the time they made their decision to attack, such was not Nasser's perception.

These points are important because the task of the model in the 1967 case is to predict the crisis outcome, namely war initiation by one of the players. Yet war initiation is not a strategy in the crisis game. Rather, war is an implicit possibility in the DD outcome. Therefore, the model may be seen to predict war only to the extent that it predicts the final crisis outcome to be DD.

However, because the players may not share the same game perception—and because war may come about as a result of a unilateral decision on war initiation by one of the players (in contrast to mutual compromise)—it is sufficient that the model predict for only one of the players a game perception in which DD is perceived to be the final outcome.

Such a prediction is not as strong as would be possible with a model in which the strategy of war initiation is explicitly modeled. It does, however, provide an explanation for the behavior of the war-initiating player, because the preference rankings of the players are based on the assumption that war is an implicit possibility in the DD outcome. A player's choice to stay at this outcome stems from that player's relative ranking of DD—and therefore of war—over any other crisis outcome to which the player could move the game.

LEVELS OF ANALYSIS

Empirical applications of game-theoretic models involve the specification and justification of preferences of concrete players. When the players are individual decision makers rather than states, the problem of units and levels of analysis does not arise, because an aggregation of those individuals' preferences into a group preference is not an issue. However, when a group is involved in making a decision, the nature of the preferences that give rise to the decision becomes problematic.

By and large, game-theoretic and rational-choice applications have circumvented this problem by means of the unitary-actor assumption. This assumption has been interpreted in two different ways. First, it has been taken to imply that a single, concrete decision maker can represent, and substitute for, the group or the state as a whole. Such a powerful individual is assumed capable of imposing his or her preferences on the group, so that the preferences of the individuals composing the group no longer matter (*see* Bueno de Mesquita, 1981).

The second use of the unitary-actor assumption is more ambiguous. The researcher specifies the preferences of the "state" by ignoring its components altogether. If any aggregation of preferences takes place, the rules underlying it are not discussed and remain implicit. What happens, in effect, is that the prior actions of the state are assumed to reveal its aggregate preferences, or that the statements of key decision makers are taken as evidence for the ranking of outcomes for the state, without additional explanations of the role and status of these individuals vis-à-vis the group.

The advantages and drawbacks of these approaches cannot be dealt with here, but the issue of group preferences is important in our case for conceptual and empirical reasons. To begin with, the concepts of attitudes and perceptions are applicable to individuals. Even if a case could be made for the application of these concepts to the group, the problem of aggregating individual attitudes and perceptions would remain.

This difficulty would not have mattered had the crisis decisions of both Egypt and Israel been made by single individuals.[19] This condition was closely approximated in Egypt's case, since by most accounts, Egyptian decision making was strongly dominated by Nasser. In this case, then, the application of the unitary-actor assumption does not present conceptual difficulties.

The same, however, cannot be said of Israeli decision making during the crisis. This is the empirical problem in the present case. According to Stein and Tanter (1980: 78), three of Israel's five key decisions were made by a group—the cabinet.

The issue, then, is how to aggregate the attitudes and perceptions of individual decision makers in the Israeli cabinet into a single preference type that is representative of the cabinet as a whole. Unfortunately, a satisfactory solution to this problem is not yet within the reach of social-choice theory. Nor do we have, in the present study, a model that specifies the political process by which multiple preference sets compete for dominance through coalition building.[20] Therefore, the empirical application of the model will be conducted at the individual level of analysis, with the emphasis being on individuals' *policy recommendations*.

Specifically, rather than predict the strategy choice of the Israeli government as a whole, the task of the model will be the following: to specify the set of individuals and their respective policy preferences from which came the winning individual-policy combination, that is, that policy—and the individual(s) associated with it—which actually prevailed in the internal group debate. That is, the model will be used to derive a set whose members are paired elements, consisting of individuals and the policy recommendations deductively associated with them. Once this set is specified, the actual strategy choice of Israel will be observed. A consistency will then have to be established (1) between the actual strategy choice and one or more members of the set, and (2) between that member or members of the set and the actual individuals and policy recommendation that prevailed in the internal debate.

This procedure accords with the predictive powers of the model. In the presence of multiple preference sets and in the absence of a "dictator," the model cannot predict which of several competing policy preferences will be chosen by the decision-making unit. The model can, however, predict—on the basis of the attitudes and perceptions of key individuals—the set of policy positions, and the coalitions that will form around them, from which the winning coalition and policy will be drawn (that is, the structure of the internal debate). Moreover, the model can predict—on the basis of changes in individual attitudes and perceptions—how the set of policy positions will evolve over time.

THE LOGIC OF INFERENCE IN SINGLE-CASE STUDIES AND THE EMPIRICAL CASE[21]

The testing of the propositions suggested by the model is a test for consistency between the values predicted for the dependent variables and the observed behavior and crisis outcome. That is, after establishing by means of historical data the attitudes and perceptions of the crisis actors, the actual strategy choices of these actors must be examined to determine their consistency with the behavior predicted by the model from the established attitudes and perceptions. The same is done with respect to the crisis outcome. (This is the "congruence procedure" described in George [1979] and George and McKeown [1985].)

With respect to each form of behavior, one needs to define what is to be considered consistent and what is not. This issue is addressed below. If consistency between the predicted and the actual behavior cannot be established, then the proposition is falsified. If consistency is discovered, the proposition is not rejected, but one cannot automatically conclude that a causal relationship is at work: An important question in an empirical setting is whether the observed behavior (choice of strategy) is in fact influenced by the actors' game perception, or whether the consistency is only apparent or even spurious.

Confidence in a causal interpretation of the evidence is enhanced if there is a firm theoretical basis for expecting that a certain form of behavior will result from a certain game perception. The section entitled What Is to Be Explained, and Figures 4.1 and 4.2, explicate the theoretical reasoning by which the predictions of the model have been derived.

As argued earlier in this study, the strictly dichotomous choice between cooperation and defection—required for purposes of simplification—results in predictions of behavior that are not as discriminating as would be possible with models that allow players to choose among levels of cooperation and defection. In this sense, the model is underdetermined: It differentiates among five types of players, but predicts essentially two forms of behavior. The result is that several different preference types are consistent with the same behavior.

This problem is perhaps less acute than it appears to be. First, the model provides a theoretical reasoning for the consistency of different types with the same form of behavior. Second, the inferences drawn from the empirical case can be qualified by arguing that although the observed behavior would also be consistent with other specified types of players, it would not be consistent with each and every type. (Thus, for example, a cooperative strategy may be consistent with two of the five decision-maker types, but it would be inconsistent with the other three.) Third, to the extent that deception has taken place, the model is more discriminating by predicting four different types of behavior (*see* discussion above).

Confidence in a causal interpretation of consistency can be also enhanced if it is established over a period of time for a sequence of decisions. The 1967 case provides ample opportunity to examine consistency, because more than a single decision was taken by each of the players throughout the course of the crisis (*see* below).

Even if consistency is both supported on theoretical grounds and observed repeatedly over time, the explanatory power of the independent variables is still not clear. Two questions need to be asked, and we will deal with each in turn.

1. Had the specified values of the independent variables been different, would the behavior/outcome have been different as well? In other words, are the specific beliefs a necessary condition for the occurrence of the particular behavior/outcome?[22]

Ideally, we could hold all other antecedent variables constant and change only the value of our independent variable in order to observe the effect of this change on the dependent variable. In nonexperimental social science research, control is difficult to achieve. In a single-case study, moreover, even variability in the variables under study is not guaranteed. The 1967 case offers several advantages and several drawbacks with respect to variability.

To begin with, the empirical study of any crisis presumes its occurrence, which precludes variability in the dependent variable of initiation. Morrow (1986) has written that "the mere fact that a crisis is observed means the case is not typical of all dyadic relations." This problem of selection bias is also addressed in Achen and Snidal (1989), who point out that deterrence studies have focused overwhelmingly on cases of deterrence failure (for example, Lebow, 1981).

The problem of selection bias is of course particularly acute in inductive studies, since such studies base their findings on a biased sample of cases. Deductive theories of crisis, on the other hand, provide for noninitiation by specifying *a priori* the conditions under which actors choose not to initiate a crisis. The problem comes up in empirical application and testing, because noninitiation (if chosen by all relevant actors to a conflict) implies that a crisis will not be observed.

Possible solutions to this problem cannot be addressed here. The point to note is that the model developed in the previous chapters does specify the conditions—in terms of types, valuation of the status quo, and the perception of the opponent—under which initiation will or will not take place. The 1967 crisis is of course a case of initiation, and the burden of the next chapter is to examine whether the conditions for initiation specified by the model are met in this particular case. This is a minimal test: If the theoretical conditions did not exist in reality, the model in this respect fails, but if the conditions did exist, we cannot legitimately conclude that in the presence of different conditions, the crisis would not have been initiated (but *see* below).[23]

Next, the 1967 crisis naturally does not provide for variability in the crisis outcome—it is a case of a crisis that ended in escalation to war. This is certainly a crippling problem for theory-generating case studies (*see* Lijphart, 1971). In our case, it provides a test for the escalation-to-war conditions specified in the model but, again, only in the sense of possibly disconfirming them: Even if the conditions did exist in reality (that is, the model would not be disconfirmed), we cannot conclude that the conditions are necessary ones and that in their absence the crisis would have ended differently.

There is, however, a procedure whereby an artificial variability can be introduced into the case. George (1979: 108) refers to this procedure as "mental experiments," whereby the investigator engages in "mental rehearsals in which he varies critical variables in order to estimate variance in outcomes." This will be done by means of argumentation from the available historical materials, for both crisis initiation and crisis outcome.

The 1967 case provides (natural) variability in two important variables: preference type and strategy choice. To begin with the former, Israel's decision makers were not monolithic in terms of their preferences. Rather, throughout the crisis, the Israeli cabinet was locked into a harsh debate between soft-liners, middle-liners, and hard-liners, who made different policy recommendations to Prime Minister Eshkol. Thus, we have *prima facie* evidence that different values of the preference-type variable do produce different policy preferences. What needs to be established is whether these differences are predicted by the model.

The problem of control remains, however, because the variations in policy advocacy may have been the result of differences in factors other than types (for example, roles). Some level of control, however, can be assumed if it can be shown that individuals of identical decision-maker types and policy recommendations differed in other respects, such as role, status, rank, and departmental affiliation.[24]

The 1967 case also provides variability in strategy choices. Brecher (1980) has documented seventeen decisions made by Israel over the course of the crisis. Certainly not all decisions were of equal importance—Stein and Tanter (1980) consider five key decisions only—and there is little variability in the nature, coercive or accommodating, of these decisions. Still, some of them were escalatory, whereas others could be seen as conciliatory.

Variability in Egyptian strategy choices is quite pronounced: After a series of escalatory steps—between May 14 and May 30—Nasser attempted to de-escalate the crisis (May 31 to June 4). This change in Egyptian strategy has not been satisfactorily explained in the literature on the crisis, which has analyzed Nasser's decision making primarily from a cognitive perspective. Providing an alternative explanation—and testing the predictions of the model in this respect—is an important objective of the next chapter.

2. Would not a behavior/outcome different from the observed one have been also consistent with the specific beliefs?

This problem arises in terms of the theory itself, which may be indeterminate in some of its predictions. (If the problem is acute, the theory cannot be falsified, and there is no sense in testing its propositions.) The issue bears on the present model, because in some cases, a single preference type is consistent with more than one form of behavior and, therefore, more than one crisis outcome. This difficulty is the result of indeterminacy in the game solutions, an obstacle to the scientific testing of game-theoretic predictions in general.[25]

Although the indeterminacy is inherent in the theory underlying the model, it applies to very few games in the composite matrix and is therefore not acute. Also, as far as the exploratory aspect of the case study is concerned, the occurrence of indeterminate game situations in reality provides an opportunity to study the behavior of actors (that is, their actual strategy choice) under such circumstances.

Having examined the two questions that relate to inferring causality from consistency, it is important to note an additional method—"process tracing"—that may be used to supplement congruence (*see* George, 1979). Process tracing consists of establishing the sequence of intervening steps between attitudes/perceptions and action. By providing the full context of the decision-making process, the researcher can trace the influence of attitudes and perceptions at each stage of the process leading to a decision.

The use of process tracing has been implied in the previous discussion, with respect to Israeli decision making, where the extensive data required for the procedure are available in the existing literature. Thus, beyond establishing consistency between attitudes/perceptions and action, the next chapter will also examine the internal debate that took place in the Israeli cabinet prior to decisions on strategy.

To summarize, the selection of the 1967 crisis as a case for study is justified by the variability it provides in key variables. Equally important is the wealth of data that exist for this crisis, primarily for the Israeli side, which has been studied extensively over the years. This aspect of the case is essential for a model that requires detailed information (for example, in order to establish preferences).

There are two additional attractive features to this particular crisis. First, it was relatively short (three weeks), thus enabling an in-depth study. Second, the crisis literature is heavily biased in favor of Western and superpower-related crises.[26] This bias is also evident in the theoretically oriented studies of the 1967 case: The focus of inquiry has been Israel, a country then dominated by Western culture. It is essential, therefore, that the study of crisis encompass more non-Western and nonsuperpower crises. Examining the Egyptian side in 1967 is a step in this direction. Moreover, the study of a crisis between culturally diverse states allows us to examine the impact of culture on crisis behavior, provided equal attention is devoted to both sides. It is in the nature of a strategic-interactive model that such a symmetry is called for.

NOTES

1. On the different functions and types of case studies, *see* Lijphart (1975; 1971) and Eckstein (1975). This chapter is written with an additional objective in mind: to set down guidelines for the empirical application of the model in general, beyond the specific case at hand.

2. For a discussion of external and internal validity, *see* Nachmias and Nachmias (1981).

3. For a comprehensive discussion of this topic, *see* Elster (1986) and Moe (1979).

4. For the sake of the present discussion, I assume a single decision maker on each side. Therefore, no distinction is made at this point between policy advocacy and crisis behavior (that is, the crisis strategy that is actually implemented), which may differ in a group setting. Similarly, problems of implementation are ignored.

5. Here and later it is understood that players are assumed to be rational. Thus, a strategy choice can be explained on the basis of a player's motivation to obtain the best possible outcome, subject to a certain game perception.

6. In this relationship, the crisis strategies of the players are the independent variables.

7. We could also say that the crisis strategies of the players are intervening variables, between the independent variables of attitudes and perceptions and the dependent variable of crisis outcome.

8. The double-headed arrow indicates the relationship that exists in some cases that are specified in the model between a player's choice of strategy and what it expects the opponent's choice to be. (Here and subsequently, "expectation" should not be taken to imply probabilistic calculations.)

9. This is not to say that the role played by the other direct and indirect participants will be ignored, but their impact will be taken into account in terms of the perspectives of the two major participants.

10. As we saw above, attitudes exert their influence on strategy choice through the intervening variables of type and game perception.

11. Harkabi (1972: xviii) reminds us that "even an ostensible attitude is not devoid of significance, for it reveals the opinions which the spokesmen wish to be given credit for holding, or those they desire to impart to their listeners."

12. It is easy to confuse policy preferences with preferences for outcomes at this point. Therefore, it is important to stress that although an individual may believe that the state will be weaker if forced to wage a defensive war and stronger if it initiates war, this assessment does not imply that the player will necessarily recommend a war-initiation strategy.

13. It is of course also possible that a policy maker will perceive his or her state to be unconditionally stronger, with the expected cost of victory fluctuating with varying circumstances.

14. Stein (1982) has pointed out that information about the opponent's type does not affect the strategy choice of players whose preferences yield dominant strategies, but it does affect these players' expectation of outcomes.

15. This is not to say, however, that such players will necessarily initiate a crisis: Recall that the decision to initiate depends on how the status quo is ranked relative to the expected outcome of a crisis.

16. This is not to say that *casi belli* are always clearly defined, structured, and articulated, or that their function and use are uniform across states. States may differ, for example, in the explicitness with which they employ *casi belli* and integrate them into their security policies.

17. Thus, for example, Sadat initiated the 1973 war in order to get the Israelis to negotiate, after a long period during which the peace process in the Middle East had been stalled.

18. Only these shifts in type are predicted by the model.

19. Bueno de Mesquita (1981), who uses the unitary-actor assumption in the first sense mentioned above—namely, as justified by the presence of a strong leader—would not consider this to be a problem, because "it is ulimately the responsibility of a single leader to decide what to do [with respect to war initiation] and how to do it" (p. 28). This argument, however, confuses the responsibility for a decision with its determinants.

20. This is one possible way in which the crisis model could be further developed in the future.

21. This section is based on the discussion of causal inference in single-case studies in George (1979) and Stein and Tanter (1980).

22. As George (1979) and Stein and Tanter (1980) note, given the complexity of decision making, it is unlikely, even if theoretically possible, that a single variable would be a sufficient condition.

23. In the next chapter, we will argue that the 1967 crisis was a case of unilateral initiation. To recall, the task of the model is not only to predict initiation by the initiator, but also to predict noninitiation by the defender. Hence, the empirical case does provides some opportunity to deal with the problem of noninitiation, though not with respect to the same actor.

24. This argument neglects the influence of decision makers' perception of the opponent, but as I shall argue in the next chapter, there was in the 1967 case a correlation between types and the perception of the opponent, so that individuals belonging to the same policy group perceived the opponent in a similar way.

25. This problem, however, is not restricted to game-theoretic studies. George (1979: 106–7) discusses it in the context of ambiguities found in empirical studies of operational codes.

26. For example, Lebow (1981) has studied twenty-six crises, out of which only two (less than 8%) did not involve Western states or the superpowers.

5

Decision Making in the 1967 Middle East Crisis

In May 1967, the status quo in the Middle East changed dramatically as a result of three major decisions made by Gamal Abdoul Nasser in the course of a week: (1) the decision to place the Egyptian army on alert and move its forces into Sinai (May 14); (2) the decision to request the withdrawal of United Nations Emergency Force (UNEF) troops (May 16); and (3) the decision to blockade the Straits of Tiran (May 22). In making the third decision, in particular, Nasser appeared to challenge a repeated Israeli *casus belli* knowingly. Meir Amit, then head of *Mossad*, the Israeli intelligence service, later recalled that "until May 23, I thought there was a possibility for maneuvers, that there is a leeway for alternatives. But when Nasser closed the Straits, I said: 'This is it, there is no way to avoid war'" (Brecher, 1980: 104).

Mohamed Heikal, the noted Egyptian journalist and confidant of Nasser, wrote in *Al-Ahram* on May 26 that "Israel cannot accept or remain indifferent to what has taken place," and "hence, I say, that Israel must resort to arms... An armed clash... is inevitable" (quoted in Shamir, 1971: 198). After the Tiran blockade, when Israel still failed to attack, Nasser escalated once again by signing a defense agreement between the United Arab Republic and Jordan (May 30). Six days later, on June 5, 1967, Israel launched its preemptive strike.

What explains the behavior of Egypt and Israel in the crisis? Why did Nasser choose to confront the Israelis after a decade of restraint? Why did he challenge Israel's *casus belli* over the Straits of Tiran? Why did Israeli decision makers, who were unwilling to tolerate less acute provocations by the Syrians, react so slowly and indecisively to Nasser's escalation? Why did the crisis end in war when neither side expected it or desired it only a few weeks earlier?

These are some of the important questions that will be addressed in this chapter. The answers will be provided in terms of the crisis model developed in Chapters 2 and 3. Hence, the decisions and events of the 1967 crisis will be explained from a rational-choice perspective. Whereas this approach has been applied to Israeli decision making in earlier studies of the crisis, the present study is a first attempt to view Nasser's behavior from such a perspective.

In fact, the contention of the existing literature on Nasser's 1967 decision making is that the Egyptian leader acted irrationally. Thus, of the two broad explanations that this literature suggests, the first focuses on Nasser's psychology and points to pathologies in his decision-making process, citing the intrusion and influence of irrational factors, inadequate cognitive processing, emotionally biased interpretations of reality, and personality deficiencies. Nasser's disastrous decisions are then variously explained by his cognitive rigidity, his tendency to succumb to wishful thinking, his inability to withstand the pressures of the situation and of his advisors, and his basic passivity and lack of foresight.

The second, more prevalent type of explanation glosses over the decision-making process itself, concentrating instead on the strategic implications of Nasser's behavior. The pattern that emerges is perceived to conform to the characteristics of a "brinkmanship crisis" (*see* Lebow, 1981). Nasser's failure is then explained as a case of brinkmanship that went out of control, as a result of deficient information processing on the part of the Egyptian leader.

The contention of this chapter is that both accounts of Nasser's decision making are unsatisfactory: By making the outcome of the crisis the starting point of their analysis, these accounts produce explanations that are partial and biased. The chapter attempts to provide an alternative explanation of Nasser's behavior by arguing that, contrary to the conventional wisdom on the crisis, Nasser's decision making was not only rational but strategically so. His failure, moreover, resulted primarily from impediments to crisis learning that were exogenous and unrelated to the nature of his decisional process or to loss of control on his part.

Apart from providing an explanation of the 1967 crisis, this case study is designed to evaluate the crisis model. The testing procedure to be used was outlined in the previous chapter. The case is also exploratory in nature—by applying the model to an empirical case, we wish to discover its weaknesses and to suggest ways in which it could be further refined and expanded.

This chapter is organized as follows. The first section seeks to establish the crisis preferences (types) of Israel's principal decision makers by evaluating their attitudes and perception of relative capabilities at the start of the crisis. The second section repeats the procedure for Nasser. The third section turns from preferences to crisis game perceptions, by establishing each side's perception of the other. In the fourth section, we take a close and critical look at the existing literature on Nasser's crisis behavior. The purpose of this review is to facilitate the comparison between earlier explanations of Nasser's behavior and the explanation provided by the crisis model. This explanation is presented in the fifth section, which proceeds chronologically from Nasser's crisis initiation to Israel's decision to preempt. Finally, our conclusions are offered in the sixth section, both for the specific case and for the model in general.

Before we proceed, it is important to draw attention to several assumptions upon which this case study rests. First, the case focuses exclusively on the Egyptian-Israeli confrontation in May–June 1967. Thus, it examines the events that transpired between May 14—when Nasser decided to mobilize his troops—and June 4, when Israel decided to go to war. The Israeli-Syrian confrontation of the months (and years) prior to May 14—which is viewed by some scholars as an integral part of the 1967 crisis—is referred to only occasionally. This time frame of the case reflects the assumption that the crisis between Egypt and Israel can be studied by itself, as a distinct event. This is not to say that the broader historical context of the crisis can be ignored, but the flow of history makes the beginning point of any analysis somewhat arbitrary, and therefore it is not evident that the starting point of the crisis must be located in earlier months or years.

Second, the case looks exclusively at Egyptian and Israeli decision making, even though the crisis was not strictly bilateral and other actors played an important role as well. This focus reflects the assumption that Egypt and Israel were the key players, and that the crisis can be explained by their actions. Therefore, the role of other players is introduced in terms of the impact it had on the perceptions, decisions, and actions taken by the key participants.

Third, Nasser is assumed to be the sole player on the Egyptian side—by most accounts (for example, Amos, 1979: 28; Safran, 1969: 304), he enjoyed uncontested authority, which allowed him to impose his preferences on his advisers. Israeli Prime Minister Eshkol, on the other hand, neither had such an authority nor sought to attain it. On the contrary, he insisted that critical issues be discussed openly and voted upon by his cabinet members. In Israel's case, therefore, it is necessary to examine the perceptions and preferences of its principal decision makers—Levi Eshkol, Abba Eban, Yigal Allon, and Moshe Dayan (*see* Chapter 4 for a more detailed discussion).

Finally, the case is organized around Nasser's, rather than Israel's, crisis decisions. The reason is that Nasser was the actor who continually raised the ante, with Israel playing a largely reactive role, until its decision to preempt.

THE PREFERENCE TYPES OF ISRAEL'S CRISIS DECISION MAKERS

Attitudes Toward the Opponent[2]

Eshkol

Eshkol's attitude toward the Arabs was a distinct product of two interacting components: his personality and his background. To begin with the former, if Eshkol's personality had to be characterized by a single phrase, the apt one would be "a man of compromise." Brecher (1972: 295) writes that he was "the prototype of compromise" and "known for his skill at bargaining and conciliation." According to Sachar (1979: 549), "[Eshkol's] talents as negotiator and conciliator ranged over the entire field of government" and, together with his brilliant organizational skills, made him a natural and logical successor to David Ben-Gurion in 1963. Sachar concludes: "Israel never had a better-liked politician, down-to-earth, kindly, and tolerant." Prittie, Eshkol's biographer, writes (1969: 207) that "allied to [Eshkol's] modesty were realism, moderation, and human sensitivity," and Eban (1977: 294) describes him as a warm humanist who "sought not to dominate, but to persuade."

Eshkol's personality, then, predisposed him to perceive his opponents—the Arabs included—in a more benign light than did his predecessor, the charismatic and visionary Ben-Gurion. This is not to say that Eshkol had a sophisticated view of the Arab world. His East European "ghetto mentality"—which consisted of a sense of self-sufficiency and isolation from the outside world—continued to dominate his outlook after he had arrived in (then) Palestine. Thus, "he lacked knowledge about 'the Arabs' as a people, culture, and society" (Brecher, 1972: 301), and viewed Israel's existence in the Middle East from an "us-versus-them" perspective.

Despite Eshkol's monolithic perception of the Arabs, which was coupled with a belief in their hostile objectives vis-à-vis Israel, his faith in the ability of human understanding and intelligence to resolve even the most intractable of problems led him to optimism about the prospects of a Middle East peace. Eshkol's first foreign policy statement as prime minister, made on July 12, 1963, called on Nasser to engage Israel in direct talks: "If only we can meet face to face, the Arab leader would soon find that peace is in the best interests of all, and that differences can be ironed out by negotiation and discussion" (quoted in Prittie, 1969: 211). In a later, major speech before the Knesset (May 17, 1965), he appealed to the Arab states for "a mutual undertaking to refrain from aggression, so that our justified apprehensions and vain Arab fears may be dissipated at one and the same time" (ibid., p. 237). He then outlined in detail his vision of a peaceful and prosperous Middle East.[3]

Finally, Eshkol did not seem to be interested in changing the status quo, and he opposed Arab attempts to do so by force. Prittie (1969: 238) contends that Eshkol's conception of peace consisted primarily of Arab recognition of Israel's existing borders: "Eshkol argued for the status quo and only that."

Eban[4]

Eban's attitude toward the Arabs was affected by his Cambridge education in classical and Oriental literatures, and by his long diplomatic service. In a 1966 interview as Israel's foreign minister, he rejected the opinion according to which the Arabs could only understand force: "Such kind of talk and thought is fundamentally wrong. As Jews we must be sensitive to any national 'typology,' to any attempt to give a whole people a negative appearance. It is our duty to educate the young generation towards an attitude of respect towards this region and its culture, languages, and strivings for advancement. It is our duty to screen public speeches from insulting innuendoes and any derision of Arab culture" (cited in Brecher, 1972: 352).

Eban's view of the Arabs did not prevent him from perceiving an Arab hostility toward Israel, and yet he was critical of the Ben-Gurionist approach, according to which only Israel's strength and resolve would bring the Arabs to negotiate. In his memoirs, Eban recalls his assessment of Arab-Israeli relations upon his appointment as foreign minister in Eshkol's government (February 1966):

> While our international relations appeared stable, I thought it useful to look hard at the weaker points. Since 1956 there had been very little development of contacts with the Arab world. Ben-Gurion had concluded that there was no chance of reconciliation until Israel's strength and stability became so manifest that the Arab states would reconcile themselves to our permanence. In the meantime, he had not thought it wise to invest very deeply in contacts throughout the Arab world.

> I began to build a series of informal Arab connections... In general, opportunities beckoned us wherever we looked. Every seed of new effort seemed to bear some fruit. (Eban, 1977: 306, 310)

Thus, if Eban was dissatisfied with the status quo, it was in the sense that in his opinion not enough had been done by Ben-Gurion's government to open up opportunities for arriving at an understanding with the Arab states.

Allon[5]

Allon's attitude toward the Arabs was shaped by Israel's inability since 1948 to secure a peace treaty with its neighbors, despite its military victories. In a 1960 interview, he told Brecher that he had urged Ben-Gurion during the War of Independence not to terminate the fighting until Israel was assured of a peace treaty. Moreover, he revealed in 1969 that he had refused to participate in the postwar Rhodes Conference, because he was opposed to accepting an armistice agreement instead of a peace agreement. Similarly, at the end of the 1956 Suez War, he opposed Israeli withdrawal until satisfactory political arrangements were secured (Brecher, 1972: 363). The lesson Allon drew from Israel's experience in the 1948 and 1956 wars was that "we cannot stop the war before we achieve full victory, the integrity of the country and a peace treaty which will guarantee normal relations between Israel and her neighbours" (quoted in Brecher, ibid., pp. 364–65).

Allon perceived the Arabs during the 1956–67 period to be implacably hostile to Israel. Summarizing his views at that time in a volume published after the 1967 war, he wrote: "As the decade advanced, it became clear that the tremendous stock-piling of arms by the Arab states, and by Egypt in particular, could mean only one thing: that they wanted non-aggression [which Allon supported as a possible interim arrangement] no more than they wanted peace; that what they did want was military superiority for another all-out war against Israel, under conditions ensuring an Arab victory" (1970: 76). Thus, Allon perceived the 1956–67 stability along the Egyptian-Israeli border as "two-fold realism" on the part of Nasser: observance of the post-1956 agreements, coupled with careful military preparations for a future strike. The presence of UNEF could be used as an excuse for inaction on Tiran (that is, the closure of the Straits to Israeli shipping), a policy with which Egyptian hawks were becoming impatient (Allon, 1970: 69–70).

Allon's view of Arab aggressiveness and intransigence, together with his perception of Israel as "uniquely isolated," shaped his thinking about the requirements of Israeli security. More than any other Israeli policy maker, Allon contributed to the development of the military-strategic doctrine that guided Israel's behavior during the pre-1967 period. He viewed the security of Israel to be unconditionally tied to its military capability. This capability had to be not only superior to that of the combined Arab powers but, moreover, supported by a political will to employ it effectively in order to assure credible deterrence (Allon, 1970: 70).

Although Allon believed that Israel could deal with the Arabs only from a position of strength, he did not call for preventive war. Thus he argued: "It would be morally wrong... to precipitate a war as long as war could be put off without endangering the State of Israel: there was always the hope, after all, that conditions might change and that war could be avoided for many years if not forever. A general Arab attack was a possibility, perhaps even a probability, but it was not a certainty; one should therefore do nothing to change this uneasy status quo" (Allon, 1970: 77).

Dayan[6]

Dayan's attitude toward the Arabs was a product of empathetic reflection. His biographer writes that "listening to [Dayan] talk of his childhood, one cannot but sense that his attitude toward the Arabs is imbued with a love for their culture and way of life; that it was only the quirks of history and the bitter destiny of the Jewish people that placed him at the head of troops who recurrently fought the Arabs" (Teveth, 1972: 114).

Brecher (1972: 354–55) writes that Dayan's empathy with the Arabs "could coexist in the same man with a severe indictment of 'illusionism' in [their] perceptions." Thus, Dayan argued that the Arab mentality was such that reality was wished away by means of illusion: "It often seems to me that the Arabs—and on all levels—act as though under the influence of drugs. Yet illusion is worse than a lie. You make a lie consciously and you dominate it, while the illusion will finally dominate you" (cited in Brecher, 1972: 355). This defining aspect of the Arab mentality, as he saw it, appeared to Dayan to explain why the Arabs continued to oppose reconciliation with Israel even though they did not want war. In political terms, then, the structure of the Arab mentality implied a protracted conflict.

In a 1968 lecture to the graduating class of the IDF Staff and Command College, Dayan reviewed the political thinking of Dr. Arthur Ruppin, one of the major pre-Independence Zionist leaders.[7] Ruppin's views on the Arab-Israeli conflict evolved from a belief in the possibility of finding a political formula that would be mutually acceptable to Arabs and Jews to a belief in the zero-sum nature of the conflict—there was no formula that would satisfy the demands of the Arabs without thereby "ceding the fundamentals of Zionism." Ruppin's answer was that negotiations were useless as long as the Arabs sought to end the Zionist enterprise; only "the weight of facts" would finally lead to Arab acceptance.

Dayan cautioned his listeners that "the weight of facts" could be a factor that the Arabs were counting on as well. He summarized his lecture as follows:

I fear that [the facts] have not yet convinced the Arabs to accept us, or our political existence, to regard us as an acceptable neighbor state with equal rights. Perhaps Ruppin's error on this point stemmed from the fact that he thought in rational categories, whereas Arab opposition stems from emotions.

Despite all our efforts—including a willingness for far-reaching concessions—to bring the Arabs to the peace table, the things which Ruppin said thirty-two years ago still seem sound. It was during the 1936 riots that he wrote: "The Arabs do not agree to our venture. If we want to continue our work in Eretz Israel against their desires, there is no alternative but that lives should be lost. It is our destiny to be in a state of continual warfare with the Arabs. This situation may well be undesirable, but such is the reality." (p. 417)

Attitudes Toward the Opponent: Summary

Two conclusions can be drawn from this review of attitudes toward the opponent among Israel's key decision makers in 1967. First, Israel's political elite shared a consensus on the eventual possibility and desirability of a peaceful settlement of the Arab-Israeli conflict. The second conclusion, however, is that there was a basic difference between Eshkol and Eban on the one hand, and Dayan and Allon on the other, about the appropriate way of inducing the Arabs to cooperate.

Dayan and Allon believed that the Arabs could be brought to negotiate only if their aggressive designs were frustrated time and again by Israel's military might. Thus, both foresaw a long period of struggle in which Israel would have to prove its invincibility beyond doubt.

Eban and Eshkol were not impervious to power considerations, and did not underestimate the importance of Israel's military capability. Neither, however, did they see the solution to Israel's predicament as a direct function of the region's military realities. Rather, they sought to establish understanding and cooperation on the basis of respect and equality, by appealing to reason rather than inducing fear and resignation on the part of the opponent.

We can summarize these differences in terms of our model by associating the "peace through victory" attitude (A1) with Allon and Dayan, and the "peace without victory" attitude with Eshkol and Eban (A2).

Attitudes Toward Loss and Perceptions of Relative Capabilities

Two additional components are needed in order to establish the preference types of the four decision makers: their attitude toward loss and their perception of relative capabilities on the eve of the crisis.

Brecher (1980: 38–39) argues that in the 1967 crisis, the Israeli elite's attitude toward defeat was defined by the so-called *Holocaust syndrome*, or the perception that Arab victory would entail the annihilation of Israel. Geist (1984: 278) suggests that whereas other states have at various times agreed to marginal or even significant restrictions on their sovereignty, Israeli decision makers have tended to view such restrictions as "the beginning of the end" because of the memory of the Holocaust and their perception of implacable Arab hostility.

What these arguments imply is that Israel's decision makers saw little difference, in the long run, between capitulation to Nasser's political demands and a defeat by the Arab armies. In an address to the Security Council at the end of the war, Eban referred to Nasser's inflammatory speech of May 28, and said: "Here, then, was a systematic, overt, proclaimed design at politicide, the murder of a state" (cited in Brecher, 1980: 97). Similarly, on the occasion of the fifth anniversary of the war, Rabin wrote in *Ma'ariv*: "I said at the time [of the crisis]: 'We have no alternative but to answer the challenge forced upon us, because the problem is not freedom of navigation, the challenge is the existence of the State of Israel, and this is a war for that very existence'" (ibid., p. 39).

It is clear, then, that Israel's decision-making elite viewed the prospect of defeat—political or military—in the most ominous of terms, and the possibility of "cutting costs" (L2 attitude) did not appear to be relevant given the stakes involved. Allon argued that had the Arabs won, "they would have committed genocide." He therefore viewed Israel's alternatives in the crisis as a choice between life and death ("to live or perish") (Brecher, 1980: 39). A similar perception was shared by Eshkol, and by Eban as we have seen.

The perception that Israel could not afford to lose must be related, however, to the perception of Arab threat; this perception, in turn, depended on the crisis intentions attributed by Israel's decision makers to their opponents. Therefore, we cannot say that the Holocaust syndrome exerted its effects on the perceptions of Israel's elite at the start of the crisis, when, as we shall see, Nasser's objectives were seen as limited.[8] Still, the syndrome defined their attitude toward defeat once the perception of Arab threat made such an outcome relevant to the decision-making process. In other words, the syndrome lay "dormant" until triggered by the perception of threat.

To summarize, the attitude toward loss among Israel's decision makers was the L1 attitude—"make opponent pay." It would not be entirely accurate, however, to characterize this attitude in these terms: Israeli decision makers simply could not conceive of a situation wherein they could "cut costs," given their perception of the consequences of Israeli defeat.

We turn now to the perception of relative capabilities. Here, as in the case of the attitude toward loss, we find unanimity of opinion among Israel's principal decision makers: They all considered the Israeli Defense Forces capable of defeating the Arab opposition (though estimates of the costs that would be involved varied from individual to individual, and over time). Brecher (1980) writes that "like his colleagues, the Prime Minister was optimistic about the outcome of war" (p. 96); "[Eban] perceived Israel's military capability in positive terms, though he devoted little public attention to it" (p. 98); "Allon, as always, was very optimistic about a military victory: 'I have no shadow of a doubt as to the final outcome, nor the outcome at each stage... It is in our power'" (p. 100). Finally, Dayan wrote in his memoirs (1976: 392) that he was confident of Israel's ability to "put the Egyptians to rout."

It is important to note that although all the principal decision makers expressed confidence in Israel's ability to defeat the Arab armies, they were at the same time highly concerned with the cost that would be required to achieve military victory. Eban (1977: 371) wrote that "the expectation of victory was overshadowed by fear of terrible casualties." This fear, as we shall see, influenced some decision makers to support a prolonged search for nonmilitary solutions and led others to advocate immediate military action, but no one suggested that Israel would not win the war eventually. Thus, the balance-of-capabilities perception among Israeli decision makers was C1, the perception that Israel was stronger than its opponents.

Decision-Maker Types in Israel's Cabinet: A Summary

The preference types of Israel's principal policy makers can now be derived. We saw before that: (1) Eshkol and Eban had an A2 attitude toward the opponent, whereas Dayan and Allon had an A1 attitude; (2) all four decision makers had an L1 attitude toward loss; and (3) all four decision makers had a C1 perception of relative capabilities. Since the L1 attitude affects only the preference ranking of individuals who expect to lose at DD (that is, a C2 perception of relative capabilities), the preference types of the four decision makers are determined by the A and C parameters only.

Thus, Eshkol and Eban, with an attitude-perception combination of A2-C1, were decision-makers of an ML2 type (*see* Figure 2.2). On the other hand, Allon and Dayan, with an attitude-perception combination of A1-C1, were decision makers of an HL type.[9]

We will return to these individuals later, in order to determine their perceptions of the opponent—and hence their crisis game perceptions—throughout the course of the 1967 crisis. We turn next to an evaluation of Nasser's preference type.

THE PREFERENCE TYPE OF EGYPT'S NASSER

Nasser's Attitude Toward the Opponent

We begin the analysis with a brief review of Harkabi's (1972) comprehensive work on Arab attitudes toward Israel, which devotes significant attention to Nasser. Although Nasser was not the most extreme of Arab leaders in his hostility toward Israel, the record of his public and written statements, as compiled by Harkabi, indicates a fundamental and intense antagonism toward the Jewish state. Several themes repeated themselves over the years in his speeches, and a sample of quotes is sufficient to convey their content.[10]

Nasser often expressed his view of Israel's basic criminality, which began with the circumstances of Israel's establishment in 1948. In a letter he sent to King Hussein on March 1961, he wrote: "We believe that the evil which has been introduced into the heart of the Arab world must be eradicated, and that the rights which have been usurped from the Arabs must be returned to their owners" (p. 5). Of Ben-Gurion, Nasser said (March 1960), "[he] is the greatest war criminal in this century. Some say that it is Hitler, but did Hitler liquidate the nation of a State as Ben-Gurion liquidated an entire nation-state?" (p. 62).

Israel's victory in the 1948 war was presented by Nasser as an affront to Arab honor, justifying the call for action to restore Arab pride: "The armed forces are getting ready for the restoration of the rights of the Palestinian People because the Palestine battle was a smear on the entire Arab Nation. No one can forget the shame brought by the battle of 1948" (August 1963; p. 72).

Nasser also perceived Israel's existence and policy as a threat to the cause of Pan Arabism: "Israel tries by her broadcasts to divide the Arabs, because their division strengthens her" (June 1962; p. 333). Israel's Middle East policy is designed not only to divide, but also to conquer and rule: "Israel has a certain policy, and it is that she must establish the State of Israel, the Holy State, from the Nile to the Euphrates, and take parts of Lebanon, Syria, Iraq, Jordan and Egypt" (February 1959, p. 74).

In operational terms, Nasser viewed the solution to Israel's criminality, its humiliation of the Arabs, and its divisive and aggressive policy, in the following terms, which he specified in a speech before the UN Assembly (September 1960): "The only solution to Palestine... is that matters should return to the condition prevailing before the error [Israel] was committed—i.e., the annulment of Israel's existence" (p. 4).

Did these statements reflect Nasser's sincere attitudes toward Israel, or were they propaganda for internal consumption? Harkabi suggests the following in his book: "Even though his references to Israel were generally brief, and he refrained from invectives, a listener to his speeches would gain the impression that he was imbued with a cold hatred. His view of Israel as part of imperialism and one of the factors obstructing Egypt's progress is not simulated, and no doubt grew in intensity after the events of 1956 and, even more, after the defeat of 1967" (pp.

431–32).

There was certainly a gap—particularly in the 1956–67 period—between Nasser's behavior toward Israel and the type of action implied by his statements. This gap, however, cannot be taken as evidence for the strictly propagandistic intention of his public pronouncements. Harkabi notes that Arab ideology "does not indicate what they are going to do, it describes what they would like to do" (p. 419). The barrier to action is reality, at least as far as Israel's liquidation is concerned. This reality is Israel's relative strength, and as such it is not static: "fluctuations in... [Arab] strength and the opponent's [that is, Israel's] acts of omission and commission affect the degree to which this ideology is realistic" (p. 420).

Harkabi's point (though not in such stark terms) is supported by other observers of Nasser. In his biography of the Egyptian leader, Stephens (1971) argues that Nasser's hostility to Israel was derived from his perception of the injustice done to the Palestinians, from Israel's existence as a land barrier between Egypt and the Asian Arab states, and from what he considered to be Israel's expansionist policy and connections with Western imperialism. Yet whatever his attitude toward Israel, "Nasser was neither eager to rush into a war of Arab reconquest nor in any hurry to make a permanent peace settlement, except at the price of radical concessions from Israel" (p. 439). This policy was dictated by practical considerations, such as the military strength of Israel and its allies, and the disunity in the Arab world.

Nutting (1972) contends that Nasser's 1965 rift with Tunisian President Habib Bourguiba, following the latter's call for Arab moderation and reason in dealing with Israel, was designed to please Arab militants. Nasser himself was realistic enough to understand that the Arab states were not ready to challenge Israel militarily, and "his plan was to use such popularity and prestige as his political posturing might win for him to inject a further dose of realism into Arab thinking" (p. 367). Thus, in a speech in Cairo to the members of the Gaza Legislative Council (February 1962), Nasser expressed his belief in the irresponsibility—even treason—of those who call for war when they are unprepared for it: "Whoever says that we should go to war without getting ready for it, is a traitor to his country and his people" (cited in Harkabi, 1972: 501). Likewise, when the Arab Summit conference met in Casablanca in September 1965, he urged the Arab leaders to prepare themselves well for the eventual showdown with Israel, instead of resorting to empty rhetoric (Nutting, 1972: 367).

In summary, Nasser perceived his relations with Israel strictly from a military balance-of-power perspective: If he had the power, he would deal Israel a crushing blow (whether this would entail genocide, as Allon thought, or an incorporation of the Jewish population into a newly formed Palestinian state); if he did not have the power, he would prolong the status quo until he acquired it. This argument supports an A1 attitude toward the opponent: Nasser was unwilling to concede anything to Israel voluntarily, and by depriving the Israelis of a pretext to attack him, he sought to prevent a situation in which he would be coerced into concessions.

Nasser's Attitude Toward Loss and His Perception of Relative Capabilities

From Nasser's statements reviewed above, it is reasonable to assume that as long as he perceived the Arabs as militarily inferior to Israel, he had no desire to squander Egypt's resources on confrontations he was bound to lose. Thus, as we have already mentioned, during the Arab summit meetings of 1964–65, he decisively opposed a Syrian proposal to launch large-scale guerrilla attacks against Israel, out of concern that such a strategy might provoke Israel to attack (Nutting, 1972: 367; Safran, 1969: 273). Riad (1981: 16) writes of the early months of 1966 that "in his determination not to be drawn into an armed conflict with Israel and with the pressing demands of Egyptian development, Nasser had brought pressure to bear on the Palestinians to refrain from commando raids, whether from across the Egyptian borders or the armistice lines in the Gaza sector."

Later in 1966, Nasser did not intervene when Israel launched a raid against the Jordanian village of Samu (November 13). Nasser's inaction triggered a verbal assault by King Hussein, who accused him of being a "political tightrope-walker" and of hiding behind the protection of UNEF (Mansfield, 1969: 79).

Then, only a little more than a month before the May–June 1967 crisis—and despite the Egyptian-Syrian joint defense agreement (in effect since November 1966)—Nasser did not come to Syria's assistance when, on April 7, Israel bombarded Syrian positions in the Golan Heights and the Israeli air force shot down six Syrian Migs (*see* Yaniv, 1987). This time, as Lacouture (1973: 294) writes, "the Damascus protestations took an even greater violence than had those of Amman after the Samou affair. Was Gamal Abdel Nasser really that 'friend of the Zionists' whom Akram Hourani had denounced?"[11]

Thus, we see that Nasser's restraint vis-à-vis Israel was very costly for the Egyptian leader in terms of his status and prestige in the Arab world, yet he was unwilling to be dragged into a conflict with Israel and sought to avoid Egyptian sacrifices for a futile cause. Nasser's attitude toward loss on the eve of the crisis was therefore L2—"cut costs."

Turning to Nasser's perception of relative capabilities, it is clear from the discussion so far that he perceived Egypt to be weaker than Israel at the time of the crisis. On September 25, 1964, Mohamed Heikal described in an *Al Ahram* article the conditions under which Nasser believed Egypt could successfully engage Israel in war. These conditions were: "the concentration of superior military power; the isolation of Israel; Arab unity" (Safran, 1969: 292; *see* also Draper, 1968: 71). None of these conditions existed on May 14, when Nasser mobilized.

Sharabi (1969: 111) writes that "in May and June 1967, Egypt was not in a position to go to war. For one thing, some 50,000 UAR troops were committed to Yemen, including some of the best trained. President Nasser had no illusions as to the military capability of the Arab world. In 1963 at Port Said, he put it plainly: 'I am not in a position to go to war; I tell you this frankly, and it is not shameful to say it publicly. To go to war without having the sufficient means would be to lead the country and the people to disaster.'" Sharabi uses this argument to cast the responsibility for the war on Israel. Whether Nasser's perception of the relative military strength remained as static as Sharabi implies is a question we will return to later. The point to note here is that at the start of the crisis, Nasser had a C2 perception of relative capabilities: He perceived Egypt to be the weaker party.[12]

We conclude that Nasser had an A1 attitude toward the opponent, L2 attitude toward loss, and C2 perception of capabilities. This makes him an SL1 player type (*see* Figure 2.2) at the point of initiating the crisis.

CRISIS GAME PERCEPTIONS

In this section, we seek to establish the game perceptions of Israel's principal decision-makers and of Nasser at the start of the crisis. To do so requires that, in addition to the preference types already derived, we also ascertain each side's perception of the other's crisis preferences.

The prevalent view in Israel on the eve of the crisis was that Nasser was not ready for war and would not allow himself to be dragged into one. This is evident from a speech to the Knesset given by Eshkol in the fall of 1968: "The experience of the Six Day War has shown that the concept of deterrence is a relative one. As you may remember, it was the general view in 1967—not only here but among experts abroad—that no Egyptian assault was to be expected before 1970" (cited in Stein and Tanter, 1980: 137, fn. 3).[13]

According to Prittie (1969: 249), both Eshkol and Eban, though conscious of Arab hostility, did not expect an armed conflict to occur in 1967. Brecher (1972: 39), too, argues that Israel's decision makers—including Eban, Allon, and Dayan—did not anticipate Nasser's mobilization of May 14, because they did not perceive the circumstances at that time as favoring such a move by the Egyptian leader. Furthermore, Safran (1969: 266) writes that "both Egypt... and Israel seemed to be in agreement that full-scale war was not likely as long as the kind of politico-military balance that prevailed during that period continued to exist."

All this suggests that Israel's decision makers were of the opinion that Nasser, however dissatisfied he was with the status quo, still preferred it to war with Israel. Moreover, as Israeli military analysts proposed at the time, Nasser's fear of war instilled in him a sensitivity to the risks involved in escalation from local incidents (Stein and Tanter, 1980: 138).

This evidence, however, is not sufficient to determine precisely how—in term of our preference types—Israel's policy makers perceived Nasser. Yet several points raised previously in our discussion combine to indicate that, with the exception of Nasser's ranking of the status quo, Israel's decision makers perceived his other preferences (type) accurately—that is, as SL1: They believed that Nasser's hostility toward Israel was checked by Israel's strength, that Nasser would not hesitate to confront Israel if he perceived himself to be stronger, and that for the time being he would do everything in his power to avoid war with Israel, even at the cost of great ridicule at the hands of his Arab foes. These perceptions are consistent with the contingent, tat-for-tit preference structure of the SL1 player.

We shall return to the Israeli perception of Nasser's type when we discuss Israel's response to his May 14 move. We now turn to Nasser's perception of Israel's preferences on the eve of the crisis. (Here, too, the evaluation must rest to some degree on conjecture, because direct evidence of Nasser's perception of his opponent is hard to come by.)

Nasser's behavior during the decade preceding the 1967 crisis is suggestive of his perception of Israel's preferences. That he refrained from any serious challenge to the Israelis over such a long period of time testifies to his understanding that Israel certainly had the resolve to protect its interests, even at the cost of war. Israel's tough policy with respect to the Syrians since 1964 provided ample evidence of its leadership's determination to face up and retaliate decisively to external provocations.

The other side of the equation, however, was equally plain: Israel appeared just as interested as Nasser to preserve the status quo along the Israeli-Egyptian border. This was evident in Israel's conduct during the January 1960 Rotem crisis when, in reaction to an Israeli strike against the Syrian village of Tawfik, Nasser mobilized and moved 50,000 troops and 500 tanks into Sinai. Israel responded with a discreet counter mobilization, and after thirty-two hours Nasser withdrew his troops from Sinai (*see* Yaniv, 1987: 118–19, and the discussion in the next section).

The Rotem crisis showed that Israel—under the leadership of the resolute Ben-Gurion—was not interested in a conflagration along its southern border. There was no reason to suppose, therefore, that an Israel led by Eshkol and Eban would rush into a war with Egypt, especially when tensions with Syria were at their highest. Additional testimony on this point is provided by Nutting (1972: 408), who recalls that in his conversations with Nasser during the last days of the crisis, the Egyptian leader indicated that "he could ride out the storm provided he offered Israel no further provocation." Earlier on, then, he must have believed that Israel was not interested in war with Egypt.[14]

Thus, Nasser's perception of his opponent was most likely the following: on the one hand, an Israel that had a low preference for war with Egypt and would therefore tolerate some level of Egyptian escalation before striking, and on the other hand, an Israel that had superior military capability and the resolve to use it if escalation went too far. These two elements are combined in the middle-line player, that is, ML1 or ML2. However, it is unlikely that Nasser perceived Israel as a player whose first preference was compromise (ML2): Israel's strategy of massive retaliation vis-à-vis the Syrians, and its quick and decisive response to his mobilization in the Rotem crisis, indicated that Israel was not inclined to accept a restructuring of the status quo that would accommodate either Egypt's or Syria's interests. Hence we can conclude that Nasser perceived the preference type of Israel's decision makers to be ML1.

To summarize the analysis in this section, Israeli decision makers perceived Nasser's type to be SL1. For Eban and Eshkol, with an ML2 preference type, this perception of Nasser implies that they considered the game played in early May 1967 to be 14(72) (*see* Figure 3.3 and assume Israel to be the row player).[15] Nasser, with an SL1 preference type and an ML1 perception of Israel, perceived the crisis game to be 9(39) (assume Nasser to be the column player).

COMPETING EXPLANATIONS OF NASSER'S CRISIS BEHAVIOR

Introduction

Before we turn to an analysis of the crisis behavior of Egypt and Israel, a review of the existing literature on Nasser's decision making in the crisis is in order. As noted in Chapter 4, an objective of our case study is to present an alternative explanation to Nasser's decisions in May–June 1967. The contribution of the crisis model developed in this study to the understanding of the 1967 crisis will be better appreciated if the explanation it produces can be compared to the explanations that have been suggested in the literature to date.

Of the voluminous literature on the 1967 crisis, none is available that deals specifically and exclusively with Nasser's decision-making process. There is no equivalent, for the Egyptian side, to Brecher's (1980; 1975; 1972) and Stein and Tanter's (1980) comprehensive studies of Israel's crisis behavior. Moreover, to our knowledge, there are no *rational-choice* studies of Nasser's crisis behavior, whereas there are a few such studies of Israeli decision making.[16]

The literature to be reviewed in this section is thus derived, for the most part, from works that deal with the Six Day War in general and in a variety of contexts. A microlevel comparison of these studies reveals important differences of interpretation on many key issues. At the macrolevel of comparison, however, most (though by no means all) studies may be seen as falling into two groups, in accordance with the type of explanatory variables they employ and emphasize. One group of studies focuses on the individual level (that is, Nasser's psychology), whereas the other is concerned with the interstate level (that is, the dynamics of brinkmanship). The critical evaluation presented in this section addresses these two kinds of studies.

Two caveats are in order before we proceed. First, the division of existing studies into two groups of explanations is hardly clear-cut. Few of the works cited below fall clearly in one of the two groups. In fact, most scholars shift back and forth between the individual and interstate levels of analysis.[17] The second (and related) caveat is that the following discussion is not meant as a criticism of individual works. The studies mentioned below are not reviewed in their entirety; rather, they are assessed in the context of the two broad explanations to which they contribute in their analysis.

The Psychological Explanation

A psychological explanation of Nasser's behavior has been offered by two of his foremost biographers. Lacouture (1973) argues that serious deficiencies in Nasser's cognitive abilities and general character prevented him from correctly assessing the consequences of his decisions. Specifically, he was incapable of distinguishing between fact and fantasy, and "seemed not to understand the relation between an act and its consequences, the fall of a hammer and the sound it makes" (p. 310). He was unable to foresee the opponent's reactions to his own moves and succumbed to wishful thinking, not the least because he "allowed himself to be seduced by the gobbledygook dispensed by his own radio" (p. 301).

These pathologies resulted in serious errors in estimating Israel's reaction to the Tiran blockade as well as America's ability to restrain its ally from attacking. When the Egyptian hawks (Minister of War Shams Badran and Commander in Chief Marshall Abdel Hakim Amer) stepped up their pressure on Nasser to escalate, he was forced to make rash moves (p. 305).

Nutting (1972), who draws a generally sympathetic portrait of Nasser, nevertheless argues that, during those critical weeks in May and June, he was prone to wishful thinking, and resisted all information or advice that seemed to counter his tenaciously held views of the crisis. This cognitive rigidity led him to exclude his ministers from the decision-making process; in the one case in which his recent decisions were discussed by the cabinet, he refused to be drawn into the discussion (p. 410). His unshaken confidence in his perception of the crisis led him to believe, until the end, that Israel would not attack, that Egypt would prevail if Israel did attack, and that the Soviets would support him, "even if this involved another world war" (p. 409).

Amos (1979: 49) argues that Nasser was drawn into escalation as a result of the charges of cowardice that were leveled against him by the conservative Arab regimes. His own rural origins had made him particularly sensitive to such insults. He also harbored a paranoid suspicion of the United States, which led him to interpret events and formulate preferences in the context of a perceived collusion between the United States and Israel (p. 52). Bar-Zohar (1970) and Kimche and Bawly (1968) argue that the impulsive side of Nasser's personality took over as the crisis progressed. Though initially moderate and responsible, the Egyptian leader gradually became intoxicated with his own successes. By the time of the Tiran decision, his euphoric condition clouded his ability to appreciate correctly the direction the crisis was taking.

The influence of Nasser's initial successes on his subsequent preferences and actions is mentioned in several other studies, including those which generally espouse a brinkmanship explanation. Safran (1969), for example, suggests that Nasser allowed "his pride in his tactical virtuosity to blind him to strategic imperatives" (p. 267). Similar arguments are made by Laqueur (1969: 124) and Dawn (1968: 223).[18] Draper (1968) writes that the Tiran decision was influenced by the fact that the Egyptian deterrent force concentrated in the Sinai could easily be used to make offensive demands on Israel. The making of these demands was in turn facilitated by the sheer presence of the force which, according to Heikal, "dazzled" the Egyptians (cited in Draper, ibid., pp. 76–77). Lebow (1981) views this effect of the concentration of force as the primary reason for Nasser's overconfidence in his military power, which in turn conditioned his assessment of the risks involved in a more bellicose policy.[19]

Other scholars cite the influence of the Arab propaganda machine, which fed on Nasser's initial successes. Laqueur (1969) concludes that "it influenced not only the masses but also, in the long run, the leaders, whose judgment was likely affected" (p. 107). Dawn (1968), Amos (1979), and Yost (1968) suggest that the Arab slogans eventually had the effect of limiting policy options.

There are three difficulties with the psychological explanation. First, it fails to account for Nasser's initial successes, because it focuses almost exclusively on his subsequent failure. In fact, the entire course of the crisis is interpreted in terms of its outcome, and one cannot but conclude that the gains Nasser managed temporarily to secure were obtained by luck or, at best, as a result of Israeli weakness. Lacouture (1973), for example, through a form of backward induction, concludes that even the initial steps on May 14 and 16 were mistaken (p. 302), thus suggesting that there was an inexorability to the course of the crisis.

This argument presents a methodological difficulty. If one assumes an inexorable and inevitable chain of events, then the explanatory problem reduces itself to identifying the first link in the chain. If, in addition, the final outcome is known to have been disastrous, all subsequent decisions are taken to be *a priori* mistaken and are explained in terms of "what went wrong."[20] This focus inflates the importance of certain factors by assumption, rather than by examination of the facts, and puts a premium on the evaluation of decisions and not on their explanation. In addition, there is the implicit assumption that bad outcomes are necessarily the result of faulty procedures or personality-related pathologies. The latter factors may or may not be responsible for the failure of strategies; this is, above all, an empirical question.[21]

Empirically, too, there is no conclusive evidence to suggest that Nasser's initial decisions sealed the fate of the entire crisis. The facts do not necessarily suggest that his mobilization decision, or even his UNEF decision, made war inevitable. In fact, the opportunities to arrest the crisis existed throughout its course, even as late as May 30.[22] Therefore, the psychological thesis is unwarranted in concluding that Nasser's failure occurred with his initial decisions.[23]

The second difficulty in the psychological explanation concerns its inability to account for the variability over time in Nasser's behavior—having escalated throughout most of the crisis, why did he stop escalating in June?[24] Why the sudden caution after "so many rash moves" (Lacouture, 1973: 305)? It is unclear, in other words, why deficiencies in Nasser's character and decisional process led first to impulsive escalatory moves, and then to cautionary restraint. Neither is it clear why "this grand master who had triumphed in so many close chess mates" (ibid., p. 304) fell victim to so many inherent flaws in his personality in the months of May and June, 1967. Why did these same flaws not lead him to reckless escalation in January 1960, when he mobilized and moved 50,000 troops and 500 tanks into Sinai during the Rotem crisis?[25]

The third difficulty in the psychological explanation relates to Nasser's ability to revise his probability estimates of Israeli attack in response to incoming information. The psychological explanation argues that he displayed cognitive rigidity in resisting such revision, despite the availability of evidence requiring it (Nutting, 1972: 408–10). This suggests that he could not correctly assess the consequences of his own decisions and actions in terms of their likely effect on the probability of Israeli attack (Lacouture, 1973: 310).

This argument is again strongly influenced by the knowledge of Nasser's subsequent failure. Working from the known outcome back to the decision, it is clear that at some point something went wrong. In fact, though, Nasser not only revised his probability estimates several times during the course of the crisis, as he himself reported in his speech of July 23, 1967,[26] but his estimates themselves were not far off the mark, as we shall see. Moreover, Nasser's estimates were not groundless—they were based on a certain strategic conception, which Heikal elaborated on in an *Al Ahram* article published in September of 1964 (*see* Safran, 1969: 292, and the discussion in the section entitled Nasser's Attitude Toward Loss and His Perception of Relative Capabilities).

The Brinkmanship Explanation

In contrast to the psychological explanation, the main thrust of the brinkmanship explanation lies not in the idiosyncratic characteristics of the Egyptian leader or his decision-making process, but rather in his manipulation of risk and, more generally, in the dynamics of escalation. Yost (1968) argues that "by May 17 the crisis had already acquired a momentum which seemed inexorably to sweep all parties toward and over the brink" (p. 315). Khouri (1968) and Draper (1968) mention Tiran as the critical turning point, at which the cycle of escalation went out of control.

Stein (1988) argues that the deterrent strategies used by Egypt and Israel were the catalyst (rather than the solution) to the process of "miscalculated escalation." The success of Nasser's deterrent strategy unleashed a series of demands from his domestic public, and from Arab allies and foes, that he could not resist or control.

On the Israeli side, "the failure of its deterrent strategy dictated a military response, sooner or later" (p. 2).

Amos (1979) points out that at a certain point in the crisis—the removal of UNEF—the localized Egyptian-Syrian-Israeli conflict became intertwined with the intra-Arab conflict, as waged in the Arab media; these two conflicts "began to cycle together, building up a dynamism of their own" (p. 57). Dupuy (1978), too, writes that both sides blundered into the crisis and contributed to its escalation: "It was a case of tragic, and classic, escalation" (p. 225).

The brinkmanship thesis, then, maintains that as the crisis progressed, the rush of events became an autonomous force that neither side could control. In terms of Nasser's decisions, the argument appears to be that by asking for the removal of UNEF, or by imposing the blockade, he inadvertently relinquished control over factors decisive for the subsequent development of the crisis, namely Israeli perception of available options, and domestic and Arab pressures for further escalation.

The first problem in the brinkmanship explanation concerns the symmetry of the crisis-dynamics argument—the contention that both parties were overtaken by events and that both parties, once beyond a certain point, could no longer exert control over the cycle of escalation. It is curious that those who advance this argument also make abundant simultaneous references to Nasser's psychological shortcomings, and to the impact of nonrational (or irrational) elements on his decision-making process.

The symmetry of the argument in fact makes idiosyncratic factors irrelevant. If neither Nasser nor Israel's decision makers could control the rush of events after Tiran, then Nasser's own shortcomings should not have mattered—he could no longer avert disaster even if he were a paragon of rationality. Elaborating on the ways in which he departed from rational decision making tends to confuse rather than enlighten, because it implies that had another leader been at the helm at this point, the crisis would have ended differently. If this conclusion is drawn, however, it necessarily undercuts the force of the "uncontrollable momentum" argument and elevates the psychology of the individual leader to the status of the primary explanatory factor.

The second and related difficulty in the brinkmanship explanation lies in its failure to document convincingly the thesis that after the UNEF or Tiran decision, the crisis acquired its own uncontrollable momentum. Vague as it is, this argument must be at least refutable. Looking at the Egyptian side of the (symmetric) equation, could it be maintained that in making the UNEF or Tiran decisions, Nasser pulled the trigger to war? A negative answer could be given if it were shown that, even at this stage, the Israeli government could not reach a consensus for a preemptive strike.

We will examine the evidence on this point later. For now, suffice it to say that the unwarranted attention to the Israeli *casus belli* over Tiran has led several observers to assume on this basis alone that Nasser's blockade of the Straits predetermined the outcome of the crisis.

CRISIS BEHAVIOR

Crisis Initiation

The 1967 crisis is one of those cases in which the identity of the initiator is not immediately evident. The question is whether or not Nasser's May 14 decision on mobilization constituted crisis initiation. The answer depends on the precise meaning of the question and the perspective from which initiation is viewed.

Most observers agree that Nasser, at least initially, did not want war with Israel (Khouri, 1968: 224–25; Yost, 1968: 304; and Dawn, 1968: 202), nor did he think it very likely on the eve of the crisis (Safran, 1969: 267–71). That, in itself, is not evidence against the argument that Nasser initiated the crisis. The point these writers wish to make is that the outbreak of a war that Nasser did not want indicates that he did not intend to initiate the crisis that preceded it. This argument presumes that Nasser could know in advance that the crisis would end in war and, therefore, would not have initiated it deliberately. The logic of this argument from the crisis outcome was examined and evaluated in the previous section.

It is possible, however, that Nasser viewed himself as responding to crisis initiation, which would make him, from a perceptual perspective, the defender in a crisis initiated by Israel. Some writers in fact trace the origins of the May–June crisis to an earlier crisis that had begun along the Israeli-Syrian border on April 7, 1967, with the aerial battle between Israeli and Syrian planes; others trace the May–June crisis even farther back in time, perhaps as early as the fall of 1966, when the local incidents along the Israeli-Syrian border escalated beyond control, and brought about stern and provocative Israeli warnings to Syria (*see* Yaniv, 1987, for an analysis of the Israeli-Syrian confrontation).[27]

After the war (on July 23, 1967), Nasser stated that it was Israel, rather than Egypt, that initiated the crisis:

The first point that should be clear to us all is that we were not the first to create the Middle East crisis. We all know that this crisis started with Israel's attempt to invade Syria.

The information we had about the invasion of Syria came from different sources. We had information from our Syrian brothers to the effect that Israel had mobilized eighteen brigades. We investigated this information and were assured that Israel was mobilizing no less than thirteen brigades on the Syrian border.

Our parliamentary delegation which was headed by Anwar Sadat and which was visiting Moscow at the time was informed by our Soviet friends that the invasion of Syria was about to take place. But what could we do? We could have maintained silence; we could have waited; we could have only issued verbal statements and cables of support. But if this country had accepted to handle the situation in that way, it would have renounced its mission, role and personality. (cited in Burdett, 1969: 201)

Nasser's statement is related to three controversial issues that loom large in the literature on the Six Day War. The first has to do with Israel's intentions vis-à-vis Syria in mid-May. The second concerns Nasser's sincerity when he stated that he believed the rumors (or information) about Israeli troop concentrations along the Israeli-Syrian border, and Israel's impending invasion of its neighbor. The third relates to the role played by the Russians in spreading the rumors of an imminent Israeli strike.[28]

We cannot go into these issues here, but two points should be noted. First, as already mentioned, Nasser did not intervene in the April 7, 1967, confrontation between Israel and Syria. Those who argue that he was dragged into the May–June crisis should explain why he was able to refrain from action at that point.[29] Second, the debate on whether or not Nasser believed the rumors of Israel's impending strike against the Damascus regime is to some extent academic: Nasser's dilemma between May 8 and May 13—when he presumably received the Syrian and Soviet information—was independent of his belief in its accuracy. Nasser could easily foresee the consequences of a nonintervention strategy: Whether Israel in fact attacked Syria or not, Egypt would be faulted for not coming to the assistance of its Syrian ally. This would have constituted a serious personal blow to Nasser: Not only had he for a long time now been taunted by his foes in the Arab world for having agreed to the stationing of UNEF troops on Egyptian territory (*see* Draper, 1968: 44; Khouri, 1968: 244–45; and Yost, 1968: 303–4), but his cautious strategy with regard to Israel contributed to his decline in prestige in the Arab world (Safran, 1969: 282). On the other hand, if Nasser escalated and Israel attacked Syria nevertheless, this would represent a failure of Egyptian deterrence, a point we will return to shortly.

We can say, then, that the situation along the Israeli-Syrian border modified Nasser's valuation of the status quo. Whereas until the first week of May he was satisfied—in the short run!—with leaving Egyptian-Israeli relations as they were and concentrating on Egypt's domestic problems, toward the middle of that month the situation had changed sufficiently for him to reconsider his strategy of restraint, whose costs were now mounting rapidly.

As we saw earlier, Nasser had good reasons to believe that Israel was not interested in a confrontation with Egypt; Israel's crisis with Syria, therefore, was not a prelude to an Israeli-Egyptian clash. Nasser's move on May 14 was not a defensive act designed to respond to Israeli crisis initiation against Egypt. It also was not an altruistic move for the sake of Syria, whose plight Nasser ignored only a month or so before, even though the two countries were pledged to a joint defense. Rather, Nasser's move was designed to forestall a further and perhaps disastrous decline of his prestige in the Arab world. He initiated the crisis in order to prevent an adverse change in the status quo.

We turn now to our model in order to provide an explanation for Nasser's May 14 mobilization move. Recall that Nasser was an SL1 player who perceived his opponent as ML1. According to the analysis of initiation in Chapter 3 (and specifically Figure 3.5), SL1 players do not initiate crises against ML1 players, no matter what their level of dissatisfaction with the status quo. Thus, if we argue that Nasser initiated the crisis, the model fails to predict his initiation.

There is, however, a more complex explanation that is suggested by the model. Consider first Nasser's valuation of the status quo on May 13. We can assume with a high degree of confidence that he did not rank the status quo lower than war with Israel, which he knew he would lose. Certainly, however, a crisis outcome wherein Israel would be deterred from attacking Syria (or at least appear to be deterred if it had no intention of attacking), or possibly some compromise agreement (tacit or overt) to that effect, would have been better for Nasser than the status quo. Therefore, he most likely ranked the status quo below Israeli capitulation and below a compromise settlement. Hence, as an SL1 (column) player, Nasser's relative ranking of the status quo on May 14 was CD > CC > SQ > DC > DD.[30]

If we turn to the game solutions of Figure 3.3, we see that the ML1-SL1 game (#9[39], which, as we said before, was Nasser's crisis game perception) ends with capitulation by SL1. (This is the reason that SL1 players do not initiate against ML1 opponents.) Thus, the problem Nasser faced as an SL1 player was that he could not obtain the CD or CC outcomes against an ML1 (row) opponent: Israel was not expected either to capitulate or compromise. As we said before, Nasser had to consider the possibility that Israel would attack Syria nevertheless, in which case he would be dragged into a war he sought to avoid.

Could Nasser not rely on his performance in the Rotem crisis to predict that the present crisis would also end in a mutual withdrawal of forces (that is, a compromise outcome)? The situation this time was different, however. First, Nasser's restraint during the Samu incident (November 1966) and during the April 7, 1967, Israeli-Syrian clash did not enhance Egyptian credibility, to say the least—even Egypt's Arab allies recognized Nasser's weakness and taunted him for it. Second, Israel was now publicly committed to confront the Syrian menace, as it saw it. These facts were plain enough for everyone to see. Therefore, as Brecher (1980: 46, fn. 32) has observed: "One of the psychological problems facing Nasser was to show that this time he meant what he said and was prepared to back up words with deeds."

How, then, can Nasser's May 14 mobilization be explained? The answer could lie in a *deceptive move* by the Egyptian leader. From Figure 3.9, we know that SL1 players have an incentive to deceive ML1 opponents by simulating an ML2 type.[31] The incentive exists, because if deception succeeds, the outcome of the game is CC (as can be seen in Figure 3.3), which is better for the SL1 player than the outcome (DC) it can expect to obtain in the ML1-SL1 game.

A possible explanation of Nasser's May 14 decision, then, is that Nasser attempted to deceive the Israelis by projecting, on the one hand, a more conflictual type and, on the other hand, a type amenable to compromise. The ML2-type simulation thus had two advantages for Nasser: He could signal that he was serious about deterring Israel from an attack on Syria, and at the same time, he could signal his willingness to compromise, by which he hoped to avoid war.

Given what was said above about Nasser's injured credibility, how could he have expected to deceive the Israelis? The answer, it appears, is that Nasser gambled on the success of his deception strategy. In a speech at the Cairo University auditorium on July 23, 1967, Nasser stated: "When we concentrated our forces I estimated that the likelihood of war breaking out was 20 per cent" (cited in Laqueur, 1968: 197–207). The condition for deception specified in our model—that is, that the deceiver believes its opponent does not know its true type—is not stated in probabilistic terms, but Nasser may have thought probabilistically.

Is there any evidence to suggest that Nasser in fact engaged in deception and projected an ML2 type? The actual decision-making process leading to Nasser's decision on mobilization remains obscure. There were, however, two aspects to the Egyptian mobilization that made it a peculiar operation. First, Egyptian troops were paraded in broad daylight and with much fanfare (Burdett, 1969: 212). Second, the troops were deployed in the center of Sinai rather than near the permanent Egyptian division, which was stationed along the Egyptian-Israeli border (Slater, 1977: 121). We can only speculate that the public procession of the troops—in plain view of the entire Arab world—was designed to signal Nasser's seriousness by committing Egypt to some form of resistance against Israel; however, away from the public eye, the backward deployment of the Egyptian troops was intended as a signal to the Israelis that Nasser was not interested in further escalation.

The Israelis, in any event, were much surprised by the Egyptian mobilization. The military assessment, however, was that Nasser was bluffing and that Egypt would not go to war (Brecher, 1980: 46–47; Stein and Tanter, 1980: 138). The Israelis, then, thought that Nasser was resorting to deception and that his move was designed for demonstrative purposes only. The Israeli chief of staff, Yitzhak Rabin, perceived the Egyptian mobilization as a replay of the Rotem crisis (Slater, 1977: 121). Interestingly, Heikal (1973) has argued that Rotem was precisely the analogy that Nasser had hoped would be invoked by his May 14 move.[32] If Heikal is correct, then the Israelis were deceived, but the simpler explanation is that both sides viewed their Rotem strategy as successful: The Israelis thought that their countermobilization exposed Nasser's bluff (*see* Brecher, 1980: 46, fn. 32), whereas Nasser thought that his mobilization proved his resolve, and his withdrawal indicated his strictly deterrent intentions.

The model, then, suggests an interesting interpretation of Nasser's crisis initiation. The evidence available at present, however, is not solid enough to confirm the proposition of deception; this part of the analysis, therefore, remains tentative.

Nasser's initiation move is described in Figure 5.1:[33] The arrow points from Nasser's true game perception to the game perception he hoped to induce by his

Figure 5.1
The 1967 Middle East Crisis: May 14–16

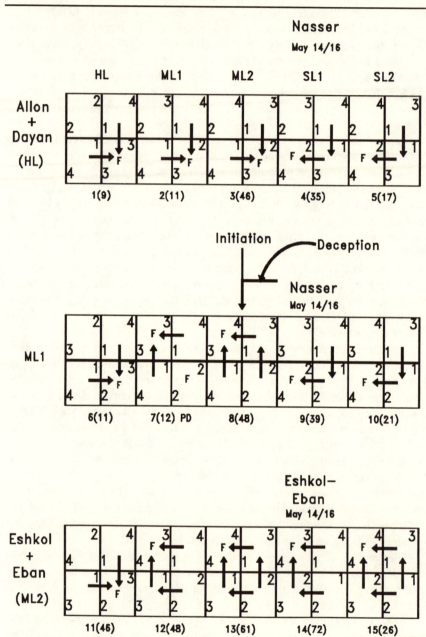

deception. The Israelis, however, were not deceived, as we have just seen, and therefore their game perception did not change (that is, remained at 14[72]).

We turn now to the response of the Eshkol-Eban team. Arguing from the model (Figure 5.1, game 14[72]), we can expect such players (1) to respond in kind, and at the same time (2) to suggest the possibility of compromise, conditioned upon a similar and prior move by the opponent.

The strategy of Eban and Eshkol was in fact two-track. Eshkol (together with Rabin and Chief of Operations Ezer Weizman) decided to alert regular army units and move some of them to Israel's southern border. On May 16, in response to continuing Egyptian mobilization and deployment, the regular army was put on alert and a reserve regiment of armor as well as some artillery were mobilized.[34] At the same time, Eban informed Egypt through UN Under Secretary-General Ralph Bunche that Israel did not intend to invade Syria (Brecher, 1980: 47). Our model, then, predicts quite accurately the reaction of the Eshkol government to Nasser's crisis initiation.

Nasser's UNEF Decision: May 16, 1967

Nasser's next move came on the evening of May 16, when the Egyptian government requested the withdrawal of UNEF.[35] This decision presents a problem for the model, because the expected outcome in the game Nasser was trying to induce the Israelis to play—8(48) in Figure 5.1—is CC. Yet Nasser did not reciprocate the Israeli conciliatory strategy; instead, he escalated the crisis even more.

Yaniv (1987: 118–19) has suggested that the strategy of the Eshkol Government, "rather than signaling moderation and strength... projected weakness and indecision[.] Israel spoke softly and carried a big stick. To Nasser, however, Israel appeared to be speaking softly because it was carrying a hollow reed." Specifically, although Eshkol employed the same strategy as did Ben-Gurion in the Rotem crisis, there were nevertheless two important differences between the 1960 and the 1967 situations. First, Ben-Gurion's handling of the Rotem crisis was "singularly discreet," in contrast to "the publicity that attended Eshkol's moves." Second, Ben-Gurion enjoyed a reputation for resolve on which Eshkol could not rely. Therefore, "Eshkol's strategy either convinced Nasser that the incumbent Israeli prime minister was made of softer fabric than was Ben-Gurion, or unwittingly created situations that made it difficult for Nasser not to escalate the crisis." Yaniv's conclusion, then, is that Nasser was tempted, perhaps even forced, to seek greater gains before extricating himself from the rush to the brink.[36]

Another possible explanation follows from our earlier argument concerning Nasser's deceptive initiation strategy. Thus, upon observing the reaction of the Eshkol government to his initiation, Nasser could easily conclude that his deception had succeeded: Israel appeared to be deterred and its countermeasures

were strictly defensive. Yet if his true preferences were known to his opponent—whom Nasser perceived as an ML1 player—the response should have been
unconditionally coercive, as expected in the ML1-SL1 game (9[39]). Instead,
Israel behaved exactly as Nasser had expected it to behave if it were deceived—that is, in accordance with the ML1-ML2 game (8[48]).[37]

This explanation in effect says that on May 16 Nasser decided to play another
round of the ML1-ML2 game, so as to derive the maximum benefits that could
be had from his successful deception. In this sense, Yaniv is correct: Had Eshkol
responded more firmly—as demanded by the opposition members during the May
16 debate in the Knesset Foreign Affairs and Security Committee (Brecher, 1980:
49)—Nasser may have concluded that his true preferences were known to Israel
and would not have escalated the crisis further.

There is still a third explanation, suggested by Bar-Zohar (1970: 32–33), that
is consistent with our argument of deception and with the contention that Nasser
did not intend the entire UNEF force to be withdrawn. According to this
explanation, Nasser's attempt to make his deterrent threat credible could not have
succeeded with the UNEF forces deployed between Egypt and Israel. During the
1960 Rotem crisis, the Egyptians demanded that UNEF troops leave their forward
positions and move into their encampments at the rear. UN Secretary-General Dag
Hammarskjöld agreed; when the tension subsided, the UNEF troops returned to
their former positions along the border.

On May 16, 1967, Nasser sought to repeat the exercise. Thus, his move on
UNEF could be considered part of his deception strategy, and should be viewed
in conjunction with the revealing pattern of Egyptian troop mobilization and
deployment.[38] The letter handed to General Indar Jit Rikhye, the commmander
of UNEF, did not ask for the withdrawal of his troops but only for their redeploy-
ment in backward positions. The letter did not mention the UNEF troops at Tiran
(or Sharm el Sheikh), because Nasser did not want his move to be interpreted as
a prelude to the closure of the Straits or to a war with Israel. It was only after UN
Secretary-General U Thant presented Nasser with an ultimatum—all troops or
none—that the Egyptian leader was forced to choose the former alternative.

The reaction in Israel to Nasser's UNEF move consisted, once again, of a
"mixed" strategy. Thus, on May 17, Eshkol and Rabin decided on further
mobilization of reserves, and Eban suggested that Israel's ambassador to the UN
(Gideon Raphael) contact U Thant in order to convince him to visit Cairo and
Jerusalem. On May 18, when it became clear that Nasser intended to request the
withdrawal of the entire UNEF force, more reserves were called up. This was
followed, on May 19, with a decision on a large-scale mobilization of reserves
and the planning of a preemptive strike into Sinai. At the same time, Eban called
in the Soviet ambassador and suggested "a reciprocal de-escalation of troops in
the South." He added that the outcome of the crisis depended on Egypt, and that
"there will be no war unless the Egyptians attack our territory or violate our rights
of free navigation" (cited in Brecher, 1980: 110).

Eshkol and Eban also sought to tone down all official statements, so as not to contribute to the Arab pressure on Nasser to escalate further. It was decided to adhere officially to the earlier evaluation that Nasser was engaged in a demonstrative move and to project a "business-as-usual" attitude (Brecher, 1980: 109–11).

On May 22, only a few hours before Nasser announced the closure of the Straits of Tiran, Eshkol delivered a speech to the Knesset, in which he called all parties to return to the status quo. The speech was drafted after the recommendation of Yaakov Herzog, the director-general of the Prime Minister's Office, who argued that its tone should be mild so as not to inflame Nasser (Burdett, 1969: 237). Thus, no mention was made of Tiran. Eshkol's speech drew sharp criticism from several members of the Knesset, who demanded stronger measures and a reiteration of Israel's commitments. Segev (1967: 49) contends that Eshkol's speech was taken as an indication of Israeli weakness in the Arab world.

The Eshkol-Eban team, then, once again reacted in consistence with its game perception (14[72]): Although stronger defensive measures were taken and the planning of a preemptive strike begun, there was also an attempt to induce the CC outcome by calling on the opponent to de-escalate and by indicating that such a move would be reciprocated. At the point of Nasser's announcement on the Straits, the Israeli intelligence estimate was that an Egyptian attack was not likely and that the Egyptian army was still deployed in a defensive formation.[39] Eban and Eshkol were of the opinion that international diplomacy had a chance.

Nasser's Tiran Decision: May 22, 1967

In the period between Nasser's UNEF and Tiran decisions (May 16–22), the strategic picture in the Middle East changed dramatically. At the time Nasser mobilized, and even at the point of his request for the withdrawal of UNEF, Egypt did not seem capable of successfully challenging the status quo, and Israel still enjoyed a reputation for decisiveness and resolve.

With the removal of UNEF, however, the two armies stood face to face, and the question of the Straits loomed large once again. Khouri (1968: 245–47) writes that once Nasser mobilized his forces, the removal of UNEF followed logically, and the blockade followed logically from UNEF. Nasser himself, in his May 28 conference, stated that he "had to ask for the withdrawal of UNEF, and since the UNEF withdrew it was inevitable for us to go to the Gulf of Aqaba and restore the pre-1956 conditions there" (cited in Draper, 1968: 228).

Nasser's UNEF decision had an immediate impact on Arab expectations. Leaders and masses alike perceived the connection between UNEF and the Straits as inexorable, and the pressure on Nasser to pursue this logic to its end kept mounting. Hightened expectations soon turned into mass hysteria, fanned by the provocative and inflammatory broadcasts of Cairo Radio and its counterparts throughout the Arab world.

We saw earlier that several observers have argued that Nasser's judgment was clouded by the euphoria that swept the Arabs. As a result, he reached the conclusion that his military power was now sufficient to challenge the Israelis. This argument, however, is not supported by Nasser's subsequent behavior, a point we will return to later.

It is important to note that Israeli weakness did not induce Nasser to change his perception of the opponent. Rather, it signaled to him that he still had some room for maneuver before arriving at the brink. It appears that Nasser had no illusions about Israel's eventual response. Throughout the crisis, he updated and upgraded his probability estimates of Israeli attack, and saw clearly the connection between his own moves and Israel's war calculus. Thus, in his July 23, 1967, speech in Cairo, he stated: "Before we closed the Gulf of Aqabah, we convened a meeting of the Higher Executive Committee... We discussed the closure of the Gulf of Aqabah. That meeting took place on [the] 22nd [of] May. At that meeting I told them that the possibility of war was 50 per cent" (cited in Laqueur, 1968: 197–207). Thus, Nasser did not think he could escape an Israeli strike if he reached beyond a certain red line, although Israel's mild response changed his perception of where this red line would be drawn.

What is quite probable, however, is that Nasser's early successes modified his perception of the stakes involved in the crisis: He had achieved too much to back down without some substantive gains. At some point between UNEF and Tiran, then, Nasser's attitude toward loss may have changed from L2 to L1: he was now willing to incur some cost in order to protect his diplomatic achievements. Whereas at the point of mobilization he perceived this cost in terms of a crushing defeat, by May 22, his military position had changed sufficiently for him to believe that this cost could be somewhat reduced, at least long enough for the UN to intervene and stop the fighting. Nutting (1972: 408) recalls from his own talks with Nasser during the last days of the crisis that such was the thinking of the Egyptian leader.

If this argument is correct, then by the time Nasser made the Tiran decision, his preferences had already shifted from SL1 to ML1 (*see* Figure 2.2). Hence, his game perception was now 7(12)—the Prisoners' Dilemma—with the players at the DD outcome (*see* Figure 5.2). The game solution indicates that if the players arrive at DD, they stay there, and it becomes the final (Pareto-inferior) outcome. Nasser was aware of this trap, as is clearly evident in his subsequent behavior (*see* below). However, he judged that escalation could proceed some more before the Israelis attacked. Thus, he decided "to stay at DD," although at considerable risk, if we are to believe his postwar testimony concerning his probability estimate of Israeli attack at that point.

Our model of deception (*see* Figure 3.8) indicates that an ML1 player whose crisis game perception is ML1-ML1 (7[12], or PD) will simulate an ML2 type in order to avoid the DD outcome. As we shall see, this is precisely what Nasser did during the last week of the crisis. Our model, however, does not tell us how long a player will stay at the DD outcome in PD before attempting to induce an ML1-

Figure 5.2
The 1967 Middle East Crisis: May 22

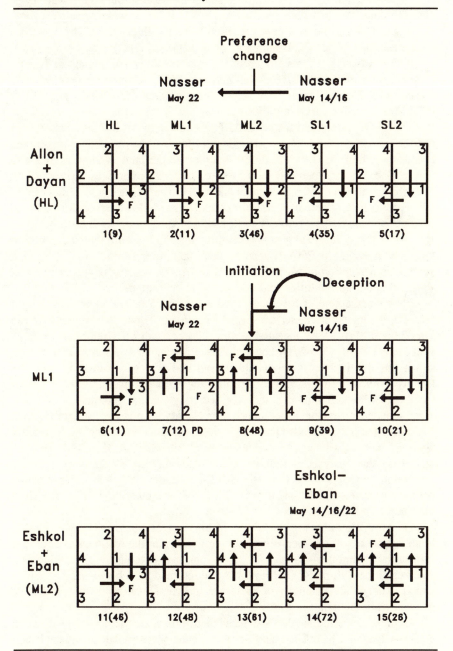

ML2 game perception on the part of the opponent. Apparently, Nasser estimated on May 22 that he still had a few available escalatory moves before the inevitable shift to the ML1-ML2 game had to be made. In the meantime, he would try to alter the status quo in such a way that would allow him to maintain at least some of his gains and to be in a better position to define the terms of the postcrisis settlement (that is, the CC outcome in game 12[48]/8[48]).

If this was Nasser's perception of the crisis on May 22, nothing in Israel's response thereafter could have alerted him to revise his estimates—between May 23 and May 30, the Israeli government decided twice (on May 23 and 28) to delay action and to pursue a diplomatic way out of the crisis.

There is no doubt that Eshkol and Eban's perception of Nasser's preferences changed at some point between May 19 and May 23. They no longer considered Nasser to be bluffing, which indicates that their earlier image of him as SL1 was now replaced by the perception of more conflictual preferences. Prittie (1969: 253) writes that "until May 23 Eshkol had hoped that Nasser could be induced to defer irrevocable action at Sharm el Sheikh [Tiran]." However, on May 26, his perception changed, as a result of further inflammatory statements by Nasser and Heikal. At that point, Eshkol was "becoming unhappily aware that war could no longer be averted" (p. 256). It appears, then, that on or around May 26, Eshkol shifted his perception of Nasser from SL1 to HL: Nasser was now serious about war, and could not be influenced or induced to compromise.

Eban's perception of Nasser changed in stages. We shall argue later that on May 30, his image of Nasser converged with that of Eshkol. However, between May 22 and May 30, he appeared to view Nasser as an ML1 player. During his visit to the US (May 26–27), Eban told President Lyndon Johnson that "there was still a possibility that Nasser would retreat, and a victory would be won for legality without war." He later met in New York with Ambassador Arthur Goldberg, who told him that the UN Secretary-General returned from Cairo empty-handed, apart from an assurance from Nasser that no Egyptian armed attack was planned. Eban responded that he "found this assurance convincing. Nasser did not want war; he wanted victory without war" (Eban, 1977: 356, 360).

Given this analysis, it follows that around May 26, Eshkol's crisis game perception changed to 11(46) (the ML2-HL game), whereas Eban's game perception changed to 12(48) (the ML2-ML1 game), most likely after the Tiran blockade (*see* Figure 5.2).

On May 23, following the advise of his director-general (Herzog), Eshkol invited leaders of the opposition to participate in the deliberations of the Ministerial Committee of Defense. Dayan took part in the May 23 meeting as a member of the Rafi party. On May 24, Allon returned from his visit to the Soviet Union. The policy positions of these key decision makers therefore become relevant from this point onwards.

Arguing from the model, the game perceptions of the four key decision makers—Eshkol, Eban, Allon, and Dayan—predict an internal debate in the Israeli government at this (post-Tiran) stage of the crisis. Regardless of their perception of Nasser, Allon and Dayan, as HL players, have a dominant strategy of defection. They are expected, therefore, to support coercive action—whether unambiguous Israeli escalation or war initiation—and oppose as useless further diplomatic efforts. Eshkol's game perception makes a coercive strategy rational as well (from about May 26). Eban's game perception, on the other hand, still provides room for compromise, although the opponent, as before, should be the one actually to make the first move toward conciliation. This analysis implies the existence of two competing coalitions: The first, led by Eshkol, Allon, and Dayan, advocates a coercive strategy; the second, led by Eban, recommends further diplomatic activity to induce the opponent to cooperate.

The record of the internal debate in Israel's now enlarged government generally confirms this argument from the model. The Ministerial Defense Committee, which met on May 23 with Dayan (but not Allon) present, agreed to delay military action for forty-eight hours and opt for diplomatic action.[40] Eban argued in favor of the delay, and his presentation, according to Brecher (1980: 120), "contained elements that would satisfy everyone—the hawks and doves, even Ben-Gurion's followers." Dayan and Shimon Peres expressed their doubts about the success of the diplomatic effort. Dayan later wrote (1976: 378): "My own view, which I put to the meeting, was that we should give the US the forty-eight hours she wanted... at the end of forty-eight hours, we should launch military action against Egypt with the aim of inflicting heavy losses on her armed forces." Also, on Eshkol's position in the meeting, he wrote: "Eshkol maneuvered so as to secure an agreed formula which would permit him not to take military action in response to Egypt's blockade of the straits. He spoke of a "device"—an American destroyer escort for an Israeli ship." Thus Eshkol, Eban, and Dayan expressed positions consistent with their game perceptions.[41]

On May 26, in a meeting of the Ministerial Committee on Defense, Allon argued that a further delay of action courted disaster. After the meeting ended, he met privately with Eshkol in order to convince him to launch a military strike. It seemed to Allon that by the end of the conversation, Eshkol had made up his mind to go to war (Brecher, 1980: 135).

On the evening of May 27, the cabinet met for a session that lasted until the early hours of the following day. Eban returned from his visit to the United States while the deliberations were on their way. He suggested, once again, that the Cabinet delay action, in order to allow the Americans to try to restrain Nasser. Allon, on the other hand, argued that Eban's trip was a mistake and that Israel should strike. Eshkol sided with Allon. When a formal vote was taken, the outcome was a deadlock: Nine ministers favored immediate action, including Eshkol and Allon; nine ministers voted for a further waiting period, including Eban. Eshkol, being prime minister and defense minister, could have cast the tie-breaking vote. Instead, he proposed that deliberations be adjourned until the following day (Brecher, 1980: 144).[42]

The cabinet session that convened on May 28 was short. By then, a note containing a stern warning from President Johnson had arrived: "Israel just must not take pre-emptive military action and thereby make itself responsible for the initiation of hostilities." The cabinet decided in favor of a two- to three-week delay in action in order to give the United States an opportunity to pursue its efforts to open the Straits. Allon expressed his reservations about the utility of further delay and voiced concern over the military situation (Brecher, 1980: 146–47; Nakdimon, 1968: 128–29).[43]

In summary, during the May 23–30 period, Israel's key decision makers made policy recommendations that were generally consistent with those that can be predicted from the model. However, two factors—Eshkol's concern for consensus decision making and the position taken by the United States—influenced the behavior of these policy makers in ways that were not anticipated by the model. It is important to note, though, that on May 29, in a speech to the Knesset, Eshkol made a firm statement that reflected his new assessment of Nasser and, hence, his shift in policy preference: "The Government of Israel has repeatedly stated its determination to exercise its freedom of passage in the Straits of Tiran and the Gulf of Aqaba, and to defend it in case of need. This is a supreme national interest on which no concession is possible and no compromise is admissible" (cited in Brecher, 1980: 152).

Nasser's Pact Decision: May 30, 1967

On May 30, Nasser made his final escalatory move in the crisis—the signing of the Egyptian-Jordanian Defense Agreement in Cairo. Judging by his behavior in the following days, it appears that Nasser viewed this move as his last available one before going over the brink.

The signing of the pact, besides its strategic value to Egypt, had the no less important significance of symbolizing the restoration of Nasser's status as the undisputed leader of the Arab world. It was the crowning achievement in a long and dazzling sequence of moves that brought leaders and masses alike to a state of frenzy. In Arab cities all over Middle East, Nasser was called upon to take the final step—to consummate the process with Israel's destruction.

The pact decision should be viewed in conjunction with Nasser's subsequent attempt to de-escalate the crisis. In terms of our model, the pact move was the last escalatory move in game 7(12) (PD). As noted above, the model predicts that an ML1 player in the PD game will project an ML2 type so as to avoid the DD outcome (*see* Figure 3.8). If deception succeeds, it modifies the opponent's perception of the game from PD to the ML1-ML2 game (8[48]), in which the players are expected to reach the compromise outcome.

Such was precisely Nasser's behavior after May 30: following a series of escalatory moves—the last of which was the pact decision—he now attempted to convince the Israelis that he was willing to settle the crisis through diplomacy (*see*

Figure 5.3
The 1967 Middle East Crisis: May 30–June 4

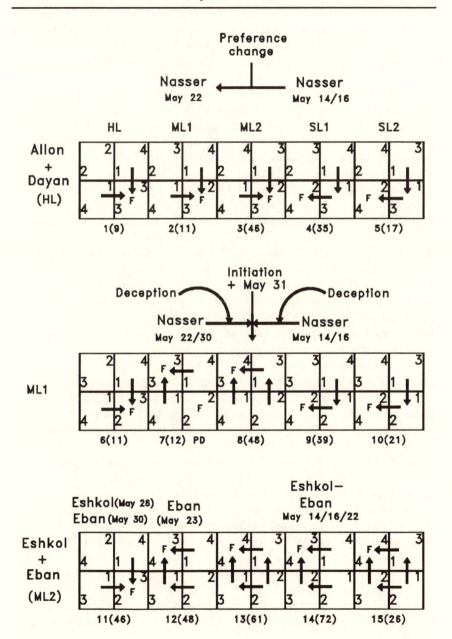

Figure 5.3).

There is in fact substantial evidence that Nasser attempted to stabilize the crisis after May 30. Nutting's personal testimony has already been mentioned. In a conversation he had with Nasser during the last day of the crisis, the Egyptian leader told him that he still believed war could be avoided, provided there were no further provocations (Nutting, 1972: 408). Nasser acted on this belief by instructing Egyptian forces in Sinai to abstain from any provocation of the Israelis. Defensive positions were taken despite the objections of Shams Badran and Abdel Hakim Amer, who pressured for a preemptive strike.[44] According to Bar-Zohar (1970: 176), when the Egyptian High Command met on June 2, Nasser instructed that, in light of indications that the crisis was subsiding, no excuse should be given to the Israelis for attacking. Khouri (1968: 247), too, argues that "as soon as he had achieved his most immediate political objectives, Nasser was content to sit back and go no further."

There is also the record of Nasser's diplomatic activities during the last days of the crisis: his pledge to Johnson and Charles De Gaulle that Egypt would not be the one to attack (*see* Riad, 1981, and Heikal, 1973); his response to a question put forth to him (on June 2) by British M.P. Christopher Mayhew that Egypt had no intention of attacking Israel; a similar assurance he gave Johnson's envoy, Charles Yost, when the latter visited Cairo at the beginning of June;[45] his decision to send Vice President Zakaria Mohieddin on a visit to Washington on June 5; and his agreement to a return visit by Vice President Hubert Humphrey (*see* Riad, 1981; Heikal, 1973; and Yost, 1968). On May 31, Egypt's ambassador to the United States suggested a formula for a compromise solution to the issue of Tiran (Stephens, 1971: 307).

Bar-Zohar (1970: 176) argues that when the Egyptian High Command met on June 2, the view of the participants was that Dayan's appointment to the post of defense minister (June 1) was an Israeli domestic matter. Therefore, it "created no undue excitement." He also points out that the Egyptian commander of the Sinai front, General Abdel Muhsin Murtagi, was vacationing in Ismailia when the Israeli attack was launched.[46] Dupuy (1978: 236) argues that Nasser's decision to retain Amer as his commander in chief and first deputy—despite deteriorating relations and rumors that the latter was planning a coup—"seems ample evidence that he did not expect a war to eventuate in 1967."[47]

In Israel, however, the outcome of the crisis had been sealed. Eban (1977: 380) writes that "by his journey to Cairo on May 30, Hussein made it certain that war would break out and that it would not necessarily be limited to the Egyptian-Israeli front." Eban understood the significance of the pact, namely that Israel would now have to fight on three fronts. Accordingly, in a May 31 meeting with heads of departments in the Foreign Ministry, he argued that "the assumption of two weeks' respite [decided on by the government on May 28] must now be revised, and that our dialogue with the United States must be modified accordingly" (p. 381).[48]

Stein and Tanter (1980: 218) write that "Israel's leaders were stunned by the joint defense pact," but understood its significance. They "quickly jettisoned the prevailing hypothesis that Arab unity was insufficient to permit an attack... and drastically updated their estimate of the likelihood of joint Arab military action" (p. 219). It was in response to this development that Eban, who led the dovish coalition, decided to reopen the May 28 decision to delay military action by two additional weeks (p. 220). Kimche and Bawly (1968: 154) argue that, together with the growing evidence that the United States was getting nowhere in its diplomatic efforts, the pact was decisive in leading to the collapse of "Eban's antiwar front" (p. 155). At that point, "there were no more doubters" in the government (p. 154). (*See* also Dayan, 1976: 373, and Churchill and Churchill, 1967: 52.)

On June 3, in a meeting at Eshkol's Jerusalem home, a unanimous decision was taken to recommend to the cabinet the following day that Israel should go to war.[49] On June 4, after further cabinet discussion and review of Israel's situation, Eshkol called for a formal vote. The decision on war was unanimous (Brecher, 1980: 164–68).

CONCLUSIONS

The above analysis suggests that whereas in the last week of the crisis Nasser perceived the game played to be 8(48) (*see* Figure 5.3)—and therefore believed that a compromise agreement was still within reach—Israeli decision makers perceived the crisis game differently. In fact, it was Nasser's pact decision that removed the last obstacle to unanimity of opinion on war initiation among Israel's principal decision makers. At that point, they were no longer receptive to Nasser's conciliatory signals.

Why did Nasser fail to realize that his pact decision would have such an effect on Israel's policy makers? The answer appears to be somewhat paradoxical: Nasser failed because up to that point he had succeeded so well. He managed, within the course of three weeks, to escalate with impunity and secure for himself gains that only a month before appeared to be beyond his reach. Throughout the crisis, his expectations were met or surpassed at each round of escalation. Yet if learning requires a negative discrepancy between expectations and outcomes,[50] we may argue that in the case of Nasser in 1967, there was no trigger to learning and therefore no reason for him to change his strategy.

This naturally turns attention to the Israeli behavior. Did Israel's decision makers in fact fail to "teach" Nasser that he was approaching the red line? Several participants and observers have argued precisely that. Ezer Weizman (1976: 215), for example, writes: "I don't hesitate to number our government's hesitancy and apprehensions as direct causes of Egyptian escalation." This also appears to be the view of Safran (1969), Cohen (1988), Quandt (1977), Amos (1979), Bar-Zohar (1970) and, as we saw earlier, Yaniv (1987).

Cohen (1988: 14) writes that "the measured warnings and unobtrusive military dispositions preferred by Israel either failed to register with the Egyptians or were simply taken as proof of weakness." Bar-Zohar (1970: 65) argues that in the meeting in which the decision to close the Straits was taken, Nasser's advisers reasoned that even Ben-Gurion took no immediate action when Egypt proceeded to close the Gulf in September 1955. It was hard to believe, therefore, that Eshkol would risk war over Tiran. There was nothing in Israel's behavior during the period thereafter that could have convinced Nasser that he had been wrong.

If the conclusion is that the success of Nasser's strategy provided no trigger for revisions, then it appears to be an interesting variant of a more general empirical observation on learning, namely that "nothing fails like success." Jervis (1976) discusses this paradox with respect to decision makers' learning from history, when analogizing to the past leads to the adoption of a strategy that worked then even if does not apply to the present. This case study suggests that the paradox may also operate within a given conflict. The mechanism that produces it, however, appears to be somewhat different—the analogy drawn is not from the present to a past event, but rather from an intermediate crisis outcome to an earlier expectation.

In Nasser's case, the parallels between the actual events of the crisis and his expectations were strong enough to produce a repetition of the previously successful strategy. These parallels would have appeared far less reassuring to Nasser had Israel managed the crisis differently. Instead, Israel's behavior could only have convinced him that his earlier estimates were rather conservative.

When seen in a broader perspective of crisis escalation in general, this conclusion points to the importance of *teaching* in crisis. From the perspective of the defender who is interested in preserving the status quo, sharp escalatory moves—such as were initiated by Nasser in 1967—may appear to be the product of resolve, boldness, or recklessness. In some crises, this is in fact the case, and the defender may then justly perceive that its only alternatives are capitulation or attack. This study suggests, however, that bold escalation may also be the result of insufficient indicators for strategy revision. This occurs when a challenger's expectations are met, or even surpassed, by actual events.

If the challenger is simply interested in provoking the defender to attack,[51] then the defender must decide whether to capitulate or attack. However, if the challenger's objective is to achieve a maximal revision of the status quo short of war, then it is paradoxically interested in being "taught" by the defender about the latter's preferences. If the defender fails to do so, it may bring about an outcome that is inferior for both parties.[52]

We turn now to the evaluation of the model itself. The model predicted well the Israeli behavior, across time and across individual actors. By tracing midcrisis changes in decision makers' perceptions of the opponent, the model was able to predict changes in individual policy recommendations. Moreover, the model proved accurate in specifying the structure and nature of the coalitions that formed in the Israeli government during the crisis.

The use of the process-tracing procedure (*see* Chapter 4) indicated that the consistency between the predictions of the model and the actual behavior of the actors was not spurious. The argumentation of individual policy makers during the internal decision-making process shows that revisions in the perception of the opponent in fact influenced behavior, and in the direction specified by the model.

The explanation of Egyptian crisis decisions proved to be more difficult. The model failed to predict Nasser's initiation, but when the possibility of deception was introduced, it specified a deceptive initiation strategy as rational for Nasser's type and his perception of the opponent. The evidence in support of this point was not conclusive but certainly suggestive of the possibility of deception. In fact, by anticipating the occurrence of deception, the model drew attention to, and suggested an explanation for, the peculiar mobilization and deployment pattern of Egyptian troops.[53]

The model failed, however, to predict Nasser's Tiran decision. In order to explain this development in the crisis, we had to argue, on the basis of factors exogenous to the model, that Nasser underwent a preference change.

It is important to define precisely the nature of this failure of the model if correct conclusions are to be drawn. First, the model did not anticipate the change in the attitude-toward-loss parameter, which, we argued, was responsible for the shift in preferences. Once this change in attitude was detected in the empirical data and "fed" into the model, the prediction of Nasser's subsequent behavior—including the anticipation of deception toward the end of the crisis—proved quite accurate.

Second, the research design in Chapter 4 called for the assessment of the four independent variables of the model—including the attitude-toward-loss variable—at each stage of the crisis and for each actor. This procedure was followed for the attitude-toward-loss variable just as it was followed for the other three variables. In this sense, the model was not expected to provide an explanation for the change in the attitude-toward-loss variable any more than it was expected to provide an explanation for the perception-of-the-opponent variable, which predicted the changes of behavior in the Israeli case.

The difference, however, is that the perception-of-the-opponent variable is endogenous to the *game component* of the crisis model, whereas the attitude-toward-the-opponent variable is exogenous to it. In its own terms, then, the game component failed to predict the occurrence of preference change. The model at large, however, did predict this change by detecting the shift in the attitude-toward-loss variable.

What this argument in effect says is that the game component of the model performed well as long as the variables exogenous to it remained constant. That, in fact, is precisely what occurred in the Israeli case, where the evidence shows that there were no changes in the attitude parameters and in the perception of relative capabilities. Hence, the explanation of Israeli crisis behavior could be provided strictly in terms of the game-theoretic component.

This is an important result, because it indicates, at least for the 1967 case, that decision makers do think strategically and moreover nonmyopically. Even more important for our agenda in this study, the argument for the necessity of a game component in a broad theory of crisis appears to have been justified by the case.

On the other hand, the failure of the game component to explain on its own terms the Egyptian behavior in the crisis indicates that there is a role for psychological variables in a broad theory of crisis. We specified three such variables, one of which—the attitude-toward-loss variable—proved useful in predicting the direction and nature of Nasser's preference change.

In fact, the "contact point" between this psychological variable and the game-theoretic component appears to have been well specified. Once the change in the psychological variable was observed, it enabled the game component to generate new predictions of behavior, which turned out to be accurate.

The incorporation of the psychological variables, then, did not detract in any way from the deductive power of the game component. Because these variables were specified as determinants of preferences, once the new preference set was defined and combined with the opponent's perceived type, the deductive power of game theory could be applied again to generate predictions.

Despite the overall accuracy of the predictions of the crisis model, it could not provide an explanation for the changes in perceptions and attitudes that were noted in the empirical case. That this failure was expected—given the specification of the attitude and perception variables as independent variables—does not alter the fact that some of the most intriguing questions about the crisis behavior of the decision makers were left unanswered. Thus, for example, we could not explain why Israeli decision makers changed their perception of Nasser's type over the course of the crisis, though we know the consequences of this change. Neither could we explain why Nasser changed his attitude toward loss in midcrisis, though, again, we know the effects of this change on his behavior.

The explanation, we suggested, lies in a learning process that involves inferences drawn by decision makers from discrepancies between expected and actual outcomes. The model detected the consequences of this learning process and predicted quite accurately its implications for crisis behavior. However, once the behavior yielded a new outcome, the model could not predict its effects on the subsequent game perceptions of the actors.

This conclusion suggests that the next stage in the development of the model could be the incorporation of a learning component, or a feedback mechanism between intermediate crisis outcomes and subsequent attitudes and perceptions. This mechanism should be able to predict the reaction of actors to the outcomes they obtain, in terms of shifts in attitudes and perceptions.[54]

This extension of the model, however, should be balanced against its presently economical nature. The model has successfully predicted some of the most important aspects of the 1967 crisis and has done so by means of a relatively simple theoretical structure. The weaknesses of the model could be remedied by introducing additional variables, but the increment in explanatory power will have to be bought at the cost of parsimony. Therefore, a future elaboration and expansion of the model will have to weigh the importance of the theoretical questions that remain unanswered in relation to the advantages of a parsimonious model.

As argued in Chapter 1, this problem of simplicity versus explanatory power lies at the heart of, and constitutes the challenge to, the development of an integrative theory of crisis. Whereas this problem cannot be resolved here, it is important to note that the model presented in this study has three advantages from the perspective of a future grand theory: First, despite its simplicity, it offers a description of crisis that is sufficiently rich and discriminating to be built upon in the future; second, it permits integration with psychological variables without impairing the deductive power of game theory; third, as the 1967 case demonstrates, it has a good chance of performing well empirically in other cases as well. Hence, the crisis model can serve as a basis for a comprehensive theory of crisis.

NOTES

1. Parts of this chapter are drawn from Mor (1991). I would like to thank the *Journal of Peace Research* and its editor, Nils Petter Gleditsch, for permitting me to use this material here.

2. The following discussion does not presume to constitute a comprehensive assessment of decision makers' attitudes toward the Arab-Israeli conflict. Only those aspects relevant to crisis preferences—as defined by the attitude-toward-the-opponent parameter—are examined.

3. Prittie (1969) argues that Eshkol's peace overtures were entirely sincere: "Eshkol's offer was not a maneuver. He was a man of peace, incapable of Ben-Gurion's clarion call to arms." Also, elsewhere: "Eshkol's personal desire for peace was beyond doubt" (pp. 211, 239).

4. Eban was Israel's foreign minister during the 1967 crisis.

5. Allon was minister of labor during the 1967 crisis.

6. Dayan was minister of defense from June 1, 1967.

7. Dayan's speech is reproduced in Gendzier (1969: 406–17).

8. By "the start of the crisis" we mean the introduction of Egyptian troops into Sinai on May 14. Brecher (1972), however, treats the May 14–16 period as the precrisis period for Israel and argues that the crisis period began on May 17, when Nasser's removal of UNEF increased Israel's threat perception significantly. Nevertheless, he discusses the Holocaust syndrome as part of the "shared psychological setting among Israeli decision-makers... during the 1967 Crisis as a whole" (p. 37).

9. Eshkol's contingent preference structure was perhaps the cause of his tendency to ponder problems at length before making up his mind. Drawing a comparison between Eshkol and Dayan, Allon remarked: "When Dayan is hesitating, his admirers say that he is thinking; but when Eshkol is thinking, his critics say that he is hesitating" (cited in Prittie, 1969: 207).

It is important to note that the Eshkol government's policy with respect to Syria in the years preceding the May–June 1967 crisis was consistent with the tit-for-tat preference type of the prime minister. That the retaliatory aspect of this policy eventually became dominant was the result of Eshkol's democratic decision-making process, which allowed the military far more influence on policy making than it had enjoyed under the authoritarian Ben-Gurion (Yaniv, 1987: 114).

10. All citations of Nasser's statements in this part of the discussion are taken from Harkabi's book. I thank Prof. Harkabi for permitting me to quote extensively from his work.

11. In June 1962, Akram Hourani, leader of the Syrian *Baath* party and a former UAR minister, published a pamphlet in which he described Nasser as an "ally of Zionism" (*see* Lacouture, 1973: 289).

12. This perception, in fact, has constituted one of the "prize questions" with which the literature on the Six Day War has occupied itself: Why did Nasser take the risks he took when he very well knew of Egypt's weakness? In a later section, we will look at some of the answers provided by various scholars to this question.

13. A short time before the crisis, Israel's military intelligence (AMAN), estimated that there was no chance of a war in the coming year because of Egypt's deep involvement in the Yemen conflict (Haber, 1987: 147).

14. Israel Lior, the aid-de-campe to Prime Minister Eshkol, noted in his diary that when Egyptian Chief of Staff Muhammad Fawzy visited Damascus after the May 14 mobilization, he demanded that the Syrians abstain from any action that would provoke Israel further (Haber, 1987: 148–49).

15. In effect, Eshkol and Eban did not perceive a crisis situation (and hence a crisis game) with Egypt prior to Nasser's mobilization on May 14. However, we shall argue later that Nasser's initial move did not change Eshkol and Eban's perception of his type.

It is important to note that Allon was not present in Israel until May 24, when he returned from a visit to the Soviet Union. Similarly, Dayan was not party to the internal deliberations initially—he became defense minister only on June 1. However, as Brecher (1980: 95) remarks, "throughout the week before he [Dayan] entered the Government, he was the focus of personal-political attention; his images are therefore relevant from about May 23."

16. *See* Wagner (1974), Zagare (1987; 1984a; 1981), and Stein and Tanter (1980). Maoz (1990c) uses the dollar auction game to analyze the 1967 crisis, which he offers as an instance of "the paradox of crisis escalation"—confrontations that end in war, contrary to the wishes of the parties involved and because of their efforts to prevent it.

17. Unfortunately, this practice does not result in explanations that integrate the two levels and specify their interrelationships. One consequence of this is that, within single studies, explanations offered at one level are often inconsistent with explanations offered at another level, as we shall argue below.

18. Sadat (1977), too, writes that Nasser "was carried away by his own impetuosity" (p. 173).

19. Stein (1988) argues that Nasser's overestimation of Egyptian military capabilities was the result of motivated error: Having committed himself to a challenge of Israeli deterrence, Nasser and his advisers now engaged in "wishful thinking and *post hoc* bolstering of their decision" (p. 10).

20. On the necessity of evaluating the expectations of crisis initiators independently of the outcome of the crisis, *see* Lebow (1981: 91–92).

21. *See* Chapter 1, The Pychological and Rational-Choice Approaches: A Critical Appraisal, for a discussion of this point.

22. Most writers argue that the decisive step, in terms of the outcome of the crisis, was Nasser's decision to close the Straits (May 22). Later on, the argument will be made that war became inevitable only after the signing of the Egyptian-Jordanian Pact (May 30).

23. One wonders what the historical verdict would have been had the United Nations, or the major powers, taken successful steps to stabilize the crisis. One suspects that Nasser's decisions would have been heralded as the product of an ingenious strategic mind.

24. Both Lacouture (1973) and Nutting (1972) supply ample documentation for Nasser's cautious policy after May 30. More on this point will be said later.

25. Stein (1988: 5) argues that Nasser's restraint in the 1960 crisis was the result of his then secure position at home and abroad. In 1967, on the other hand, he was a weak leader who could not resist the pressures exerted on him. This reasoning is not entirely convincing. It presupposes that insecurity and weakness breed aggression, whereas strength yields restraint. This relationship, however, is not logically necessary: A weak leader may realize that he or she cannot afford to take the same risks that a strong and secure leader can. In fact, despite his weakness, Nasser showed remarkable restraint during the years immediately preceding the 1967 crisis, as well as toward the end of the crisis itself, as will be argued later.

26. This claim was later substantiated by the Egyptian Minister of Defense Shams Badran during the course of his postwar trial and by Anwar Sadat in his memoirs. Badran's statement is mentioned in Safran (1969: 300). Sadat (1977) recalls a meeting of the Supreme Executive Committee toward the end of May 1967, in which Nasser discussed his probability estimates of Israeli attack. (There is a difference, however, in the versions given by the three men.)

Excerpts from Nasser's speech are reproduced in Draper (1968, appendix 14) and in Laqueur (1968: 197–207).

27. Maoz (1982a) classifies this crisis in the category of "unintended crises," which occur when "the initiator is unaware of the implications of its actions for the defender" (p. 222).

28. On the question of Israel's intentions with respect to Syria, *see*, for example, Shamir, 1971: 187; Laqueur, 1968: 74–75; Badeau, 1968: 110; Derogy and Carmel, 1979: 207–22; and Yaniv, 1987: 115–17. Dawn (1968: 209) and Yost (1968: 303–4) argue that Nasser believed an Israeli attack on Syria was forthcoming. Safran's (1969) view is that even if he had doubts about the reliability of the information, "in a certain particular sense he believed it to be *essentially* true" (p. 278; original emphasis). For an in-depth analysis of the Russian role in the crisis, *see* Burdett (1969). Bar-Joseph and Hannah (1988) provide a comparative perspective on Soviet crisis behavior in the 1956, 1967, 1973, and 1982 Arab-Israeli wars.

29. In November 1966, following criticism by Jordan's prime minister of Nasser's failure to intervene in the Samu incident, Heikal wrote in *Al Ahram* that according to the plans of the United Arab Command, it was the responsibility of individual states to cope with Israeli raids—Egypt was bound to intervene only if Arab territory was occupied. A week before Heikal noted that the same condition applied to the Egyptian-Syrian Joint Defense Agreement (Safran, 1969: 273).

It is important to note that whereas on April 7, 1967, there was an actual clash between Israel and Syria, on May 14, 1967, there were only rumors of Israeli troops concentrations in the north. Laqueur (1968: 88) argues that "the record shows that between May 1966 and May 1967 there was hardly a week without news in the Syrian and Egyptian press about major Israeli troops concentrations on the Syrian border."

30. For the purpose of presenting the crisis by means of the composite matrix (*see* below), assume henceforth that Nasser is the column player and Israel the row player. Thus, the CD outcome represents Israeli capitulation, whereas the DC outcome represents Israeli victory.

31. In Chapter 3, we did not consider explicitly deception strategies in crisis initiation, though their use was implied by several of the empirical examples that were discussed. In terms of its exploratory function, then, the case study of the 1967 crisis draws attention to that aspect of the crisis model.

32. On the role of the Rotem analogy during the initial stages of the crisis, *see* Amos (1979: 55), Stein (1988: 4, fn. 29), Stein and Tanter (1980: 138), Dupuy (1978: 230), Kimche and Bawly (1968: 84–85), Brecher (1980: 46), Quandt (1977: 39), Eban (1977: 323), Weizman (1976: 209), and Rabin (1979: 68).

33. Note that this figure is actually the composite matrix, with the soft-line row players omitted.

34. At that point, Eshkol was of the opinion that Nasser's intent was deterrent rather than offensive (Stein and Tanter, 1980: 139). Still, cautious as he was, he also sent emissaries abroad to secure the delivery of arms and began to make arrangements for the transfer of money from world Jewry (Brecher, 1980: 48).

35. There is an ongoing debate in the Six Day War literature on whether Nasser intended the entire UNEF force to be withdrawn or was forced to do so only following an ultimatum by UN Secretary-General U Thant. Riad (1981: 17–18) goes as far as to suggest that the idea to demand the withdrawal of UNEF came from Abdel Hakim Amer, the commander general of the Egyptian forces, who acted independently. Prittie (1969: 251), on the other hand, argues that such a move could not have been taken without Nasser's knowledge and approval. Nasser, in any event, said on May 23 that had the Egyptian request been rejected, "we would have regarded it [UNEF] as a hostile force and disarmed it" (cited in Laqueur, 1968: 103).

36. Ben-Gurion himself was highly critical of Eshkol's management of the crisis. He viewed (at least until May 19) the Egyptian concentration of troops as demonstrative and contended that Eshkol's reserves mobilization was a grave error—had Eshkol not done so, Nasser would have withdrawn his troops (Bar-Zohar, 1970: 64). On May 22, Rabin met with Ben-Gurion, who accused him of compromising Israel's security by escalating the crisis when the army was not sufficiently ready and by acting without the support of an outside ally (Stein and Tanter, 1980: 158; Haber, 1987: 174).

37. According to Draper (1968: 70), "the evidence is overwhelming that Israel acted exactly as Nasser expected it to act."

38. The rapid succession of moves on the part of Nasser may also be indicative of the integral nature of the May 14–15 mobilization and the May 16 decision on UNEF.

39. After the war, General Matityahu Peled argued that the military's intelligence estimate up to May 22 was that Nasser's moves were diversionary. Peled concluded that the size of the Egyptian force in Sinai—which by May 19 was only somewhat larger than it had been during the Rotem crisis—was not sufficient to threaten Israel's security (cited

in Stein and Tanter, 1980: 157, fn. 1; Reuveni, 1972, discusses the debate concerning this estimate).

Israel Lior (Eshkol's aide-de-camp) wrote in his diary that when Rabin attended the Ministerial Committee on Defense on May 21, he reported that "the Egyptian deployment is strictly defensive and does not pose a danger to our forces" (Haber, 1987: 162; my translation). However, later that day, in a cabinet meeting, the chief of staff argued that although Egyptian deployment was defensive, it did constitute a "serious threat." Ezer Weizman, then chief of operations, argues (1976: 211, 213) that the general staff "was perplexed and confused," and that its doubts concerning the necessity of an Israeli strike were eliminated only around May 26.

40. The forty-eight-hour delay was requested by President Johnson, and delivered to the Israelis through Under-Secretary of State Rostow.

41. Recall that Eshkol's game perception until May 26 was 14(72).

42. Brecher (1980) argues that Eshkol's method of decision making "was to achieve broad consensus, particularly on momentous decisions" (p. 144).

43. That same evening of May 28 Eshkol delivered a stuttering and hesitant national radio address, which left a harsh impression on the public and ignited the political process that was to culminate only a few days later with Dayan's appointment as minister of defense.

That same evening, too, Eshkol had a bitter confrontation with the general staff of the Israeli Defense Forces (IDF), which vehemently objected to the decision on further delay (for an account of this dramatic meeting, *see* Haber, 1987: 194–98). The severity of the conflict between Eshkol and the general staff found expression in yet another serious incident. Following the May 28 decision, Eshkol instructed the IDF to begin releasing reserves. Not only was the prime minister's instruction not carried out, but additional reserves were called up (ibid., p. 193).

44. Nutting (1972: 416) also suggests that the deployment of Egyptian aircraft near Egypt's civilian airport was that of "sitting targets for enemy attacks." Much has been written about the deployment pattern of the Egyptian forces. The best analyses are those of Dupuy (1978) and Stein (1988). This issue resulted in a sharp division of opinion between the Israelis and the Americans during the course of the crisis. Israel argued that the Egyptian deployment suggested a likely attack. The Pentagon, however, did not find evidence for this claim. Later on, when head of the *Mossad*, Meir Amit, visited Washington, he found it difficult of convince Pentagon officials that Israel's estimate of Egyptian intentions was correct. (*See* Eisenberg, Dan, and Landau, 1979, for details on this meeting.)

45. Yost reached an agreement with Nasser to put the issue of Tiran before the International Court at the Hague (Lacouture, 1973: 307).

46. Churchill and Churchill (1967: 75) write that on June 4, "Egyptian generals were seen on the tennis courts of Cairo."

47. Derogy and Carmel (1979)—relying on the testimony of the Soviet diplomat Vladimir Sakharov, who was stationed in Cairo (1968–1970) before defecting to the West—argue that the Soviets knew of Israel's plan to attack on June 5, but did not inform Nasser of this so as "to prevent his backing out" (p. 218).

In his July 23, 1967, speech, Nasser claimed to have correctly assessed the implications of Dayan's appointment. In the same speech, he also indicated that on June 2, in a meeting with senior military officers at the Supreme Command HQ, he told his listeners that he expected an Israeli attack to take place within forty-eight to seventy-two hours, and even specified that the attack would begin on June 5 with a strike against the Egyptian Air Force. The same account is repeated in Sadat (1977) and Riad (1981).

These accounts cannot be easily reconciled, and further research is required in order to establish the correct picture, but the evidence is perhaps not as contradictory as it appears to be at first sight. To begin with, it is possible that Nasser was simply uncertain about the implications of Dayan's appointment. There were, after all, quite a few indicators that the crisis was in fact subsiding. Primary among them was the American diplomatic effort, which appeared to be gaining momentum with the visits of Robert Anderson and Charles Yost, the imminent departure to Washington of Zakaria Moheiddin, and the expected return visit of Hubert Humphrey. It is not surprising therefore—but somewhat inconsistent with his claim to have predicted the onset of war—that in the same speech of July 23, Nasser lashed out at the Americans for having engaged in deception prior to the Israeli attack.

Nasser's statement of June 2 to his military officers may well have been a warning rather than a prediction. Given the officers' overconfidence in the Egyptian army's capabilities and level of preparedness, Nasser may have felt it necessary to jolt them into action. In this he apparently did not succeed, as revealed subsequently by the poor alertness level of the Egyptian forces.

48. It appears that at this point, Eban's perception of the crisis game finally converged with that of Eshkol. There was no longer any doubt that a compromise agreement of any kind could be worked out. Therefore, on June 3, Eban joined Eshkol, Dayan, and Allon in voting for war (*see* Figure 5.3).

The pact decision appears to have changed the perception of the crisis in Washington as well. Bar-Zohar (1970: 157) reports that upon hearing of Nasser's move, "the Americans realized that they had been on the wrong track"; Walt Rostow called Ephraim Evron, Israel's minister in Washington, and "confessed for the first time that he could see no solution."

49. Present in that meeting, besides Eshkol, were Allon, Dayan, Eban, Rabin, Zvi Dinstein (deputy minister of defense), Yigal Yadin (Eshkol's link to Dayan and the general staff), Meir Amit (head of *Mossad*), Aharon Yariv (director of military intelligence), Yaakov Herzog (director-general of the Prime Minister's Office), Arye Levavi (director-general of the Foreign Ministry), and Avraham Harman (Israel's ambassador to the United States).

50. On this point, see Bandura (1977) and Maoz (1990b).

51. Lebow (1981) refers to such crises as "justification of hostility crises."

52. In Israel's case, an interest in conveying to Nasser the limits of Israeli tolerance made sense as long as Nasser did not conclude the pact with Jordan. However, once Israel's decision makers failed to deter this further escalation of the conflict, and once this development triggered their decision to go to war, they became interested in keeping Nasser in the dark about their true intentions so as to maintain strategic surprise. Paradoxically, their earlier failure at signaling may have helped them to project a consistent pattern of moderation even as they were preparing for war: Dayan's press conference of June 3, in which he indicated that war was not imminent; the pictures of Israeli soldiers (several thousands of whom had been granted leave) resting on the beaches; and the routine communiqué issued by the cabinet on June 4, made the "right" impression in Cairo (*see* Churchill and Churchill, 1967: 74–75, and Brecher, 1980: 165). Lior wrote that "the

prolonged attrition involved in the endless anticipation for war lulled the senses of intelligence agents, the press, the foreign delegations, and perhaps the armies surrounding the state of Israel" (Haber, 1987: 221; my translation).

53. The case suggests that crisis initiation may be accompanied by a deceptive shift on the part of the initiator to a more conflictual type. This observation, which requires further empirical confirmation, was possible because the model was used in an anticipatory way. It is important that the model be applied in such a fashion to other empirical cases of crisis initiation, because the literature on strategic surprise—which deals by and large with war initiation—predicts that preinitiation deception will take the form of a shift to a less conflictual type. In fact, this argument is confirmed in our case—Israel did attempt to project moderation from June 3 until its preemptive strike. It is possible that deception operates differently in crisis and war initiation; more research is needed to establish and analyze this difference.

54. This is one possible role for the psychological approach in the integrative framework. The literature on learning is rich enough to provide insights into the process by which discrepancies between expectations and actual outcomes affect the perceptions of actors. Thus, for example, studies of personality argue that learning depends on the structure and content of belief systems. Findings drawn from these studies can be stated in probabilistic terms, that is, as the likelihood that different types of players will revise their perception of the opponent as a result of discrepancies between expectations and intermediate crisis outcomes.

Elsewhere (Mor, 1990), I used probabilities in a multistage game model to predict Nasser's crisis behavior in 1967. These probability estimates were derived from Nasser's July 23, 1967, speech, in which he specified his perception of the likelihood of an Israeli attack at each stage of the crisis. It should be noted, however, that the probabilities were exogenous to the model and were applied to a single player type.

6

Summary and Conclusions

This study undertook the development of a game-based model of crisis that could (1) explain the initiation, development, and termination of international crises, and (2) serve as the core element of a broad theoretical framework within which game-theoretic and psychological variables could be integrated. The present chapter briefly reviews and summarizes the theoretical concerns of this study and evaluates the crisis model in light of the objectives it was designed to meet. The emphasis of the discussion will not be on substantive conclusions, which have been adequately addressed in earlier chapters, but rather on the formal, logical, and theoretical aspects of the model, and on its normative implications.

We began (in Chapter 1) with the argument that crisis theory has suffered from the continuing breach between the psychological and rational-choice approaches to crisis research. A close examination of the literature produced by each approach revealed competing but equally deficient conceptions of crisis. Thus, we maintained that the psychological approach reduces crisis actors to isolated centers of information processing, thereby neglecting the strategic-interactive aspect of crisis that is essential to a theory of interstate conflict. The game-theoretic approach, on the other hand, focuses on strategic interaction to the neglect of actors' psychology, which limits its ability to explain crisis dynamics, in particular transitions over crisis games.

We argued further that a more satisfactory conception of crisis should combine and integrate elements from both approaches, so as to benefit from the explanatory potential that each approach has to offer. A comprehensive theory of crisis can be embedded within such a framework.

More specifically, the theoretical framework suggested in this study rests on the belief that an essential and central aspect of the empirical phenomenon of crises is strategic interaction. This conception implies that the focal point of an integrative framework consist of a game-theoretic component. The challenge in the development of this component is twofold: It must provide a rich and differentiated description of crises so as to reflect the variability found in the empirical population, and it must include explicit contact points with psychological variables.

The development of this game component was the task we confronted in this study. In Chapter 2, we specified a basic crisis game, reflecting the notion that all adversarial crises present decision makers with similar basic dilemmas. The variability among crises was then conceived to be a function of differences in actors' preferences and in the information they possess. This reasoning led us to depart from existing game-theoretic studies—which rely by and large on a "generic crisis" (for example, Chicken or Prisoners' Dilemma)—by developing a game-based typology of crises.

The typology was based on a deductive derivation of players' preferences. We ventured outside game theory to hypothesize that the source of crisis preferences lay in the attitudes (toward the opponent and toward loss) and perceptions (of relative capabilities) of the players. In this way, an explicit link was established between psychological variables and the crisis game, reflecting the conception of preferences as one possible contact point between the psychological and rational-choice approaches. The utility of this conception was demonstrated by tracing the effects of changes in the attitude and perception variables on the crisis preferences of players. Thus, for example, Woodrow Wilson's strategy change vis-à-vis Germany in March–April 1917 was traced back to a change in his attitude toward the opponent, which in turn resulted in a shift in preferences and a new game perception.

The derivation of crisis preferences yielded five preference sets, or decision-maker types, corresponding to the belief system concept that is well established in the psychological literature. The interaction of the different types in a single composite matrix resulted in a typology of crisis games. This typology, we argued, reflected the variability of crisis situations found in the empirical population and, hence, enabled the subsequent analysis of crisis behavior to be cast in terms of general propositions.

In Chapter 3, the theory of moves was applied to the games of the composite matrix in order to derive optimal crisis strategies for the different player types. The nonmyopic solution concept, which we supplemented with the assumption of two-sided analysis, reflected the view of crisis actors as far-sighted decision makers who are capable of planning their moves more than one step ahead. In fact, by making the decision on initiation dependent on the crisis outcome that players expect to obtain (as well as on their valuation of the status quo), we proposed that crisis is a process whose different stages are perceived by decision makers as interrelated.

This latter conception is at odds with the view of crisis decision making that emerges from most psychological studies, where crisis behavior is described as a function of myopic, disjointed responses and deficient information processing. As argued earlier, the focus on policy failures (so evident, for example, in studies of Nasser in the 1967 crisis) leads to explanations that are biased by the search for pathologies. The crisis model presented in this study, on the other hand, is designed to provide explanations for successes as well as failures. The assumption of long-term strategic calculation does not imply that decision makers necessarily succeed, but it reflects a theoretical position that is opposed to the idea of constructing a general theory of crisis rooted in decisional pathologies.

The notion of far-sighted decision makers who calculate their moves on the basis of an integrated view of crisis provided parsimonious explanations of behavior. Thus, we derived propositions concerning initiation, crisis strategy (including deception), and crisis outcome from three independent variables: types, perception of the opponent, and valuation of the status quo.

Despite the simplicity of the model, it coped well with the complexities of the 1967 Middle East crisis. We were able to provide an explanation for the different policy positions of Israel's key decision makers and to account for changes in those positions over time. The model also suggested that Nasser's crisis behavior could be explained on the basis of strategic rationality, contrary to the conventional wisdom of the Six Day War literature. Hence, the assumption of nonmyopic rationality turned out to generate predictions that were quite consistent with the empirically observed behavior.

The test of a good model, however, is in its ability to go beyond the explanation of known events to propose hitherto unobserved patterns of behavior. The application of the model to the 1967 case indicated that deception was a rational strategy for Nasser at the outset of the crisis and toward its termination. A reexamination of the evidence in light of this surprising prediction drew attention to aspects of Nasser's behavior that have not received sufficient attention in the literature. Specifically, the odd deployment pattern of Egyptian forces on May 14–15 and Nasser's attempt at de-escalation after May 30 could very well have been instances of deception. Thus, the model suggested new and plausible explanations in a case that has been analyzed extensively in the past.

Looking to the future, this study suggests two agendas with respect to research on international crises. The first would be to expand the present theoretical framework for integrating psychological and rational-choice elements. Whereas the psychological variables in the crisis model were specified as independent variables, future expansions of the model could treat them as dependent variables. This in turn implies that more work needs to be done on the determinants of attitudes and perceptions.

In fact, the explanation of transitions over crisis games—an essential component of dynamic behavior—requires that we gain a better understanding of how and when attitudes and perceptions change in response to intermediate crisis outcomes. The empirical case demonstrated that an answer to this question is of vital importance: In the absence of a theory of preference change, we were unable to account for Nasser's Tiran decision and had to invoke factors that are exogenous to the model.

The next stage in the development of the model, then, should be the specification of a learning component. It may be easier, however, to deal initially with learning that does not affect preferences—and yet changes the perception of the crisis game, such as revisions in the perception of the opponent. We saw that this process was decisive in explaining shifts in Israel's crisis strategy.

It is important to emphasize, as we did at the end of Chapter 5, that the introduction of additional variables to account for learning is not costless. One advantage of the present model is its simplicity and parsimony, which may have to be compromised with further theoretical elaboration. A process of trial and error will be required in order to determine whether or not any particular extension of the model yields explanatory dividends that are worth the loss in parsimony. Such a process is unavoidable if a general theory of crisis is ever to emerge from the mass of individual and disconnected models.

Another agenda suggested by this study relates to normative issues that concern crisis behavior and management. To begin with, our analysis took a neutral position with respect to deception by defining it as the projection of an insincere preference type. This definition did not foreclose any of the possible objectives that such a strategy may serve. In fact, we found that rational players may employ deception for the sinister purposes that are commonly associated with such a strategy, that is, the exploitation of weak players. However, we discovered that deception may also be beneficial to crisis management by averting war and inducing compromise (*see* also Brams, 1977). Moreover, deception has such salutary effects precisely when the use of a sincere strategy would result in war.

Our study indicates, then, that deception constitutes an integral part of the range of crisis strategies available to rational decision makers. From a normative standpoint, deception should not be treated as an aberration, but rather as a legitimate crisis strategy. A position that categorically opposes the use of deception as an immoral means of waging conflict is untenable; just as sincere strategies may be employed for aggressive and expansionary purposes, so deception may be used to terminate conflict peacefully.

In addition, deception may be the only effective means of defense available to weak states. Paradoxically, then, the use of such a strategy by the weak is not only rational, but also consistent with the morally justified and endorsed practice of self-defense.

Like deception, which is often rejected as the machination of conniving minds, crisis initiation is often perceived to be the tool of aggressors. Hence, the literature on crisis and deterrence is strongly defender-oriented (*see* Maoz, 1982a), reflecting the attitude that the preservation of the status quo—or its change by strictly noncoercive means—is inherently good and justified.

Our analysis of initiation avoided this bias by taking the valuation of the status quo as given. Initiation then became a function of rational calculation only, and our results showed that every player type—even middle-liners and soft-liners—may initiate occasionally.

In normative terms, this result reminds us, as in the case of deception, that initiation may in fact be used to further aggressive aims, but it may also constitute the only available means of restructuring the status quo for players who are exploited under the existing system. That is, when the status quo does not offer established avenues for a peaceful readjustment of the existing order, states may be forced to initiate crises. In such cases, initiation does not imply an expansionary foreign policy.

This latter point, as we saw in Chapter 3, has serious policy implications for the defender. A national security policy that seeks to deter each and every initiation may undermine its own effectiveness by increasing, rather than decreasing, the threat to the state. Successful deterrence prevents initiation in the short run, but it increases the frustration of the opponent, whose grievances are not addressed, in the long run. Eventually, the opponent's dissatisfaction with the status quo will rise to a degree where initiation can no longer be deterred.

A sensible security policy, then, should not proceed from the assumption that each and every case of initiation involves unlimited demands by the opponent. Instead, a far-sighted strategy should take into account the concerns and grievances of a dissatisfied opponent; it should seek to reduce external threat by facilitating incremental adjustments to the status quo.

This is not to say that appeasement is an optimal strategy of crisis prevention or management. As we saw in the 1967 case, an effective strategy is one that signals both a willingness to consider legitimate demands and a resolve to resist excessive ones.[1] On the one hand, the possibility of compromise has to be made available to opponents with legitimate concerns so as to induce noninitiation in the long run as well as in the short run. On the other hand, red lines have to be drawn so as to deter expansionary actors and indicate the limits of tolerance to opportunists.

The latter type of actors, in particular, have an interest in learning where the red lines would be drawn. In the 1967 crisis, Israel failed to signal unambiguously its tolerance levels to Nasser. As a result, the revision of Egypt's crisis strategy occurred after Israeli decision makers had already decided that war was unavoidable.

Much additional research is required before we fully grasp the role that signaling plays in crisis management. As this book has attempted to show, such an understanding can be gained only if the interrelationship between structure and process is elucidated. Thus, game theory can provide insight into the structure of crisis situations or the strategic context within which signaling occurs. Psychological studies can unravel the process by which signals are transmitted, received, and interpreted. However, only by integrating the psychological and rational-choice approaches can we develop the kind of theory that can cope with the challenges of crisis management and war prevention.

NOTE

1. This conclusion is consistent, in general terms, with the findings of Axelrod (1984), Leng (1984), and Huth and Russett (1988).

Bibliography

Aaftink, Jan. 1989. Far-Sighted Equilibria in 2 x 2, Non-Cooperative, Repeated Games. *Theory and Decision* 27(3): 175–92.

Abelson, R. P. 1976. Social Psychology's Rational Man. In *Rationality and Social Science: Contributions to the Philosophy and Methodology of The Social Sciences*, ed. S. I. Benn and G. W. Mortimore. Boston: Routledge and Kegan Paul, pp. 58–59.

Achen, Christopher H., and Duncan Snidal. 1989. Rational Deterrence Theory and Comparative Case Studies. *World Politics* 41(2): 143–69.

Aggarwal, Vinod K., and Pierre Allan. 1988. A General Theory of Preference Formation: Statics. Paper presented at the Swiss-U.S. Joint Seminar on "Cooperative Models in International Relations Research, Graduate Institute of International Studies, Geneva, December 16–18.

Allison, Graham T. 1971. *Essence of Decision: Explaining the Cuban Missile Crisis.* Boston: Little, Brown and Company.

Allison, Graham T., and Morton H. Halperin. 1972. Bureaucratic Politics: A Paradigm and Some Policy Implications. In *Theory and Policy in International Relations*, ed. R. Tanter and R. Ullman, (eds.). Princeton: Princeton University Press, pp. 40–79.

Allon, Yigal. 1970. *The Making of Israel's Army.* London: Sphere Books Limited.

Amos, John W. 1979. *Arab-Israeli Military/Political Relations: Arab Perception and the Politics of Escalation.* New York: Pergamon Press.

Aron, Raymond. 1966. *Peace and War.* New York: Doubleday.

Axelrod, Robert. 1984. *The Evolution of Cooperation.* New York: Basic Books.

Badeau, John S. 1968. The Arabs, 1967. In *The Arab-Israeli Impasse*, ed. Majdia D. Khadduri. Washington: Robert B. Luce, pp. 97–113.

Bandura, Albert. 1977. *Social Learning Theory.* Englewood Cliff: Prentice-Hall.

Banks, Jeffrey S. 1990. Equilibrium Behavior in Crisis Bargaining Games. *Amercian Journal of Political Science* 34(3): 599–614.

Bar-Joseph, Uri, and John P. Hannah. 1988. Intervention Threats in Short Arab-Israeli Wars: An Analysis of Soviet Crisis Behavior. *The Journal of Strategic Studies* 11(4): 437-67.

Bar-Zohar, Michael. 1970. *Embassies in Crisis: Diplomats and Demagogues Behind the Six-Day War.* Englewood Cliffs: Prentice-Hall.

Bendor, Jonathan, and Thomas H. Hammond. 1992. Rethinking Allison's Models. *American Political Science Review* 86(2): 301–22.

Benn, S. I., and G. W. Mortimore, eds. 1976a. *Rationality and the Social Sciences: Contributions to the Philosophy and Methodology of the Social Sciences*. Boston: Routledge and Kegan Paul.

———. 1976b. Technical Models of Rational Choice. In *Rationality and the Social Sciences: Contributions to the Philosophy and Methodology of the Social Sciences*, ed. S. I. Benn and G. W. Mortimore. Boston: Routledge and Kegan Paul, pp. 157–95.

Brams, Steven J. Forthcoming. *Theory of Moves*. Cambridge: Cambridge University Press.

———. 1985a. *Rational Politics: Decisions, Games, and Strategy*. Washington, D.C.: Congressional Quarterly, Inc.

———. 1985b. *Superpower Games: Applying Game Theory to Superpower Conflict*. New Haven: Yale University Press.

———. 1983. *Superior Beings: If They Exist, How Would We Know?* New York: Springer-Verlag.

———. 1977. Deception in 2 x 2 Games. *Journal of Peace Science* 2(1): 171–203.

Brams, Steven J., and Marek P. Hessel. 1984. Threat Power in Sequential Games. *International Studies Quarterly* 28(1): 15–36.

Brams, Steven J., and D. Marc Kilgour. 1988. *Game Theory and National Security*. New York: Basil Blackwell.

———. 1987a. Optimal Threats. *Operations Research* 35(4): 524–36.

———. 1987b. Threat Escalation and Crisis Stability: A Game-Theoretic Analysis. *American Political Science Review* 81(3): 833–50.

Brams, Steven J., and Ben D. Mor. Forthcoming. When Is It Rational to Be Magnanimous in Victory? *Rationality and Society*.

Brams, Steven J., and Donald Wittman. 1981. Nonmyopic Equilibria in 2 x 2 Games. *Conflict Management and Peace Science* 6(1): 39–62.

Braybrook, D., and Charles E. Lindblom. 1963. *A Strategy of Decision: Policy Evaluation as a Social Process*. New York: The Free Press.

Brecher, Michael. 1980. *Decisions in Crisis: Israel, 1967 and 1973*. Berkeley: University of California Press.

———. 1975. *Decisions in Israel's Foreign Policy*. New Haven: Yale University Press.

———. 1972. *The Foreign Policy System of Israel: Setting, Images, Process*. London: Oxford University Press.

Brecher, Michael, and Jonathan Wilkenfeld. 1989. *Crisis, Conflict and Instability*. Oxford: Pergamon Press.

Bueno de Mesquita, Bruce. 1985. The "War Trap" Revisited. *American Political Science Review* 79(1): 156–73.

———. 1981. *The War Trap*. New Haven: Yale University Press.

Burdett, Winston. 1969. *Encounter with the Middle East*. New York: Atheneum.

Churchill, Randolph S., and Winston S. Churchill. 1967. *The Six-Day War*. Boston: Houghton Mifflin Company.

Cohen, Raymond. 1988. Intercultural Communication Between Israel and Egypt: Deterrence Failure Before the Six-Day War. *Review of International Studies* 14: 1–16.

———. 1979. *Threat Perception in International Crisis*. Madison: The University of Wisconsin Press.

Creary, Pat J. 1984. Contending Images of International Crisis. *International Interactions* 10(4): 401–9.

Davis, Morton. 1983. *Game Theory: A Non Technical Introduction*. New York: Basic Books (Second Edition).

Dawn, Ernest C. 1968. The Egyptian Remilitarization of Sinai, May 1967. *Journal of Contemporary History* 3(3): 201–24.

Dayan, Moshe. 1976. *Story of My Life: An Autobiography*. New York: Warner Books.

De Rivera, Joseph H. 1968. *The Psychological Dimension of Foreign Policy*. Columbus, Ohio: Charles E. Merrill Publishing Company.

Derogy, Jacques, and Hesi Carmel. 1979. *The Untold History of Israel*. New York: Grove Press.

Draper, Theodore. 1968. *Israel and World Politics*. New York: The Viking Press.

Dupuy, Trevor N. 1978. *Elusive Victory: The Arab-Israel Wars, 1947–1974*. New York: Harper and Row.

Eban, Abba. 1977. *An Autobiography*. New York: Random House.

Eckstein, Harry. 1975. Case Study and Theory in Political Science. In *Handbook of Political Science* VII, ed. F. I. Greenstein and N. W. Polsby. Reading, Mass.: Addison-Wesley, pp. 79–138.

Eisenberg, Dennis, Uri Dan, and Eli Landau. 1979. *The Mossad: Inside Stories*. New York: NAL Penguin.

Elster, Jon. 1986. Introduction. In *Rational Choice*, ed. Jon Elster. Worcester: Billing & Sons Ltd, pp. 1–33.

Etheredge, Lloyd. 1985. *Can Governments Learn?* New York: Pergamon Press.

Fearon, James D. 1991. Counterfactuals and Hypothesis Testing in Political Science. *World Politics* 43(1): 169-95.

————. 1990. Deterrence and the Spiral Model: The Role of Costly Signals in Crisis Bargaining. Paper presented at the Annual Meeting of the American Political Science Association, San Francisco, August 30–September 2.

Ferreira, J. L., I. Gilboa, and M. Maschler. 1992. Credible Equilibria in Games With Utilities Changing During Play. Discussion paper no. 9217, Center for Economic Research, Tilburg University.

Gates, Scott, and Brian D. Humes. 1989. Game Theoretic Models and International Relations. Paper presented at the Annual Meeting of the American Political Science Association, Atlanta, August 31–September 3.

Geist, B. 1984. The Six-Day War. In *Diplomacy and Confrontation* (in Hebrew), ed. Benyamin Neuberger. Tel Aviv: Everyman's University, pp. 273–85.

Gendzier, Irene L. 1969. *A Middle East Reader*. New York: Pegasus.

George, Alexander L. 1979. Case Studies and Theory Development: The Method of Structured, Focused Comparison. In *Diplomacy*, ed. Paul Gordon Lauren. New York: The Free Press.

————. 1972. The Case for Multiple Advocacy in Making Foreign Policy. *American Political Science Review* 66(3): 751–94.

————. 1970. The Casual Nexus Between Cognitive Beliefs and Decision-Making Behavior: The "Operational Code" Belief System. In *Psychological Models and International Politics*, ed. Lawrence Falkowski. Boulder: Westview Press, pp. 95–124.

————. 1969. The "Operational Code": A Neglected Approach to the Study of Political Leaders and Decision Making. *International Studies Quarterly* 8(2): 190–222.

George, Alexander L., and T. J. McKeown. 1985. Case Studies and Theories of Organizational Decision Making. *Advances in Information Processing in Organizations* 2(1): 21–58.

George, Alexander L., and Richard Smoke. 1974. *Deterrence in American Foreign Policy.* New York: Columbia University Press.

Gibson, Q. 1976. Arguing From Rationality. In *Rationality and the Social Sciences: Contributions to the Philosophy and Methodology of the Social Sciences,* ed. S. I. Benn and G. W. Mortimore. Boston: Routledge and Kegan Paul, pp. 111–31.

Haber, Eitan. 1987. *"Today War Will Break Out": The Reminiscences of Brig. Gen. Israel Lior, Aide-de-Camp to Prime Ministers Levi Eshkol and Golda Meir* (in Hebrew). Tel Aviv: Idanim.

Harkabi, Yehoshafat. 1972. *Arab Attitudes Toward Israel.* New York: Hart Publishing Company.

Harsanyi, John C. 1977. *Rational Behavior and Bargaining Equilibrium in Games and Social Situations.* Cambridge: Cambridge University Press.

Heikal, Mohamed Hassanein. 1973. *The Cairo Documents.* New York: Doubleday and Company.

Herek, Gregory M., Irving L. Janis, and Paul Huth. 1989. Quality of US Decision Making During the Cuban Missile Crisis. *Journal of Conflict Resolution* 33(3): 446–59.

———. 1987. Decision Making During International Crises. *Journal of Conflict Resolution* 31(2): 203–26.

Hermann, Charles F., ed. 1972a. *International Crises: Insights From Behavioral Research.* New York: The Free Press.

———. 1972b. Some Issues in the Study of International Crisis. In *International Crises: Insights From Behavioral Research,* ed. Charles F. Hermann. New York: The Free Press, pp. 3–17.

Hipel, Keith W., Muhong Wang, and Niall M. Fraser. 1988. Hypergame Analysis of the Falkland/Malvinas Conflict. *International Studies Quarterly* 32(3): 335–58.

Holsti, Ole R. 1989. Crisis Decision Making. In *Behavior, Society, and Nuclear War* (Vol. 1), ed. Philip E. Tetlock, Jo L. Husbands, Robert Jervis, Paul C. Stern, and Charles Tilly. New York: Oxford University Press, pp. 8–84.

———. 1972. *Crisis Escalation War.* Montreal: McGill-Queen's University Press.

———. 1967. Cognitive Dynamics and Images of the Enemy: Dulles and Russia. In *Enemies in Politics,* ed. D. J. Finlay, O. R. Holsti, and R. R. Fagen. Chicago: Rand McNally, pp. 25–96.

———. 1962. The Belief System and National Images: A Case Study. *Journal of Conflict Resolution* 6(2): 244–52.

Holsti, Ole R., and Alexander L. George. 1975. The Effects of Stress on Foreign Policy Makers. *Political Science Annual* 6: 255–319.

Huth, Paul, and Bruce M. Russett. 1988. Deterrence Failure and Crisis Escalation. *International Studies Quarterly* 32(1): 29–45.

James, Patrick, and Frank Harvey. 1989. Threat Escalation and Crisis Stability: Superpower Cases, 1948–1979. *Canadian Journal of Political Science* 22(3): 523–45.

Janis, Irving L. 1989. *Crucial Decisions: Leadership in Policymaking and Crisis Management.* New York: The Free Press.

———. 1972. *Victims of Groupthink.* Boston: Houghton and Mifflin.

Janis, Irving L., and Leon Mann. 1977. *Decision Making: A Psychological Analysis of Conflict, Choice, and Commitment*. New York: The Free Press.

Jervis, Robert. 1988. Realism, Game Theory, and Cooperation. *World Politics* 40(3): 317–49.

———. 1979. Deterrence Theory Revisited. *World Politics* 31(2): 289–324.

———. 1978. Cooperation Under the Security Dilemma. *World Politics* 30(2): 167–214.

———. 1976. *Perception and Misperception in International Politics*. Princeton: Princeton University Press.

Kahneman, Daniel, Paul Slovic, and Amos Tversky, eds. 1982. *Judgment Under Uncertainty: Heuristics and Biases*. London: Cambridge University Press.

Kavka, Gregory S. 1987. *Moral Paradoxes of Nuclear Deterrence*. Cambridge: Cambridge University Press.

Keohane, Robert O. 1984. *After Hegemony: Cooperation and Discord in the World Political Economy*. Princeton: Princeton University Press.

Khouri, Fred J. 1968. *The Arab-Israeli Dilemma*. Syracuse: Syracuse University Press.

Kilgour, D. Marc, and Frank C. Zagare. 1991. Credibility, Uncertainty, and Deterrence. *American Journal of Political Science* 35(2): 305–34.

———. 1987. Holding Power in Sequential Games. *International Interactions* 13(2): 91–114.

———. 1984. Equilibria for Far-Sighted Players. *Theory and Decision* 16(2): 135–57.

Kimche, David, and Dan Bawly. 1968. *The Sandstorm*. New York: Stein and Day.

Kinder, Donald R., and Janet A. Weiss. 1978. In Lieu of Rationality: Psychological Perspectives on Foreign Policy Decision Making. *Journal of Conflict Resolution* 22(4): 707–35.

Kirkpatrick, Samuel A. 1975. Psychological Views of Decision-Making. *Political Science Annual* 6: 39-112.

Kugler, Jacek. 1991. From Desert Shield to Desert Storm: Success, Strife or Quagmire? Paper presented at the Peace Science Society Meetings, Ann Arbor, November 14–16.

Lacouture, Jean. 1973. *Nasser: A Biography*. New York: Alfred A. Knopf.

Langlois, Jean-Pierre P. 1989. Modelling Deterrence and International Crises. *Journal of Conflict Resolution* 33(1): 67–84.

Laqueur, Walter, ed. 1969. *The Israeli-Arab Reader*. New York: Bantham Books.

———. 1968. *The Road to Jerusalem*. New York: The Macmillan Company.

Lebow, Richard Ned. 1981. *Between Peace and War: The Nature of International Crisis*. Baltimore: The Johns Hopkins University Press.

Leng, Russell J. 1988. Crisis Learning Games. *American Political Science Review* 82(1): 179–94.

———. 1984. Reagan and the Russians: Crisis Bargaining Beliefs and the Historical Record. *American Political Science Review* 78(2): 338–55.

———. 1983. When Will They Ever Learn? Coercive Bargaining in Recurrent Crises. *Journal of Conflict Resolution* 27(3): 379–419.

Levy, Jack S. 1992a. An Introduction to Prospect Theory. *Political Psychology* 13(2): 171–86.

———. 1992b. Prospect Theory and International Relations: Theoretical Applications and Analytical Problems. *Political Psychology* 13(2): 283–310.

Lijphart, Arendt (1975). The Comparable-Case Strategy in Comparative Research. *Comparative Political Studies* 8(2): 158–77.

————. 1971. Comparative Politics and the Comparative Method, *American Political Science Review* 65(3): 682–93.

Luce, Duncan R., and Howard Raiffa. 1957. *Games and Decisions*. New York: John Wiley and Sons.

Mandel, Robert. 1986. Psychological Approaches to International Relations. In *Political Psychology: Contemporary Problems and Issues*, ed. Margaret G. Hermann. San Franciso: Jossey-Bass, pp. 251–78.

Mansfield, Peter. 1969. *Nasser*. London: Methuen Educational Ltd.

Maoz, Zeev. 1990a. Choosing War, Choosing Peace: Decision Theoretic Contributions to Peace Research. Mimeo, Department of Political Science, University of Haifa.

————. 1990b. *National Choices and International Processes*. Cambridge University Press.

————. 1990c. *Paradoxes of War: The Art of National Self-Entrapment*. Boston: Allen and Unwin.

————. 1985. Foreign Policy Decision Making: A Progress Report. *The Jerusalem Journal of International Relations* 7(4): 28–63.

————. 1984. Peace By Empire? Conflict Outcomes and International Stability, 1816-1976. *Journal of Peace Research* 21(3): 227–41.

————. 1982a. Crisis Initiation: A Theoretical Exploration of a Neglected Topic in International Crisis Theory. *Review of International Studies* 8(4): 215–32.

————. 1982b. *Paths to Conflict: International Dispute Initiation, 1816–1976*. Boulder: Westview Press.

————. 1981. The Decision to Raid Entebbe: Decision Analysis Applied to Crisis Behavior. *Journal of Conflict Resolution* 21(4): 677-707.

McCalla, Robert B. 1992. *Uncertain Perceptions: U.S. Cold War Crisis Decision Making*. Ann Arbor: The University of Michigan Press.

McClelland, Charles A. 1972. The Beginning, Duration, and Abatement of International Crises: Comparisons in Two Conflict Arenas. In *International Crises: Insights From Behavioral Research*, ed. Charles F. Hermann. New York: The Free Press, pp. 83–105.

————. 1968. Access to Berlin: The Quantity and Variety of Events, 1948–1963. In *Quantitative International Politics: Insights and Evidence*, ed. J. David Singer. New York: The Free Press, pp. 159–86.

Mintz, Alex. 1992. The Decision to Use Force Against Iraq: A Multidimensional, Non-Compensatory Theory of Decision Making. Mimeo, Department of Political Science, Texas A&M University.

Mishal, Shaul, David Schmeidler, and Itai Sened. 1987. Israel and the PLO: A Game with Differential Information. Mimeo, Foerder Institute for Economic Research, Tel-Aviv University.

Moe, Terry M. 1979. On the Scientific Status of Rational Models. *American Journal of Political Science* 23(1): 215–43.

Mor, Ben D. 1991. Nasser's Decision-Making in the 1967 Middle East Crisis: A Rational-Choice Explanation. *Journal of Peace Research* 28(4): 359–75.

————. 1990. Nasser's Decision-Making in the 1967 Middle East Crisis: A Multi-Stage Game Model. Mimeo, Department of Politics, New York University.

Morgan, Clifton T. 1984. A Spatial Model of Crisis Bargaining. *International Studies Quarterly* 28(4): 407–26.

Morrow, James D. 1989. Capabilities, Uncertainty, and Resolve: A Limited Information Model of Crisis Bargaining. *American Journal of Political Science* 33(4): 941–72.

———. 1986. A Spatial Model of International Conflict. *American Political Science Review* 80(4): 1131–50.

Nachmias, David, and Chava Nachmias. 1981. *Research Methods in the Social Sciences.* New York: St. Martin's Press.

Nakdimon, Shlomo. 1968. *Toward Zero Hour* (in Hebrew). Tel-Aviv: Ramdor Publishing Co.

Neuberger, Benyamin, ed. 1984. *Diplomacy and Confrontation* (in Hebrew). Tel Aviv: Everyman's University.

Niou, Emerson M. S., Peter C. Ordeshook, and Gregory F. Rose. 1989. *The Balance of Power: Stability in International Systems.* Cambridge: Cambridge University Press.

Nutting, Anthony. 1972. *Nasser.* New York: E. P. Dutton & Co.

Oren, Nissan. 1982. Prudence in Victory. In *The Termination of Wars*, ed. Nissan Oren. Jerusalem: The Magness Press, pp. 147–63.

Oye, Kenneth A, ed. 1986. *Cooperation Under Anarchy.* Princeton: Princeton University Press.

Podell, J. E., and W. M. Knapp. 1969. The Effect of Mediation on the Perceived Firmness of the Opponent. *Journal of Conflict Resolution* 13(4): 511-20.

Powell, Robert. 1990. *Nuclear Deterrence Theory: The Search for Credibility.* Cambridge: Cambridge University Press.

———. 1989a. Crisis Stability in the Nuclear Age. *American Political Science Review* 83(1): 61–76.

———. 1989b. Nuclear Deterrence and the Strategy of Limited Retaliation. *American Political Science Review* 83(2): 503–19.

———. 1987. Crisis Bargaining, Escalation, and MAD. *American Political Science Review* 81(3): 717–35.

Prittie, Terrence. 1969. *Eshkol: The Man and the Nation.* New York: Pitman Publishing Corporation.

Pruitt, Dean G. 1981. *Negotiation Behavior.* New York: Academic Press.

Quandt, William B. 1977. *Decade of Decisions: American Policy Toward the Arab-Israeli Conflict, 1967–1976.* Los Angeles: University of California Press.

Rabin, Yitzhak. 1979. *The Rabin Memoires.* Boston: Little, Brown and Company.

Rapoport, Anatol. 1966. *Two-Person Game Theory: The Essential Ideas.* Ann Arbor: University of Michigan Press.

Rapoport, Anatol, and Melvyn Guyer. 1966. A Taxonomy of 2 x 2 Games" *General Systems: Yearbook of the Society for General Systems Research* 11: 203–14.

Reuveni, Y. (1972). Perception of Threat and the 1967 War (in Hebrew). *International Problems* 11(1–2): 8–10.

Riad, Mahmoud. 1981. *The Struggle for Peace in the Middle East.* London: Quarter Books.

Riker, William H., and Peter C. Ordeshook. 1973. *An Introduction to Positive Political Theory.* Englewood Cliffs: Prentice Hall.

Robinson, James A. 1972. Crisis: An Appraisal of Concepts and Theories. In *International Crisis: Insights From Behavioral Research*, ed. Charles F. Hermann. New York: The Free Press, pp. 20–35.

Rosenau, James N. 1967. The Premises and Promises of Decision-Making Analysis. In *Contemporary Political Analysis*, ed. James C. Charlesworth. New York: The Free Press.

Sachar, Howard M. 1979. *A History of Israel: From the Rise of Zionism to Our Time.* New York: Alfred A. Knopf.

Sadat, Anwar el-. 1977. *In Search of Identity.* New York: Harper and Row.

Safran, Nadav. 1969. *From War to War.* Indianapolis: The Bobbs-Merrill Company.

Schelling, Thomas C. 1966. *Arms and Influence.* New Haven: Yale University Press.

———. 1960. *The Strategy of Conflict.* Cambridge: Harvard University Press.

Segev, Shmuel. 1967. *Sadin Adom* (Hebrew). Tel Aviv: Tberski Company.

Sergeev, V. M., V. P. Akimov, V. B. Lukov, and P. B. Parshin. 1990. A Cognitive Approach to Modeling the Caribbean Crisis. *Journal of Conflict Resolution* 34(2): 179–207.

Shamir, Shimon. 1971. The Middle East Crisis: The Brink of War. *Middle East Record,* Vol. 3, The Shiloah Center for Middle Eastern and African Studies, Tel Aviv University. Jerusalem: Israel University Press, pp. 183–204.

Sharabi, Hisham. 1969. *Palestine and Israel: The Lethal Dilemma.* New York: Pegasus.

Shirer, William L. 1960. *The Rise and Fall of the Third Reich.* New York: Simon and Schuster.

Shlaim, Avi, and Raymond Tanter. 1978. Decision Process, Choice, and Consequences: Israel's Deep Penetration Bombing in Egypt, 1970. *World Politics* 30(4): 483–516.

Shupe, Michael C., William M. Wright, Keith W. Hipel, and Niall M. Fraser. 1980. Nationalization of the Suez Canal. *Journal of Conflict Resolution* 24(3): 477–93.

Simon, Herbert A. 1985. Human Nature in Politics: The Dialogue of Psychology with Political Science. *American Political Science Review* 79(2): 293–304.

———. 1976. From Substantive to Procedural Rationality. In *Method and Appraisal in Economics,* ed. Spiro J. Latsis. Cambridge: Cambridge University Press, pp. 129–48.

———. 1957. *Models of Man: Social and Rational.* New York: Wiley.

Slater, Robert. 1977. *Rabin of Israel: A Biography.* London: Robson Books.

Snidal, Duncan. 1985. The Game *Theory* of International Politics. *World Politics* 38(1): 26–57.

Snyder, Glenn H., and Paul Diesing. 1977. *Conflict Among Nations.* Princeton: Princeton University Press.

Snyder, Richard C., H. W. Bruck, and Burton Sapin, eds. 1962. *Foreign Policy Decision-Making.* New York: The Free Press.

Stein, Arthur. 1982. When Misperception Matters. *World Politics* 34(4): 505–26.

Stein, Janice Gross. 1988. Deterrence and Miscalculated Escalation: The Outbreak of War in 1967. Paper presented at the Annual Meeting of the American Political Science Association, Washington, September 1–4.

Stein, Janice Gross, and Raymond Tanter. 1980. *Rational Decision-Making: Israel's Security Choices, 1967.* Columbus: Ohio University Press.

Steinbruner, J. D. 1974. *The Cybernetic Theory of Decision.* Princeton: Princeton University Press.

Stephens, Robert, 1971. *Nasser: A Political Biography.* New York: Simon and Schuster.

Tanter, Raymond. 1978. International Crisis Behavior: An Appraisal of the Literature. *Jerusalem Journal of International Relations* 3(2): 340–74.

Teveth, Shabtai. 1972. *Moshe Dayan: The Soldier, The Man, The Legend.* New York: Dell Publishing Co.

Tisdell, C. A. 1976. Rational Behavior as a Basis for Economic Theories. In *Rationality and the Social Sciences: Contributions to the Philosophy and Methodology of the*

Social Sciences, ed. S. I. Benn and G. W. Mortimore. Boston: Routledge and Kegan Paul, pp. 196–222.

Tsebelis, George. 1989. The Abuse of Probability in Political Analysis: The Robinson Crusoe Fallacy. *American Political Science Review* 83(1): 77-91.

Tversky, Amos. 1972. Elimination by Aspects: A Theory of Choice. *Psychological Review* 79(2): 281–99.

Vertzberger, Yaacov Y. I. 1990. *The World in Their Minds*. Stanford: Stanford University Press.

Wagner, Abraham R. 1974. *Crisis Decision-Making: Israel's Experience in 1967 and 1973*. New York: Praeger Publishers.

Wagner, Harrison R. 1989. Uncertainty, Rational Learning, and Bargaining in the Cuban Missile Crisis. In *Models of Strategic Choice in Politics*, ed. Peter C. Ordeshook. Ann Arbor: The University of Michigan Press, pp. 177–205.

Weizman, Ezer. 1976. *On Eagles' Wings*. New York: Macmillan Publishing Co.

Welch, David A. 1989. Crisis Decision Making Reconsidered. *Journal of Conflict Resolution* 33(3): 430–45.

Welsh, William A. 1971. A Game-Theoretic Conceptualization of the Hungarian Revolt: Toward an Inductive Theory of Games. In *Communist Studies and the Social Sciences*, ed. Frederic J. Fleron, Jr. Chicago: Rand McNally and Company, pp. 420–65.

Wright, William M., Michael C. Shupe, Niall M. Fraser, and Keith W. Hipel. 1980. A Conflict Analysis of the Suez Canal Invasion of 1956. *Conflict Management and Peace Science* 5(1): 27–40.

Yaniv, Avner. 1987. Deterrence Without the Bomb. Lexington: Lexington Books.

Yost, C. 1968. The Arab-Israeli War: How It Began. *Foreign Affairs* 46(2): 304–20.

Zagare, Frank C. 1990. Rationality and Deterrence. *World Politics* 42(1): 238–60.

———. 1989. Up and Down the Staircase: Crisis, Escalation, and War. Mimeo, Department of Political Science, State University of New York at Buffalo.

———. 1987. *The Dynamics of Deterrence*. Chicago: University of Chicago Press.

———. 1984a. *Game Theory: Concepts and Applications*. Beverly Hills: Sage Publications.

———. 1984b. Limited-Move Equilibria in 2 x 2 Games. *Theory and Decision* 16(1): 1–19.

———. 1983. A Game-Theoretic Evaluation of the 1973 Cease-Fire Alert Decision. *Journal of Peace Research* 20(1): 73–86.

———. 1981. Nonmyopic Equilibria and the Middle East Crisis of 1967. *Conflict Management and Peace Science* 5(2): 139–62.

Zinnes, Dina A., Joseph L. Zinnes, and Robert D. McClure. 1972. History in Diplomatic Communication: A Study of the 1914 Crisis. In *International Crisis: Insights from Behavioral Research*, ed. Charles F. Hermann. New York: The Free Press, pp. 139–62.

Name Index

Subject Index

AMAN (Israeli military intelligence), 146 n.13, 148–49 n.39

Attitudes: and crisis model, in empirical case, 143–44; empirical assessment of, 88–90, 104 n.11

Attitudes toward loss, 36, 37, 40; and crisis model, in empirical case, 143; and Holocaust syndrome, 114, 145 n.8; of Israel's crisis decision makers, 114–15; of Nasser, 118, 134

Attitudes toward the opponent, 35–36, 37, 40; of Allon, 111–12, 113; of Dayan, 112–13; of Eban, 110–11, 113–14; of Eshkol, 109–110, 113–14, 145 n.3; of Nasser, 116–18

Attitudinal prism, 5

Belief system, 5, 154

Between Peace and War (Lebow), 4

Case studies, logic of inference in, 100–104

Composite matrix. *See* Crisis model

Congruence procedure, 100

Crisis: definitions of, 2–4, 6, 14–15, 23–24, 25 nn.5–8; general theory of, ix–x, 1–2, 31–32, 42, 144, 145, 154–55; incidence of, ix; intra-war, 3; "justification of

hostility," 4; learning in, 5, 19–20, 27 n.28, 141–42, 151 n.54, 156; signaling in, 157; teaching in, 142, 157; typology of, game-based, 31, 43 (fig.), 154. *See also* Crisis *entries*; Psychological approach to crisis; Rational-choice approach to crisis

Crisis decision making: analytic (rational) model of, 7–8, 10; bureaucratic politics model of, 26 n.16; cognitive model of, 8; "conflict-theory model" of, 9; cybernetic model of, 7–8; and "groupthink," 9; "multiple paths to choice," model of, 8; stages in, 7, 26 n.14; and stress, 6–7, 9, 25–26 n.13. *See also* Crisis *entries*; Psychological approach to crisis; Rational-choice approach to crisis

Crisis games: empirical assessment of outcomes in, 97–98; empirical interpretation of solutions to, 56; escalation in, 56; nonmyopic solution to, 49–56, 78 nn.2, 7, 79 n.15. *See also* Crisis model; Theory of moves

Crisis initiation: conditions for, and player types, 58–60, 156–57; and crisis game, 48, 57; and crisis model, 23; and deception, 151

About the Author

BEN D. MOR is Associate Professor in International Relations and teaches in the *Program of National Security of the University of Haifa and the National Defense College of the Israeli Defense Force* at the University of Haifa in Israel. Previously, he has taught at New York University and the University of Nebraska, Lincoln. He has contributed to publications such as the *Journal of Peace Research* and *Rationality and Society.*